Annette M. Ferdera
7-rr. 35.

THE ARTS OF LEISURE

THE
ARTS OF LEISURE

By

MARJORIE BARSTOW GREENBIE

New York WHITTLESEY HOUSE *London*

McGRAW-HILL BOOK COMPANY, INC.

PUBLISHED BY WHITTLESEY HOUSE

A division of the McGraw-Hill Book Company, Inc.

Printed in the United States of America by The Haddon Craftsmen, Inc., Camden, N. J.

Time

Time is so long. There is no end of it,
Nor ever was beginning. Yet I find
No time in all the day when I can sit
Alone within the deep pool of my mind,
And feel time flowing over me like water,
And see time spread like sunshine all about.
The moments goad me, and the hours slaughter
All natural joys at birth. The days leap out
In serried ranks of weeks, and months, and years,
Hounding with duties, whipping me to goals.
And still, from age to age the Eastern seers
Say time re-incarnates our driven souls!
Let me be born a child or fool or flower
That knows Eternity in its own hour.

Foreword

NEED a husband, in this age of matrimonial equalitarianism, necessarily be called upon to recognize publicly his wife's off-spring? It seems to me a bit old-fashioned. Husbands should be neither seen nor heard. Particularly when the off-spring is a book. Husbands should content themselves with being acknowledged by their author-wives in a dedication—*"To the dear companion of my typewriter"*—as in former times, husbands dedicated their books *"To the dear companion of the hearth."* But that is what makes this preface unique. To confound my unhappy lot, I must openly confess that this child of my wife's was laid at my editorial door-step as a foundling, bearing the highly suspicious paternity of one Robert Carrick. Here I am asked to give my name and my blessings to a dubious child first fathered under another name, and with which I fell in love when it was still a brat. The affection got its hold upon me. Surely this is enough to test the chivalry of the most modern of moderns.

Can any married man imagine anything less conducive to leisure than having his wife write a book about it? In a home where both husband and wife write, where a twelve year old daughter watches for a chance at a typewriter and a fourteen year old son whacks away at his own, where a farm has to be farmed and children to be educated, and lectures given, leisure is apt to be an unknown benefactor. Yet leisure is much indulged in our home, and because it was so much a part of our very substance of living, its arts were always considered, though seldom mastered. We often spoke of it, thinking of the world over which we have traveled and where we have seen its arts more or less practiced by strange peoples in strange ways. When, therefore, all primed for developing

vii

leisure as a public proposition, I sauntered into Boston and had a new-born magazine about Leisure handed over to me to be foster-fathered, god-fathered and reared, I turned to my wife, even as when our first-born came to us, with suggestions for its diet and its disciplining.

What it needs, I said, is someone to teach it the art of conversation. How few people there are in the world properly brought up on good talk. Grammar, voice, and how to wither your partner for a poor move at bridge, all that is taught; but how to talk to strangers and even to friends, *that* is embarrassingly unknown. How to dress and how to show off a pretty ankle, that, I said, was part of modern business pedagogy; but how to be at ease, how to loaf in good company, that was a thing of the past. How to "Say it by Telegram" is already a national vice; but how to write a friendly letter, only the stereotyped letter-writing book could tell. And so on. In that manner was this book conceived.

It was my notion as Editor of Leisure, to develop these arts of living from month to month, and thus there appeared the first of these articles. Unwilling to plaster the magazine with the name of the editor and his family, we agreed that such a tournament had better be entered in the armour of a male. Then Robert Carrick began to engage the attention of a book publisher. For a time I conducted the negotiations as Carrick's proxy, till it was no longer necessary to disguise the gender of the armoured knight. Let the world know that woman, no less than man, is skilled in the arts of leisure.

With that the announcer withdraws from the stage. Prefacer or chairman, his is not to write a book or make a speech. As husband, chivalry enjoins him not to criticise his wife, and pride, to let the world praise her, if it will. Let mercy treat him gently, whether he did well or ill in encouraging his housewife to wander from domestic usefulness into the dubious arts of leisure.

SYDNEY GREENBIE

Table of Contents

THE ARTS OF LEISURE

The Contrary Art of
Being One's Self—Introduction

THERE are rumors that the curse of Adam is worked off at last. No longer need man labor in the sweat of his brow. A great new holiday is coming —maybe. But now that the farmer watches the daisies grow over his ploughed-in wheat, and Wall Street sells one stock where it used to sell a thousand, and industry sees half of its great machines stand idle, and labor works three days a week where it formerly worked six, we are all as uncomfortable as if we had found ourselves in heaven, arrayed in white robes, with harps in our hands, and nothing to do but play tunes for the everlasting amusement of God.

Leisure—here it is. Or is it? And if it is, what are we to do with it? When Beatrice found Dante walking in the flowering meadows of Paradise, she sternly bent her beautiful brows and asked, "What are you doing here? Don't you know that this is the place where man knows how to be happy?" That is what will happen to us, when the new economics has made a paradise for us—if it ever does. Our homes will be rebuilt; our hours of labor will be shortened; our farms will yield a guaranteed income; our savings will be secure; we won't have to worry about unemployment or old age; and every town will have a swimming pool built by the P.W.A. But shall we know how to be happy? That is something else again.

What will make you personally happy is the one thing you cannot take any man's word for. Wall Street says you will be happy if you make a million, and the advertiser says you will be happy if you "smoke a Camel." All that they mean is that they will be happier if you do what they tell you—or they

3

think they will be. Havelock Ellis once remarked that the trouble with socialism is that we already have it in the wrong place. No one, he said, needs rugged individualism in getting his water supply, and no one ought to have socialism in his religion. Mass economics are better than mass morality and mass amusement. In the dear lamented age of prosperity which has now departed, every man was free to make his money in his own way, or he thought he was. But the minute he had made it, whether it was a fortune or a day's wage, he was swallowed up by enormous mass interests which rushed him and ballyhooed him and pressed their wares upon him, and enlisted the voices of his nearest and dearest to repeat propaganda to him, till only the toughest and most contrary ego could stand out against them.

If we are not now so enslaved to mass interests, it is only because we have less money, and these beasts eat money. What is meant by the "new leisure" is partly more time, and partly less money. The minute you have money, there is some tremendous mass interest to gobble you up. But if you have no money as a bait, you may be left alone for a few hours, and those hours are your "leisure." Having nothing to go to the movies with, or to belong to the country club with, you may, for the first time in your life, find yourself doing what you really want to do. And then you discover that there is nothing in life so cheap as joy. It runs along beneath the pavements of life, like veins of water underground. Dig a hole anywhere, and lo, there is a well of it. Almost anything you can do is fun, provided you do it because you want to, and have all the time in the world for it, and need not make any money by it, and everybody lets you alone while you are doing it.

Probably there are as many distinct ways of being happy as there will have been people on this globe when the sun burns out and the last man closes his eyes on the everlasting night. Many things which made people happy in the past are forgotten now, and much of our current machinery for joy was not known a few years ago. Believe it or not—but people were happy when they didn't have any movie to go to, nor car to ride in, nor radio to listen to. They will probably be happy in ways we cannot now even dream of when all these things will be old iron on the junk-heap of civilization.

2

Because happiness is so personal, there is only one place for a man to begin his search for it, and that is in himself. The doctors of leisure now talk of equipment for the use of spare time, endowments for community recreation, swimming pools, work shops. All these things are good. But the primary equipment for leisure consists in the possession of two eyes, two ears, two hands, and two feet, with the addition of numerous other items such as a heart, a memory, and a tongue —so long as they are all your own, and not mortgaged to any mass interest, mass habit, mass advertising, or mass hooey whatsoever. One may get along with a fraction of this equipment, if one really runs it one's self, for one's own satisfaction. But some personal possessions of this sort are fundamental, and if a man has all the Lord usually provides, he has so much equipment for having a good time that it is a wonder he ever puts himself out to get any more.

The money value of these possessions is indisputable. If a man loses his eye or his thumb through the fault of another, he is entitled to sue for a definite amount. The financial equivalent of a whole man, complete and in good running order in all his parts, is set by our courts at $50,000.00 or upwards which the family may sue for if he is killed through another's negligence.

This is what our selves are worth to us, and this valuable equipment which has already cost someone a lot of money, beginning with the doctor's bills at birth, is available for our own happiness. But who really uses it? We are like people with mansions who live in only one or two rooms. Most of us might as well be blind for all we really see, and deaf for all we really hear; and if you are a lover of good talk, you will feelingly concede that almost everybody is dumb!

Really to use one's self, to explore the possibilities of sensation, of feeling, of thought, of creative action, one must be free from the invisible social control which paralyzes our wills as with enchantment. It begins in the family, with the earliest objects of our love. Who made them propaganda agents for futile activity, and substituted petty bossing of our free time for caresses and sympathetic talk and comradeship in the whole adventure of living? And still don't we know that Auntie will feel badly if you do, and Uncle will disapprove if he hears, and Father thinks that you should not offend Mr. Z? There is always some one in a family who is running the rest of the members in this way.

Beyond the family is the community. There is much it has a right to expect from the individual, in exchange for the security it promises. But there is also the Lions' Club, and the Woman's Club, and the money one must subscribe to this, and the hours one must put in on that. Clubs are means of companionship, of union in non-egoistic interests. If you like them, enjoy them—and God bless you. But why this harrying of the barbarian beyond the gates, this house-to-house canvassing, this dragging away of our car to the picnic and our old hat to the Golf Club rummage sale? Life in many social groups is a perpetual hold-up. Political taxes are nothing to the social tax on time and purse. For what? To keep busy-bodies buzzing.

Beyond this there is the religion of success. One's success in life is supposed to depend on tolerating Mrs. So-and-So, and catering to Mr. Blank. One may not walk, because a neighbor always picks one up on the road with a pitying air, as if one did not have a car of one's own—picks one up and casually mentions that he has two cars. One may not go fishing in Canada for the summer, because all the friends on whom one's mystical "standing" depends are going to the resort on Long Island. One must belong to the country club. One must hit golf balls and doze over bridge and dance with whales in tuxedos or porpoises in backless evening gowns. And all to keep up what? The privilege of doing it all over again. Dances and games are lovely things but only for the young and the innocent and those who enjoy them for their own sake. The driving necessity of doing what the rest do will take the joy out of anything. It introduces worry and self-consciousness and competition, and these just naturally put out joy. The blight spreads far beyond those that are sentenced to well-to-do society. Thousands of middle class folk who have small salaries but every possibility of hearty personal enjoyment are sick with envy of the social chain-gangs.

The worm in the social apple is the idea that fun with one's fellows is not an end in itself but only an indirect means of making more money. In the magazine stories one learns that the young salesman put over a big order by playing golf with the magnate. But there is always the contrary story of success achieved by *not* playing with the magnate, but doing instead something odd and unpopular. One story is just as good as the other, and probably just as true.

This enslavement to mass pressure and "blah" creates physical tension and sub-conscious spiritual pain. Everywhere one sees tense, harried people, driven from one joyless activity to another by some invisible whip. In his final stab of self-realization, Babbitt confessed that he had never in his life done one thing he really wanted to. This is the tragedy of Babbitt everywhere. He is fat. He is sleek. He is a successful realtor. He has a nice house and a nice little car. *But he isn't a real person.* He is just a collection of things and gestures that have been put over on him by salesmen and national advertising, service clubs and fraternal lodges, his church, his bank, and his political party. When Babbitt really opens up, he talks only of one thing. Escape. Going to Europe maybe. Going to Alaska. Getting a farm or a ranch. But if

one asks him why he doesn't cut it all and really do what he
pleases—giving him the benefit of the doubt and assuming
that he really does know what he pleases (which is unlikely),
he shrinks and sighs and says he "can't." These things are
for other people, but not for him. He is utterly enslaved.
Yet what is the name of his slave-driver and where does he
live? The slave-driver is really non-existent. But God himself
had never such power over the free spirit of man.

3

What is the use of rugged individualism in getting more
money to spend the way the rest tell you to? Time is money,
and most of us have plenty of time, or would have if we took
our days and hours out of the hands of all who grab it and
spend it for us. Of the 168 hours in a week, only forty at most
are now commandeered by industry. The rest should be one's
own—one's own to sleep, to love, to play, to grow. Once, if
you had time but no money, you were comparatively safe.
The mass-interests only wanted you to buy something or con-
tribute something to a good cause. But now a new danger
threatens. You must use your leisure. Use your leisure to
collect stamps, to develop hobbies, to join in community
recreation. Every time some one does find an individual way
of enjoying his free time, it is seized by the crowd and
whoopeed to death. That is what happened to mah jong, to
Tom Thumb golf. As one reads the new documents on
leisure, one is seized with a bleak despair. Is this all there is
to life—this bouncing up and down on hobby horses? How
melancholy a thing is time, if all one can do with it is to kill it.

It is not in this sense that we speak of leisure. Leisure in
this book is all life that is not yet bottled and packaged and
sold by advertising. It is idling without conscience, and walking to get nowhere, and thinking that solves nothing, and
talking to hear yourself talk. It is making things that you

can't sell, and making love that gets you no wife. It is the opportunity to cut and run.

To find such leisure you must follow your own bent rather than the recommended procedures of leisure specialists. Listen to all the great doctors of leisure, but obey none of them blindly—not even me.

Arts of Solitude

"A man's life, a woman's life, can be lived like a thing of magic still, if we will only be obstinate, crafty, and lonely."
—Powys

The Noble Art of
Loafing—I

IF THE hours of leisure are those hours in the brief span of living which shine in their own right and not merely as coins wherewith to buy some other hour of hoped for happiness, one of the natural talents of man should come into its own at last. This is the talent for loafing. All men are born with it, and in boys of fourteen or fifteen, it frequently amounts to genius. But women in the form of mothers, and later of wives, have no patience with it, and weed it out with a ruthless hand. Hitherto the work-a-day world has joined with the women in the slaughter.

Yet loafing is a beautiful art, and of great value to the human race. It is the aboriginal ancestor of both poetry and science, the primitive half-sister of that art of the contemplative life which, as Aristotle and the Christian fathers believed, was the life of God and the angels. Down through the ages there have been some distinguished loafers—Socrates, for example, the street corner philosopher of Athens, and Another Whom it is difficult to name in this connection without offense, One Who might have grown old as a carpenter in Nazareth, had He not taken to loafing on the highways, and on hillsides, and in public gardens, gathering folks about Him and talking to them about things glorious and God-like. There were the monks, too, both in the East and the West, Buddhist and Christian. They are responsible for the most various additions to happy living, from the Saint Bernard dog to the drinking of tea; but they were only organized bands of loafers, as any contemporary tradesman could have told you. After a loafer becomes famous, history is usually ashamed to give him his right name. That is why we often know him only as a philosopher, a saint, or a poet.

2

There have been some Americans, however, who objected to this camouflage. Loafers they were, and they insisted on calling themselves so, flaunting their disreputable calling right in the face of industrious people. Perhaps it was only an accident which gave to the American the reputation of hustling, and set his nose to the grindstone of hard work for over a century. For one of the forms of genius in which America has thus far been rich is the genius for loafing. The most brilliant, the most original, the most ingenious, and the most persistent of loafers in modern times have been Americans. There was Walt Whitman. He stands quite at the head of the list of modern loafers, foreign or native, in the scope and determination, the philosophy and benevolence of his loafing. He was notable, too, in that he could loaf anywhere. Most loafers need a grassy bank in the sun or a lonely sand pile on a beach before they can relax and loaf. But Walt Whitman could loaf under all circumstances. He loafed up and down the noisiest and busiest streets of the noisiest and busiest city in the world— New York. He loafed on docks, amidst the shouts of sailors unloading bales of cotton and cargoes of bananas. He loafed in factories, amidst the clang of iron and steel. The more somebody else was doing something, the more serenely and grandly he just did nothing.

And thus, like all the loafers who have reported their sensations, Walt Whitman found joy—"the joy of my soul, leaning poised on itself, receiving identity through materials and loving them, observing characters, and absorbing them." Often the joy burst forth in poetic noise. The myriad activities of men played on his nerves till, stirred like a great beast in the sun, he sent his barbaric yawp ringing over the roof tops of the world. Again he was sometimes subdued by cosmic sorrow.

The consciousness of murder and rapine, the weeping of families over the corpse still on its pallet, the shrieks of mothers in the struggle of birth, fused into an outcry from the very heart of things. The rain falling on the world became tears. "Tears, tears, tears." Yet so absorbed was he in this sharing of life that he lost all sense of his own existence apart from the vast throbbing of the cosmos. He had no need of wealth, for he possessed the world, nor of personal achievement for his were the achievements of all men through sympathetic participation. To be but a drop in the rushing torrent of existence— that was enough.

In recent years there has been another American loafer of talent. He, too, was unafraid of noise, bustle, people, and machinery, and functioned best amidst conditions which make the delicate and squeamish loafers of Europe take to the tall timber for peace. This was the late Vachel Lindsay, whom time may acclaim as the greatest of our modern poets. The place where he liked best to loaf was a great highway in the West, where the cars swooped by on their way to "California and the gold sea sand." He liked to hear the distant hum growing louder and louder, to feel the sudden rush, the choking dust as they passed him, to hear their horns growing faint in the distance. Out of the illimitable East they came, like the sun, and plunged like the sun into the golden west. He liked, too, to see their great eyes glaring as they came on through the darkness. He even liked to see them lap up gasoline "from great red flagons." How amusing it was to note the cities and states they came from, to see the names of their towns flapping on pennants, to count the different cities that passed him thus in the day—Concord, Niagara, Boston, Chicago, Hannibal, Cairo. He said, as he sat on a milestone and watched the sky, that the whole United States went by him.

So he would loaf all day along a highway—nap and amble, yawn, and stare, and "write fool thoughts in my grubby book." He would tell stories to children, draw funny pictures for the boys, and in the end, "get me a place to sleep in the hay, at the end of a live-and-let-live day." At night, while he automatically continued to listen for the swoop of the cars, he would also hear the Kansas windmills "singing o'er the wells," and listen to the "wonder that the night wind tells," until the chirpings in the prairie grass would shape themselves into little words like "sweet, sweet, dew and glory, stars and rain," which seemed the expression of his own happiness.

After this it only remains for some American to write of the joys of loafing to radio. To lie on a couch on the porch of a lonely cottage on the shores of Penobscot Bay, with nothing about for miles except the pines and the birches, and the waves lapping against the shell encrusted rocks, and breaking at the roots of the timothy in the seaside pastures— to lie at ease in this sea-bright, sunlit loneliness, and, turning a switch, to have the raucous sounds of the world of men hurtling down on you from the empty sky—to hear an English girl announcing bargains in the shopping streets of London, and the German Minister snorting propaganda, and idlers dancing to the strains of the carioca in the cafes of Brazil, and the cigarette girl joshing the orchestra in a Broadway restaurant; to hear the wistful, agitated strains of a Beethoven symphony rising sweetly from Robin Hood Dell in Philadelphia, and a Methodist preacher speaking softly of prayer, and a half dozen imaginary murders going on for the advertisement of breakfast foods and laxatives, and real crimes broadcast from the flying cars of the police—to hear all this and to think how all the agitation and the folly of man is hidden as a secret in this sunshine and this sky; and then to turn off the switch, and hear again only the waves sucking in the pebbles, and the wind moving among the pines, and a loon laughing alone somewhere out there on the water. Some American might find the joy and peace of loafing in this.

Yet for all the excitement of men and mechanics, the

purest and most serene loafing is still to be enjoyed in those places where there is "only grass and the presence of God." Of this sort of loafing Henry David Thoreau was the great American apostle. After some experiment, he discovered that he could support himself by six weeks of labor a year, provided that he lived very simply, which was the way he liked to live. So he built himself a little cabin in the woods, near Concord, Massachusetts, and, having earned his keep for the year, devoted the rest of the time to loafing and looking after himself. He said that he had an advantage over people who were obliged to look to the theatre and society for amusement, in that his life was his amusement, a drama of many scenes, and never the same two days in succession. Sometimes he worked hard enough, keeping house in his cabin, hoeing his beans, making himself a fire-place, going to town and bringing back his groceries slung in a sack over his shoulder, for he was a neat and thrifty soul and, in his simple Yankee way, liked to live well. And he read and studied a good deal. But there were times, he said, when he could not sacrifice the "bloom of the day" to any work either of head or hands. On such days, after his morning dip in Walden pond, which was one of his favorite daily ceremonies, he would sit down on his doorstep in the sun and stay there, "rapt in revery, amidst the pines and hickories and the sumachs, in undisturbed silence and stillness." The birds would hop around him. The sun would move across the sky. It would be high noon, and then afternoon. Not until he noticed the sun coming in through the western window, or heard the noise of some traveler's wagon on the distant highway, would he come to and realize that a whole day was gone and nothing done. "I grew in those seasons like corn in the night," he said. "They were not time subtracted from my life, but so much over and above my usual allowance." He was happy beyond measure in such loafing. "Instead of singing like the birds I silently smiled at my incessant good fortune."

3

When one turns from Americans to loafers in Europe, one misses a great deal. Their idea of loafing is more stereotyped and narrow. They do not know how to take the whole human scene into their consciousness or to enjoy the stir and excitement of modern mechanism. They lack the expansive human benevolence, the humor, the fresh, pungent enjoyment of anything and everything that comes their way. But there are two Englishmen who have left such charming descriptions of loafing and its psychological effects that they deserve a place in this record. They were both a little outside of the scholarly, aristocratic, monkish, or pseudo-classical traditions which tend to inhibit really original and joyous loafing in Europe. Both were fascinated by the spaces of the American continent, though one knew them only at second hand, through books of travel which he read eagerly. Perhaps they should have been born Americans instead of Englishmen. One was Hudson, the naturalist, and the other Wordsworth, the poet, whose best verse is a rationalizing of loafing.

In "Idle Days in Patagonia" Hudson describes his days and days of loafing in South America. Morning after morning he would get on his horse, and taking his dog and his gun, ride out over the prairies. The dog and the gun were probably just a gesture to satisfy the convention that when a man goes into the woods it must be to kill something, for he says that he never even tried to hunt. He would just ride on and on, over the gray wastes, through the low bushes, under the chill gray sky, pausing now and then on a rise of ground to survey the desolate scene, and then taking up again his aimless course. At noon he would usually stretch out on his poncho, not to rest, for he was never tired, but just to enjoy the stillness. He would sit for an hour without moving, and "listen to the silence." During this time, and during most of his aimless riding, no thought ever crossed his mind. "In that novel state of mind I was in, thought had become impossible," he said. His brain seemed to have transformed itself from a thinking machine into a machine for some other unknown purpose. "To think," he said afterwards, "was like setting in motion a noisy engine in my brain; and there was something there which bade me to be still, and I was forced to obey." This utter stillness was accompanied by a ("strong feeling of elation.")Day after day he returned to this solitude, "as to a festival," setting forth with happy expectation in the morning, and returning only when night and hunger forced him back. (Later on, when he renewed the habit of thinking and the routines of social life, he found them by comparison, an "insipid existence.")

This sense of elation which comes when one has put off all human responsibilities and even all animal activity, when one is just content to sit—to sit and not even to think—has been described again and again by Wordsworth. He imagines a woman made beautiful by it. As she sits by the brook, where rivulets dance their wayward round, "the beauty born of murmuring sound" will pass into her face. Shaped by silence, harmonized by the great rhythms of nature,

> *Hers shall be the breathing balm,*
> *And hers the silence and the calm*
> *Of mute, insensate things.*

In these moments of bodily and mental stillness, the heavy and weary weight of all this unintelligible world is lightened. The mind and the body are laid to sleep, but something deep within wakens, and with an eye made quiet by harmony, and the deep power of joy, "we see into the life of things".

4

As one reads these many accounts of loafing, so different in detail, yet so alike in the confession of utter happiness, one wonders how it is that a certain way of doing absolutely nothing can bring such joy. Perhaps the truth is that in all our daily activities we are really pinched and shaped to compartments too small for us. We use only fractions of ourselves, and use them far too violently. We need moments when we can expand to our true stature, when all the unused areas of sensation can awake and begin to function, when the unconscious is released to the sunshine, in the fulness of its own vegetative, wordless, pulsating existence. Then the unconscious life, so foul in its confinement sometimes, takes on a strange beauty and harmony, like a wilted and rotting plant from a cellar, which, brought out to the light and set in the earth, bursts into flower. Psychologists have taught us to explore the unconscious, to pry among the faded blooms and rotted roots of yesterday, sometimes even to cut them off and throw them on the scrap heap. But some loafers have discovered another way. Let but the conscious life and will abdicate, let but the mechanism for deciding and doing be still, let the muscles relax and the conscience go to sleep, alone, out of doors, under the open sky, and the unconscious takes care of itself. Released and brought back to health, it revitalizes the whole of the conscious personality.

Intense and even mystical as is the joy some have found in the moments when, as Walt Whitman says, they loaf and invite their souls, there may be a simple explanation of it. For the consciousness of joy depends on two things—on an organic reserve of life and on the absence of checks. The fulness of life flowing harmoniously, that is joy. Wherever there is a reserve of life, there is happiness. There is happiness even in hard work, and a subtle happiness in suffering itself, so long as the superabundance of energy lasts. In the orgies of dissipation, when men spend life recklessly, there is joy, even the delirium of joy, only so long as there are vital reserves to spend. When these are gone, there is only satiety, and bleak absence of sensation, and a headache the morning after. What one feels as joy, in these moments of loafing, is the fulness of life flooding in and the organic kinship with all the life of the world—the vitality that flowers in the golden-rod, and flies with the swallow, and secretly glides through the lightless spaces of the sea. So one enters into one's own share of that life which is larger than the ego, and older, perhaps, than time.

The Special Art of
Seeing—II

ONCE upon a time there was a little boy in a Victorian house in London. He had no brothers, no sisters, no playmates, no yard to play in, and no toys; for his father and mother did not believe in toys. All day long he was left absolutely alone. If he cried, or made any other noise, or did not do as he was told, or fell down stairs, he was whipped. This was not because his father and mother were cruel. It was the way they thought a child should be brought up.

Alone in a Victorian room, disciplined to silence and immobility, the child could do just one thing. He could look. He could look at the heavy curtains swathing the windows, at the patterned carpet covering the floor, at the what-nots and the dried flowers, the dark steel engravings, the dim, flat oil paintings. He could stand at the window and count the bricks of the opposite wall, with intervals of rapturous excitement when the water cart stopped and was filled through its leathern pipe from a dripping iron post at the end of the pavement. And so he passed days "contentedly" in tracing squares and comparing colors, and examining knots in the wood. In later years John Ruskin bore no rancor against his parents for the long, still imprisonment of his childhood. He felt himself more than compensated by his discovery of the way in which the soul and the mind may escape through the eye, and the pleasure there is at all times in just looking.

Later when his marvelously trained and exercised eye was open to the whole beauty of the world, he found rapture. His pleasure in mountain landscape he could compare only to that of a lover in being near a noble and kind mistress. The beauty of cloud and lake and hill and of the forms of vegetation wrought the fervor and enchantment of first love. The sight of a mountain landscape, he said, was inconsistent with spite, anger, covetousness, discontent, or any other hateful passion. As his life matured, beautiful landscape "associated itself with every just and noble sorrow, joy, or affection". So all the privations of his childhood were compounded to him in the joy of the eye.

Probably the world is easier to look at now than it was in Ruskin's childhood. He spent his life warring on all that made that Victorian sitting room so ugly and so trivial. He set going currents of discussion which talked the curly-cues off the chairs and the draperies off the windows and the carpets off the floor, and re-dyed the brown domestic interior in all the colors of the sunset. Despairing of men, he turned to women. Standing in an art-gallery one day, he was amazed to see a fashionable young woman go by him with only a casual glance at the picture he was studying. He would not expect her to grasp the artist's thought, to throb to any emotion of wonder or beauty. But that she should not notice the lustre and texture of the fabrics painted in the picture—should not notice them and wish that her own dull garments were of that quality! Had women no eyes? Could they not want beauty in the stuff they must use and handle? Seeing women forever pricking their fingers with needles, he could not understand why every wall in England, farmer's cottage and gentleman's mansion, was not by this time covered with tapestries in pure and living colors. When he said that the primary use of the artistic instinct was to "make beautiful the articles we must perforce use," people laughed. What! Make pots and pans, dish-mops and kitchen sinks, beautiful! But many an American bathroom and kitchen now realizes this fantasy; and the simplest American housewife now often knows how to make a beautiful interior, because more than a century ago a little boy she hardly knows by name learned to *see*.

2

While Ruskin was unrolling to the dim eyes of England pageants of painting and architecture and landscape, a little boy in the south of France embarked on another great adventure in seeing. A traveler might have seen him one afternoon—a country boy about six years old, barefooted and in a homespun smock to which his grandmother for obvious purposes had tied a big handkerchief by a string. He was gazing at the sky, his whole little being alight and alert, for he had made a great discovery. Facing the sun but a moment before, and feeling his body flooded with joy and excitement by the light, he had asked himself a strange question. "How does this joy come to me? Do I get it through my mouth or my eyes?" Accustomed to good things arriving by way of the mouth—the bland comfort of warm milk, the thrill of honey on the tongue—he said, "I must get it through my mouth." He closed his eyes and opened his mouth. The light went out, and with it the joy. Blankness closed round him. No, not his mouth. He would try his eyes. He closed his mouth and opened his eyes. The world sprang back to life and color. Joy flashed down his little spine and burst in a great shout from his tightly closed lips. His eyes! His eyes! He got joy through his eyes! He ran home. He told his grandmother, his mother, and his brothers and sisters that he had found out a wonderful thing. They gathered to listen. He explained. Joy came to him through his eyes. Was that all? How they laughed!

But Henri Fabre cherished his discovery. Years later, as a poor young teacher of the classics, he was shut up in a city with only a backyard to walk around in. One day he found a bee-hive. He began to watch the bees. He kept on watching. Gradually a wonderful world opened to his sight, a world with a social economy as complicated as man's, and in many ways much better. He looked around. He saw other insects. Did they, too, have a social organization—customs, morals, ambitions, adventures? Gaudy social scenes opened to his gaze —battles, murders, sudden deaths, huge ambitions, delicate and fantastic love-making. Within a brief life between dawn and sunset he saw winged nothings compacting more experience than a man crowds into a life-time. The books he wrote on the life of the Mason bees and the social affairs of insects are now familiar to everyone. To him, as to Ruskin, no space was so small that, looking at it, he could not escape through his eyes to wonderland. Once he stood with a child in a kitchen, and looked at the humble supplies on the shelves— the vinegar, the starch, the cod-fish; and, by the time he had done talking about them, he had spun a book which now reads like a fairy tale.

3

Ruskin and Fabre—they illustrate the two great branches of the art of seeing. One saw and chose continually. "This is beautiful. I like this. I will keep this. That is ugly. Throw it away." The other looked and only asked, "Why?" He guessed the answer, and looked again. It was like another chapter of a story. Thus the first artist and the first scientist were made, perhaps, back in the unknown ages of the world. And so they are perpetually recreated.

The opening of the eyes, in dozens of such men, created the modern world. A young man in England, reading poetry in which all the birds were "feathered songsters" and all the fish "finny tribes", decided really to look at birds and fish for a change before he said anything about them. Poetry, he said, should describe the "object as in itself it really is". And with those words he created modern poetry. Instead of "feathered songsters" we began to hear of the linnet and the skylark, and how the swan on still Saint Mary's lake, floats double, swan and shadow. Instead of telling about "enamelled meadows," he wrote of the beauty of the "daisy's shadow thrown on the smooth surface of this naked stone". Generations of men, many of them amateurs amusing themselves in spare hours, looked and tinkered and looked again, and so lit our houses with electricity, and brought the voices of all the world into the most remote country kitchen, and filled the highways with motor-cars, and set the whole magnificent, terrible industrial machine going for the ultimate release of man from toil or for his ghastly undoing. Darwin, in the quiet of an English country house, looked at scraps and the odds-and-ends of remains of every conceivable species of animal collected everywhere, till his looking rocked the foundations of human thinking like an earthquake, and brought toppling to earth conceptions to which man had tied his moral life for thousands of years. Since then, other men, in the quiet of their spare hours, have been rebuilding on the wrecks a new structure of thought of which only the foundations are laid but which may yet tower higher into the heavens of man's imagining, and glow in more manifold wealth of material and of form.

There is nothing a man will not undertake, no risk he will not run, no place he will not go to, once the fascination of looking at the world has taken possession of him. Will Beebe descends half a mile into the sea, down, down, where no light has ever penetrated, into depths no human eye has pierced before—down where the fish carry their headlights before them, careening like stars gone mad, where creatures, big as man, that man never saw, move serenely to and fro, and never miss the sky. So Piccard ascends in his balloon till earth and clouds and air itself drop away, and there is nothing around him save the cold, purple blaze of the stratosphere. So Byrd, at the South Pole, sits alone in his hut beneath the snow, while the thermometer drops to eighty below zero and over him roar the storms of unbelievable winters.

This great art of seeing, so portentous for the modern world, requires no teacher, no money, and no equipment at the outset. It may be practiced alone, anywhere, and under the most severe physical handicaps. Yet it leads to a variety of activities, to far-ranging thoughts, and to ennobling and tranquillizing emotion. Much of the activity of the religious imagination in the past was due to the instinctive dissatisfaction of man with the world in which his own blindness enclosed him. He wanted something grander, more terrible, more beautiful. He wanted something endless in space and eternal. So he created heaven and hell. But as man learns to see, heaven and hell open before his eyes, and beyond each hell a deeper one, and beyond each heaven a higher. So mystery returns to the universe, and to the heart, humility and awe.

4

The greatest seers have taught themselves to see, and any one may begin at once to give himself lessons. Unique experiments of this sort are not limited to the great ones of the past. Twenty years ago there was a boy who liked to read, but who never could be content with what the book told him. "These books," he said, "were written by men who went out to see, and wrote what they saw. How do I know that they are right unless I go and look at the world, and judge what they say for myself?" So he spent the time and the money, which other youths spend getting a college education, in creating a college education for himself with the world as his campus. He travelled around the Pacific ocean. He walked two thousand miles in New Zealand, living with the shepherds, sleeping alone in the bush, prying into the cities. He ate eels with the Maori savages, and sat with the Samoans singing under the palm trees, in front of their huts, in the dusk. He lived for two years in a Japanese house in Japan. He looked. He kept notes. He organized his observations.

And only after he had done this did he read about what he had seen.

Afterwards, when he became president of the Floating University, he was shocked to see how college professors flounder when asked to take their eyes off their books and look at the very things they teach from the books. He felt as impatient with professors who could not use the world as the source of knowledge as they felt with students who could not use a library. Nothing seemed real to them until it came to them at second hand through writing. So in the learned pages of the Phi Beta Kappa magazine, this wanderer, Sydney Greenbie, now seriously proposes to the professors, that the basic exercises in all learning should not be exercises in reading but exercises in seeing. Such exercises he intends to give students, when the travelling university gets under sail again, and to give them in all the ports of the world.

Not every one has the energy to go all over the world in pursuit of an education in seeing. But simple lessons in seeing may be devised by anyone. The following are offered to the ingenious as something they may improve upon.

For the first lesson take any position looking out on any-thing—a room in your own house, a garden, a bit of woodland, a city street. Now look and look and look, registering everything. Look from right to left; from left to right. Look up and down, at the foreground, at the middle ground, at the background. Then close your eyes, and try to hear every least sound, all the hummings, buzzings, scratchings, tappings, and scrapings, the distant murmur, the nearby articulations, the orchestrated noise that makes what the human ear calls silence. Listen to them separately and in combination, and try to distinguish their sources. In a city, perhaps, this is a dangerous exercise, for the city is tolerable only for the deaf. But in the country, sometimes, when one listens so, one hears the deep, formless music of the earth.

Now close your ears as you have closed your eyes, and, deaf and blind, try to move about and distinguish each article by the touch. One might go even further and sample everything through taste. Taste was our first contact with the world. Babies and puppies bite, suck, and chew anything that comes their way, and so increase their knowledge of life. Probably we are more dependent than we realize, on a knowledge of the real properties of things which our exploring tongues and lips once lodged in the unconscious. Who does not really know the taste of varnish on furniture, the flavor of chewed paper, the crunch of burnt matches between the teeth? How do we know? The cook never served them for dinner within our memories. When one has come as near as dignity dares to the baby's knowledge of life, open the eyes and look again. How rich and varied the seeing has now become! The other senses co-operate with sight, like instruments in an orchestra. Things no longer look flat. They are round and full and vibrant. One is sensitized in every nerve.

Another lesson. Fix your eyes upon a familiar scene—one you look at every day and seldom honor with a thought or a feeling. Relax your muscles and dismiss every thought. Now, as your eyes move idly about, let your feelings respond to what you see in a natural, unforced way. This is easier than it sounds to our unfeeling generation. If you look at anything quietly, without trying to do anything about it or to think about it, you soon discover that you have a feeling about it—not enough feeling, perhaps, to make you tear your hair or look for your handkerchief, but a real feeling growing stronger and more individual and more subtly pleasant as you let it have its way. The kitten is playing on the lawn— running in circles with humped back and upright, spread tail, pursued by two enemies, its shadow and its tail. Look at it, relax—and laugh. A cloud passes over the sun. Sadness falls on you with the shadow. Let it fall, on your eyes, on your heart. It is chill but not unpleasant, like dew. The iris blooms in the garden. Your eyes follow it, tracing its lines, drinking in its color, which even when most brilliant has a ghostly and unearthly glow. There is a feeling of tranquillity barely rippling into pleasure. Such emotional responsiveness brings into the face and manner that play of feeling which is the secret of personal charm. Our usual emotional response to what we see is like jazz, monotonous and insistent. A little experiment will transform it to music.

There is a third lesson. Take one simple thing, the simpler the better, look at it for a long time, and ask yourself every possible question about it. When you have exhausted every question, leave it and try to find the answers. Then come back next day and look at the same thing again, repeating the process as long as patience lasts. This was the method of Agassiz. They say that he would place before a student at Wood's Hole a scrap of fishbone, without explanation or instruction. The student, having fooled with it a while, would finally ask what he was to do with it. Agassiz would say, "Look at it." The student would look and look. Finally he would go back to Agassiz. Agassiz would say, "Have you looked at it?" "Yes, till I could draw it in my sleep." Agassiz would say, "Look again." Day after day the student would have to look, staring down boredom and discouragement, staring till his eyes blurred and his head ached. The thing meant nothing to him. If at least he could know what kind of fish it came from!

Suddenly, when he had looked to exhaustion, there would come a flash of understanding. The shapeless scrap would take form. He would see a skeleton shaping itself around the bone. He would see a jaw-bone forming or a head. He would see the whole creature, and then its background, deep sea waters, and it scudding before other creatures that chased it, or tropical muddy waters, and reeds growing, and tigers coming down to drink. Then followed days of excitement while he verified each detail of the intuitive vision. He would see that the least fraction of this bone could belong only to one kind of creature leading one kind of life, and so the mystery of organic form and adaptation would slowly unfold. Perhaps only a certain kind of person is capable of looking thus to the point of intuitive vision. But many have reached this point in many kinds of observation. It is, they say, one of the high experiences of living.

5

All that many an American learns from such experiments is that an interval of quiet seeing winds up his nervous machinery and sets him going again. But he feels happier in the going, and if going is what he lives for, it is worth while to give it energy and direction. An American woman who tried the first experiment in what she took to be her clean, dusted, orderly, and beautiful living room spent the rest of the morning furiously moving the furniture, polishing the floor, and shopping for new curtains. But she thought she was having a good time. She next tried to look at things in her garden. She spent the next two days very cheerfully— cutting off dead flowers, trimming the grass borders, and moving the coreopsis plants out of sight of the pink phlox. When she was advised to try the woods, in the hope of finding a place she couldn't do anything to afterwards, she came home with shining eyes, with her arms full of mosses, plants, and vines which she distributed in vases. Such people are not made for the contemplative life. But, even for them, seeing makes the active life more entertaining.

The training of the eye leads to many forms of active self-amusement, highly recommended by all doctors of leisure. People who have had their eyes opened, sketch; paint; snap cameras; study insects, butterflies, fossils, or animals; build pools; start wild flower gardens; go on bird walks; buy microscopes; look through telescopes; haunt natural history museums; take summer school courses; join the Agassiz Association; study economics, sociology, or psychology; construct radio sets; stock aquariums; invent machines; make smoke prints of leaves; weave things of pine needles; make things of birch bark; and collect everything under heaven.

Of these amusements collecting is perhaps most widely appealing. Collecting re-enforces seeing with the acquisitive instinct and the combination is irresistible. A collector is one who would rather spend his money and his labor on something to look at than on something to eat, wear, or dance to. The value of a collector's article is fixed not by its usefulness, but by what the collector and others can see in it. Anything may be collected from diamonds to old nails. The typical collector is the stamp collector. Into a scrap of old paper, often poorly designed and badly colored, torn around the edges and defaced with government ink, a true collector can read a book full of history and geography. His stamps are windows into far off lands, and into the triumphs, heroism, and fads of nations. Thus through the power of the eye, the most devastating impulse of man, the impulse to grab, is turned into harmless, amusing and instructive channels. When the Golden Age comes again, all bankers, capitalists, racketeers, burglars, and alimony hunters will have become collectors.

To be a collector of things is good. To be a collector of experience is better. If the connoisseurs of experience have the gift of communication, they become the poets, the story-tellers, the artists. This is what poets and artists are for—to see something that the average man misses and to tell him about it. Then he can see it, too, and partake of their delight.

6

But beyond curiosity and the lust of the eye, beyond the impulses to do, to take, to talk, which are the first effects of increased seeing, there is another vision. It touches the greatest painting with a light which is not of the stars or the sun. It turns the greatest writing, in prose or in verse, to cadences of unearthly music. Yet many experience it who cannot put it on paper or on canvas. It is difficult to illustrate, for every experience of this sort is at once individual and evanescent. But suppose one has emerged from a night club at three o'clock in the morning, with a noisy and probably a foolish crowd. There is the din of jazz in one's ears, and smoke in one's head, and the hot mist of drinking on one's whole net-work of nerves. One is gay and idiotic, and seems to be suc-cessfully skirting some abyss that threatens to open beneath it all, bottomless and horrible. Then, for a second of time, between one noise and the next, one lifts one's eyes, and over the long gray chasms of the streets, over the twinkling towers, over all the vast, inert, slumbering city, over one's self on the curbstone, hailing a taxi, one sees the sailing moon. Only the moon—just another ball of rock and dirt like ours, circling futilely in space! Only the moon, and around her the sky, and beyond her the stars; but is not one happy, in that brief moment of seeing, happy in a high, pure, tranquil way?

Again one is having an altercation with a person one de-spises. One is enraged and humiliated. The viper—of all the despicable—Oh God! Oh God! how can such people live! Suddenly, and without warning, you see the worm before you as you might see him if he were sleeping, or if he were dead. He is comic. He is tragic. He is infinitely pitiable and unimportant. You are comic, yourself, and do not matter very much.

These moments of second sight are most impressive when they intrude thus on a disordered consciousness. But there are many who can evoke them in more normal moments. They raise their eyes to the sky. They look out of the window. They see a flower in a vase, or the face of a child. Even a trivial or ugly thing may fix the attention and the vision comes. Happy are those who can retreat at will to this strong-hold of the spirit; for in those moments you see as you would see if you were only an Infinite Eye.

The Lively Art of
Going Places—III

THE automobile age is full of people who move continually and go nowhere. Up and down the same road, round and round the same circuit, into the town and out of the town, back and forth to the same houses—like squirrels on a wheel, they are always on the move and never nearer to anything. Sometimes they go on long journeys and their mileage runs up enough figures to girdle the earth; but there is a roof over their heads all the way, and glass between them and the air, and when they stick their noses out, it is only to ascertain that around them are the same hotel walls, the same hotel verandas, and the very same golf course they left behind at the last place. People even go around the world, snugly oscillating between the steamer saloon and the hotel lounge in Hongkong, in Singapore, in Cairo, and never move except from their bridge table to the dining room and from the dining room to their beds. So they journey on a ship as we journey with the earth, which runs a strange course around the sun, but jogs no human nut out of his own shell.

Yet one may also travel a long distance, and cover little space. There was a business man in New York who used often to hop off by airplane to visit the branch office in Chicago. This was no journey at all. The office he went to was so much like the one he left that to move from one to the other was like closing one's eyes and opening them to see only that the secretary had moved the typewriter and the janitor emptied the waste basket. But one noon when he was walking back from his restaurant to his office—a distance of half a block—he passed a Catholic church. Now it happened that this man had never been in a Catholic church, having been brought up a Methodist and having, in recent years, dispensed with churches altogether. But he had a personal problem on his mind. He wanted a place to think where no one would find him and the telephone would not ring. It was very hot on the city street, and glaring. It looked cool in there. On an impulse he went in. In those few steps he travelled farther than Chicago. This incense flavored dimness, where the organ music vibrated against the vaulted roof and down the long chill aisles, where vested priests moved rhythmically to and fro, and candles twinkled against the sculptured faces of saints, was really a foreign country. Here was all that makes a land foreign: different climate, different smells, different lights and shadows, different people in different costumes going about a quite different business. He had travelled backward through centuries of time, and inward beyond space altogether. When he came out, he was astonished to see the street still sizzling and seething, and the same elevator man waiting to take him up to the same office. It seemed to him that he had been away for ages and ages—so long that all these things must have crumbled away, and a new world grown up in his absence.

When Thoreau heard merchants in Boston, in the great days of the China trade, talking of Canton and Bombay and the Sandwich Isles, he said, "*I have travelled a good deal in Concord.*" No man lives in a place so small that he could not spend a good life travelling in it. Once a man wrote a book entitled "The Next Street But One," describing the customs of a London tenement house district a block away from his own house. By the time he had recorded the slum language, superstitions, and social customs, it was as if he had told of a tribe in New Guinea. Lauren Gilfillan, the daring Smith College girl who recently visited the striking miners in Pennsylvania, at the risk of life, health, and virtue, could not have found more gaudy adventures among cannibals.

Probably each one of us could name twenty places within walking distance of his home or his office which, if he visited them, would be to him a foreign shore. There is the Dreamland Café by the roadside. John Doe, driving home at night after coaching the high school basketball team, often looks at it and listens to it and speculates. He and Dora haven't danced since they went to college together out west. Suppose he took her there? Suppose she wore an evening dress without a back, like those girls. Suppose—oh heavens—that she smoked a cigarette! And suppose, after all this supposing, that one night he did take Dora? Montmartre could do no more for him.

There are people whose sole idea in travelling is to visit all the Dreamland cafés which they don't go to at home. They seek out exact replicas of all that social opinion or "morality" or just habit denies them, and then they do it. Often this is good for them. But why pay the price of a steamship passage for it? Higher than tariff barriers between countries are the social barriers within countries. Not knowing another's language is not nearly so embarrassing as not knowing his manners. But a free and lively spirit may adventure even across these boundaries.

Any place is good to go, provided it isn't the place you are used to. When every other resource fails in life, there is still some place to go—down a different street, into a different restaurant, into a museum or a florist's shop, into a settlement house, to a Salvation Army street meeting, to a speakeasy, to a church supper. There are probably a hundred places we look at every day, and wonder what it would be like to visit them, and don't. Even in an empty Maine landscape there is that island out in the bay, and the haunted house on the shore. There is the grange hall which once a week at night springs into airy gaiety. Cars drive up. Music comes out of it. People come out of it, chattering in the night, along the lonely wood road. There is the country church, alone in a jungle of golden-rod, with a skunk-hole under it. Yet a preacher comes and preaches there every three weeks. There is Hardscrabble. The people there are peculiar. Their houses look lonely and unkempt. They eye you darkly. Dogs bark when you go near. The barren fields bear little but rocks and crags. There is the Lobster Pound. There is the crazy woman's hut on the edge of the marsh. How many places to go to—and why don't we go?

It is true that most of the places, that, unvisited, have an aura of romance, would prove tawdry and commonplace if we went into them. But this is true also of far distant lands and things famed in story or in romance. Once in a palace in Siam, looking out on marble porticoes and fountain-fed gardens, I wrote

> I journeyed twice to Singapore
>   And once to gold Siam.
> My travels show me more and more
>   Just what a fool I am—
> To put myself to toil and hurt
> To find the whole earth's made of dirt.

my sentiment exactly
m. J. R.

Yet after the shock of disillusionment, one discovers that the great advantage of going places is just that it does deliver us from the tyranny of dreams. For the dream world is a lonely one, and over it hangs, like the growing doom-shadow over Valhalla, the despair of desire which cannot, by its very nature, be realized. To take this hankering for what we have not, this charm that invests the place we have not been in, and whatever it is that we have not done, and then to go out resolutely to crash the gates is to see one's feet on a path which, if persisted in, leads at last through the wrecks of romance to wisdom and to peace. Sooner or later you seem to find whatever it is you were looking for, but what that is you may not know even in the end—you will only know that you have got it.

But to speak less cryptically, the fact is that beyond any threshold, there may always be the Big Surprise—the person or the event that will change the whole course of your life; and the more thresholds you try, especially in youth, the more you are likely to find it. Probably there are all sorts of things people miss—fortunes, heroic opportunity, glamorous brides —by just staying where they are instead of going somewhere else. But then, perhaps, they also miss disaster and sudden death.

2

Withal, there is something to be said just for locomotion. The capacity to move is the precious gift of the animal world, as distinguished from the plants that cannot move, of their own volition, from the place where they are rooted. But to move adequately one must be willing to leave one's own stage setting and properties behind. Those who insist on keeping just the same habits, on seeing just the same kind of people, and spreading about them just the same appurtenances of comfort they left behind are like the plants which will not live unless, in moving them, you take with them a large chunk of the dirt they were growing in before. Such people reduce themselves again to the condition of vegetables.

This, and this only, is the objection to the motor car. Next to the airplane it is the most marvelous invention of the most peripatetic of the animals. It gives you, as it were, a new body—so instinctively does it seem to respond to the least impulse. The experienced driver moves his car as automatically as he moves his own feet. Through it the American enters into possession of the vast land he has inherited. To us it is indispensable as horse and camel to the Arabs of the desert, as sail and keel to the dwellers upon the islands of the sea. The coursing about of Americans upon their highways is no different from the coursing of other peoples in older and smaller lands. One of the national characteristics which has made the Japanese so unified and so energetic a people is that they are always moving about and so really possess their own land and all the landmarks of their own civilization. School children are sent in hordes over the Empire to visit historical shrines. People pour out of the cities to see the cherry trees in bloom or the azalea upon the mountain side or the autumn leaves in the valleys where they are reddest. There is hardly a rock or a hill or a water-fall that has not been celebrated by some poet or artist as a place to go to, and everybody goes to it. Far into the night, in the loneliest place, you hear the endless scrape, scrape of the wooden clogs—of men, women, and children, going some-where.

The re-nationalization and revitalization of Germany after the war, which looks to us so dubious now, but seems to the people themselves something supremely worth while, was accomplished through setting a whole generation in motion, going from place to place over their own lands. "Youth-wandering" was a new religion in Germany. The moment they were released from school or work, they were to go somewhere—to set their packs on their backs and find some comrades and walk. Every little town had its youth shelters. Every one was in honor bound to look after the travelling children and to give them help. One saw them everywhere, camping in old castles, learning old dances from the peasants under the trees, solemnly filing through the cathedral at Cologne, the colored light from the great stained glass win-dows falling in rainbows on their eager, awe-struck faces. Whether all these young have now been betrayed through the very love of their own land they imbibed from its rocks and its woods and castle-crowned heights, and the ties of youthful companionship knit around camp fires—is quite another question. No one could see the youth-movement in the old days without feeling the marvelous regeneration of the individual involved in taking to his feet and going somewhere.

The American who would similarly possess his own enormous country must take to the motor car. The objection to much of the coursing about is that it is so purposeless and so continually over the same territory. The amount of time, gas, and wear on tires spent on useless going to town would really take us somewhere. The sense of locomotion is allowed to drug the impulse to explore and to experience. But these happy campers, these nomads with trailers, these crossers of the continent, these voyagers to Canada and to Florida are another matter. There are motor camps in the west which at evening have all the romance of a desert caravansary—the groups about their fires, the unfurling of tents, the visiting with strangers around the pump, the borrowing of tools, the consultations over road maps, the tales of the road.

To use a motor car for really going places, and not as a practical convenience only, one must pick places that are far away. For the nearest spots, the motor car can never equal the feet. For those a little farther, it cannot equal the canoe or the sail boat, the horse, or the bicycle. And even when it has taken one far away, one ought to re-enforce it with these more primitive appliances of motion. To become so car-bound that one cannot climb a crag or get a boat and row across a lake when the car has brought you to them is pathetic. This is the reason why hunting and fishing are so perennially appealing. One must leave the car and take to one's feet, and follow the trail of wild creatures to places where houses and furnaces, telephones and bath rooms are not. Really to go to a new place, one must discover it on all the primitive levels of sensation—bruise one's feet on its stones, tear one's flesh with its briars, build one's fire of its wood, cook what grows in its fields, and sleep only in the bed it provides.

3

When all is said, there is probably no vehicle that gives you so much for your mileage as your feet. Feet are good for any going except that whose only aim is to annihilate distance. Then anything that travels over four miles an hour is better. Feet are adjusted to our whole mechanism of sensation, of thought, and of feeling. They go just about fast enough to let you take in the whole scene without strain. They carry you along on the level with other men and above the heads of most animals—which is as it should be. They do not hold you so high that you cannot stoop to pick a flower or a strawberry. The energy necessary to move them, and the regular and rhythmical operation of putting one foot before the other, sets the blood to pumping easily and strongly, and so clears the mind and releases that mysterious happiness that comes with the harmonious functioning of the organic life. They will take you where automobiles will not go, and up heights where a Mexican burro would stumble. Anyone who walks over ground which he customarily covers by motor car will have the sensation one has when one sees a familiar object through a microscope. Every square yard of space has a thousand times as many things in it. Every thing is clearer, sharper, rounder, and yet more mysteriously interesting. There is, too, the complex of smells and temperatures, and the exposure to climate. To walk into the rain or the snow, to beat against the wind, is in itself to go somewhere, for rain and snow and wind make each its own world, and to him who fronts them bravely the elements are always friendly. Each sends him back to the tepid climate of his indoor world with its own gift to his spirit—with the peace of the falling snow on his heart, or the wild force of the wind in his purposes.

All that feet still mean in the motor age may be illustrated by two ways of visiting Crawford Notch in the White Mountains. You may, if you are a prosperous business man, drive up nicely in a closed car. Beautiful and serene the mountains will rise, tier on tier in your sight. The loneliness and the sunny quiet will reach you even through the wind-shield, as if from a picture, and sometimes through the open window the breath of mountain torrents and the scent of balsam. You will drive up to the great hotel. You will bathe and dress and sit on the veranda, or probably, finding the mountain air a little chill, in the lobby looking out through the great windows on the mountains. You may even walk a little up the neat paths leading nowhere in particular, but edged with woods and winding gently upward, coming back soon because the mosquitoes bite you, and the kind of dress one wears in a hotel does not suit the woods. So you sit down again, and watch the quiet people move quietly about. They do not speak to you, nor you to them. It is as if all were pictures in a still enchanted world. Outside the motor cars move along the road, but they are quiet, too, at that distance, and even the little railroad station and the train stopping at it are like an old colored print. You seem as one pleasantly dead, and sealed in a glass coffin and drowsing there through all eternity. Through the glass you see the mountains and dimly wonder what they are really like, and what the world would look like from that peak. But you have no feet and no wind, only wealth and clothes and a motor car, and so you stay restfully there where you are, and come to for half an hour at meals, and then go back to the veranda and sit. This is the way many a person spends a vacation in the White Mountains.

But suppose you are two college boys without a motor car and without money, but with curiosity and with feet. You stand on the spacious floor of Crawford Notch some tingling August morning and watch the dawn break like a reveillé across the ranges. Through the cool forest you climb for a few hundred feet and see with awe the bare walls of rock rising above you. Up the rocks you go on hands and feet, pausing at each crevice for breath. You strike a gulch. You scramble out and into a stunted forest. Six hundred feet up and you step off breathless on the Webster Cliff trail. You rest half an hour in a forest of balsam scrub. Then up again. You reach the top of the mountain at noon. You lie there all afternoon, dozing and talking, till in the sunset the great peak of Mount Wiley towers tall and menacing. Below in a tiny world automobiles become fire-flies and the train crawls into the station like a phosphorescent worm. Down you dive into the spruce and balsam silence of Webster Jackson Col. In the darkness you come to a shelter. You sleep there the sleep of the just, save when the owls wake you hooting from tree to tree, and a porcupine scratches at your window. Off at dawn. Lunch on the uppermost ledges of Mount Franklin, with the virgin forests of the Ammonoosuc Valley stretching out below. Shifting to the North, you follow the cold gusts of wind as they play in ripples over the tawny, grass grown slopes ahead, and swirl in eddies about the outcrops of granite. On you go, over the tops of the world, meeting a hut-master whose form detaches itself from the fogs like a ghost with a spectral black cat riding atop his high pack. On and on, and up Mount Washington, and there you find a little city in the clouds, "incredible and beautiful." So Robert Freeman, an eighteen-year-old boy, reports his adventures in the July, 1934, number of *Leisure*—"Along the New Hampshire Timberline."

4

And this brings us to one of the melancholy facts observed long ago by the author of the "Anatomy of Melancholy." The rich man, he says, cannot travel. The poor man may jog along from land to land, and everywhere be at home according to the custom of the country. He eats with the people at their board. He works with them if he has to, pitching their hay, feeding their hogs. He gets some skill with their weapons, and learns their cuss-words for the men and their love-songs for the ladies. But the rich man can only ride in his own coach, with his own servants, and his own outriders, and must everywhere be met and entertained and stared at and have his own kind of food prepared for him and his own bed spread with his own sheets. And so he never sees any country. He only sees the noise and the dust that he himself raises.

So if one has wealth, one must lay it by when one goes places. All wealth and fame are good for is now and then to get one a pass into fantastic and curious experiences, denied to the average (audiences with kings, dinners in castles, liquor in a night club). For this purpose it is good, and should be used to the limit. To be sure, after a long course of adaptation to new food and other people, the comforts one is used to assume a prodigious importance. One aches for the dear bath, and sickens with such nostalgia as the Englishman in India feels when he hears the popular songs of London. They are city. They are home. They were "all that ever went with evening dress". Then is the time to take these things for what they are good for—for a rest, a change; to take them in their most extreme and luxurious form; to bask in them and sleep in them and pose in them in one's best clothes, and dissipate in them till the whole soul cries out—as it will very soon—for the fresh air and the open road. If I had only enough money to travel comfortably and decently abroad in a middle-class way, I should save most of it and "bum" it, rattling along third class, eating snacks by the roadside, sampling black bread or macaroni or raw fish or resin wine or whatever the place offered. Then I should take what I had saved and blow it in periodically in a stay at some gorgeous place on the Lido, or the Riviera, or in Cook's hotel in Luxor. By such means you get all the lights and shades of life. But even so, I should never, never, never take a motor car in the desert, but a donkey or an Arabian steed or a camel. And I wouldn't hire a motor boat on the Grand Canal—not while there are house-boats in China.

5

But there is still the principal reason why people don't go places. They have no one to go with. To think that one must carry a friend with one is like the American's superstition that he must carry his plumbing. The best way to go places is to go alone. The friends you left behind you are all right, but there are always other friends over the horizon. If you do not believe that, you are no traveler. To know that you will find friends, and to be ready to make them, without benefit of introduction or fear of seduction, is the final mark of the true traveler. Believe it or not—but savages in the jungle are quite likely to be honest; bandits in the mountain are often kind; and a lady may travel a long distance with a gentleman she has struck up an acquaintance with, and never lose her virtue. It is true that the worst people are out there, on the highways of life, but so, too, are the best; and it is amazing how fast you learn to tell the difference. The traveler who has learned to taste any drink once, but not too many of them twice, is not the one who most needs prohibition.

The greatest lovers of men have been great wayfarers. It was the immortal vagabondage along the sunny roads of Palestine that taught the western world a new meaning for the word love. Buddha, though born a prince, made the way of the redeemed the way of the humble traveller, sending out his monks with begging bowls to get their food from house to house as they went along—an admirable device which the Christian religion later borrowed. Saint Francis, wandering ceaselessly up and down Italy, to the Holy Land and back again, found that all men were his brothers, and not men only but the beasts and the birds and even the sun and the stars. The lonely and the people who have no one to go places with are the very ones that should go. The world is so full of people that sooner or later, if you circulate in it, you are certain to find those who are for you.

The Preposterous Art of
Self-Indulgence—IV

ONE of the difficulties
for the restless modern soul is that altruism has been overdone. We have been told to love our neighbor, and to love
God, without being told what to love them with—which is
an harmonious, healthy, and well developed self. As Emerson
said, "No society can ever be as large as one man. He, in
his friendship, in his natural and momentary associations,
doubles or multiplies himself, but in the hour in which he
mortgages himself to two or ten or twenty, he dwarfs himself below the stature of one."

If every individual person were a free, self-directed, self-
sufficing, contented, and happy person, knowing what he
needed to make life good for himself, and with sufficient
skill and energy to get it, society would take care of itself.
Indeed some very good societies have been built on an ideal
of loving which never got far beyond intelligent selfishness.
To the Greeks and the Chinese, in the hey-day of their civilizations, a man's principal business in life was himself. His
first aim was to be healthy, and his next to be handsome,
and his third to be as rich as was convenient. "Give me beauty
in the inward man," was the prayer of Socrates, "and let the
outward and the inward man be at one. Give me such a
quantity of gold as a sensible man, and he alone, can bear
and carry." The ideal may need supplementing, but it is a
wholesome one to start with.

Every one of us is romantically in love with his own dear
ego. It is a love as deep as life itself. It cannot be safely denied
or repressed. Released and given its due outlet in self-enhanc-

47

ing, self-glorifying, and self-improving activities, it leaves a place for other and greater loves. Ignored and suppressed, it becomes a source of infection in the spirit, poisoning all other loves and warping them into complex forms of selfishness.

The first expression of this love is a caressing interest in one's own body. The child loves to play with himself. He gurgles with interest in his own ten toes. Sucking his thumb tastes good to him. The normal expression of this interest among all living creatures is in self-preening and self-grooming. All the higher creatures are for ever licking and setting themselves in order. It not only gives them comfort and keeps them healthy and beautiful; it satisfies some deep instinct of self love, of caressing affection directed to themselves.

Some grown-up people are ashamed to be as clean as the animals. They pretend to resent the time it takes to bathe and groom themselves. The shame is very foolish, and fundamentally insincere. Where there is a sense of irksomeness, it is merely the frustration of a normal love. If they were honest, they would admit that they thoroughly enjoy the moments of self-preening. They are rested and exhilarated thereby, and set up in their own estimation. The lady who has satisfied herself with a long perfumed bath, and all the mysteries of powder and lipstick and wave-setting and putting beautiful soft silks over her own beautiful soft skin goes forth really ready to forget herself, to be happy in the society of other people. One of the peculiar modern repressions of men, who are greater pretenders than women in these matters, is that they are ashamed of those processes by which the more ornamental males of other civilizations used to make themselves cocks of the walk. The result is that they drink and tell dirty stories, in the dear safe company of their own sex, when they ought to be strutting up and down in a velvet coat and scarlet stockings, strumming a guitar under some lady's window.

Recently some business women devoted several sessions of a club to a study of leisure. Of the eight departments into which they agreed to fit their spare time activities, one of them caused great amusement. But it was the most popular. It was entitled Super-Personal Care! In a recent magazine article a bright Beauty Editor undertook to tell the business girl what to do with a summer week-end when an invitation to a house-party was suddenly called off, and she had nowhere to go, and no one to go with. She should spend two blissful days sleeping late, getting a massage and a shampoo and a curl, taking a dancing lesson, buying some new lingerie or putting what she had in order, and luxuriating slowly through a Turkish bath. If we were doing this, we should add one or two hours in which we spread ourselves on the couch in a handsome negligee, and read about some ravishing female who conquered every heart in sight. Such orgies of self-indulgence are good for every one. They relieve a basic urge and help make one an addition to the social landscape.

Some people transfer this primitive sensuousness of bodily self-love to others—women in dressing up their children, perhaps; men in maintaining a lady for the sole purpose of wearing silks and diamonds. This looks unselfish, but it isn't. We have no right to expect other people to do our living for us. This kind of unselfishness is thieving. It is stealing another's life, and using it as if it were our own. Some people think they have rooted out such self-love entirely and substituted for it higher things. But they only change self-love into some more disagreeable and dominating form. Either they demand from other people appreciation, attention, or adulation, to make up for the attention they aren't giving themselves, and insist on it being doubled, trebled, and indefinitely multiplied; or they become self-conscious and jealous; or they fall into some ugly form of self-pampering, like eating too much. The fact is that there is a certain amount of physical self-love that can be safely used only in making ourselves handsome animals, and purring contentedly in the process. Used in this way, it is harmless, quickly satisfied, and generally ornamental. Suppressed or diverted, it spreads like a poisonous gas among all the other expressions of the personality, corrupting and blighting.

2

Another form of self-love, scarcely more heroic than the love of one's own body, is the impulse to show off. We think so well of the marvelous self that we are determined to advertise it. The only thing to do with this is to develop a self worth showing. To talk well or dance well or have some amusing "stunts" up one's sleeve is to keep the gyrations of the ego from being a pain to other people—at least within reasonable limits; for no one can stand seeing other people show off to the point of not being able equally to show off himself. This is the value of social accomplishments, and of skills in all the social games. When you beat your opponent at bridge or golf, you show how bright you are. It is true that many people waste in petty skills the energy and desire to display themselves which might lead to larger and more useful accomplishment. But almost all the really great and useful work of the world must be done by those whose motive in doing it is other than showing off. The big show-offs of history and art, like Napoleon or Byron, rendered their immense talents sterile by a vanity which should have been harmlessly discharged in small ways. The best thing to do with the impulse to show off is to get rid of it in social display that is at once idle and entertaining. Every one should acquire sufficient means of self-display, in personal accomplishments, social games, attractive dress and appurtenances to use to the full his own individual endowment of vanity.

Those who, being unable to show off adequately, feel themselves left out and neglected in a world largely inhabited by bright and beautiful beings who can do all the things they can't (and this is what the world looks like to the inferiority complex) may well spend their spare time learning anything that looks attractive in other people. Take the first person who inspires you with that hopeless feeling, "Oh if I were only like So-and-So," and list all the things that this human marvel does and you don't. Then set yourself to acquiring the nearest equivalent. In the large cities institutions like the Y.W.C.A. and the Y.M.C.A. now offer for small fees means of learning almost anything that makes life worth living. In the small towns, these things are learned individually by quietly joining in with whatever is going on—sports, public dances, plays—and keeping one's eyes open and imitating one's betters. The desire to show off which, when unsatisfied, seems unlimited and fills all the consciousness, may be quickly contented with very small and simple activities. Two or three people among whom you can shine in some sport like bridge or tennis, a dancing class once a week in which you are doing rather well, or a part in a play will keep the ego quiet for months.

In this era of national advertising the wish to show off is constantly diverted by full page displays in magazines to the acquisition of things rather than of personal accomplishments and skills. Your guests are not to admire *you*, but your new draperies or the ice-box in the kitchen. When you feed them, it is not your culinary skill they will praise, but the mustard or the ketchup in the bottle. We are to abdicate the privilege of being handsome, amusing, clever, and charming persons in favor of piling up a lot of material junk. The difference between displaying one's self in skills and accomplishments and displaying things is that in the first case the psychic energy is really used and comes to a full stop in satisfaction. In the second case it is not used, and so goes on hankering for more and more. By the time you have played through a set of tennis brilliantly or sung a song beautifully, you have spent the force of your desire. It is like a drama which comes to its climax and denouement, and ends in peace.

But in showing off *things* there is no effort, no climax—and no end.

Discharged harmlessly, in social display, the impulse to show off adds much to the gaiety of life. But suppressed and diverted it becomes a dangerous social force, with almost unlimited potentialities of evil. For all natural forms of life have their limits. They grow to a pre-determined pattern; they reach the climax of vitality; and they die. But there is something in human energy like the infinite capacity for increase in cancer, which grows and grows, destroying all that comes in its way, yet having no form or function or inherent character to correspond to its vitality—just organic chaos. So the worst showing off is not among those feeble ones who cultivate fake illnesses or "sensitive souls," or queer manners, to attract attention. It is the perversion of public business and government and activities on which the life and welfare of millions depend. Battle, murder, and sudden death have followed in the wake of some of the great show-offs of history who have, at various times, seized the governments of great peoples and with the energy not of ability and insight, but of emotional eruptions, have imposed themselves on the body politic. A universal epidemic of showing off was largely responsible for the depression. Industrial plants, banking activities, office buildings, executive forces were expanded far beyond what the genuine industrial and trade activity warranted in order that each corporation might look bigger and better than its neighbors. There is not a single public activity that is not corrupted to its soul by those who want not to do what is necessary or useful, or even profitable to themselves, but just to show off—to have their pictures in the papers, to make speeches at banquets, to be known as the promoter of something or other.

For the individual, the itch to show off takes the joy out of all genuine activity; for nothing he gets comes up to his gaudy expectations. Everywhere there are the miserable victims of "blah"—business men making a reasonable income for their families, but feeling themselves failures because they aren't multi-millionaires and wasting the means of comfort in trying to make everybody believe they are getting rich; authors and artists with sincere and devoted followings, suffering because they aren't the season's "best-sellers" or the "great popular success of the day"; women with charming homes and many friends, scanning social columns and wretched because their names aren't there. Real work and real love aren't things to show off with. They are their own exceeding great reward. What we need is to take the gas and hot air out of the real business of living, and send it sizzling off in sky-rockets for the entertainment of our idle hours.

3

A third form of self-love is a hang-over from babyhood. It is the longing for a Papa or a Mamma to love us, and take care of us, and give us everything we need. When we look for Mamma or Papa in the friend or the lover or the boss, we are looking in the wrong place. The only person who is going to love you in that way is yourself. The sooner one settles down to being one's own guardian, guide, and provider, the happier one will be. There are some people whose whole conception of love is imagining what the dear beloved can do for them, and then winning it by blandishments or demanding it as a right or as the price of affection in return. And there are some people so weak as to fall for this emotional bulldozing because, in showing kindness or giving help, they have a chance to show off. Sometimes we like to have other people be babies in relation to us because we can then show how big, and strong, and generous we are. But when some one who wants a Papa meets some one who wants to show off as Papa, the relation is bound to be disappointing to both. It is better to be Papa to one's self.

"Nobody to love me," croons the radio singer. None to love you, poor soul? What is the matter with you? Love yourself. Take whatever it is that the dear, darling, kind, loving person would do for you, and do it for yourself. What you want is not really love. It is only Mamma.

The Serene Art of
Meditation—V

WHEN I was a guest of the Hindu poet, Rabindranath Tagore, in the serene little oasis of Shantiniketan, India, I used to look across the level fields at dawn, and see on the balcony of the two-storied stucco house, occupied by the poet himself, a scene which always touched me. It was the poet seated in meditation under the paling stars, his beautiful head, with its smooth long white locks, outlined against the Indian sky as it flared into sunrise. Every morning he would sit there, in perfect stillness, while dark burst into light and the stars were blown out as by a wind, and over the tawny levels of earth rolled the molten flood of the tropical day.

There was nothing special or affected in this, for meditation is part of the cultivated Hindu's technique of life. To the Hindu it is as indispensable as the morning bath to the Englishman—a putting in order of the house of life for the day, a removal of the clutter of the previous day's experience, a mental dusting and emotional washing, and a securing within the consciousness of all that the spirit wishes to keep. Rabindranath's father, Devendranath, during the happy days he spent alone on the slopes of the Himalayas, used to meditate so all the morning, legs folded under him in the immemorial attitude of Eastern meditation, perfectly relaxed and still. So Buddha, long ago, meditated under the Bo-tree, while the forces of Maya, the evil one, taking successively the shapes of the many-formed fascinations of the world, raged around him. One after another he examined and let go the various solutions which worldly wisdom and religious asceticism had offered to the mystery of existence, till, in the moment which was ever afterward called the great illumination, there came to him what he knew to be the truth.

No doubt there are many truths in life, and millions have lived and died happily without Buddha's truth, having found some other truth of their own. But millions have been happier, too, because of that illumination, as anyone who has lived in the beautiful Buddhist lands of Siam or Burma can testify. And something there is in this serene art of meditation which might well be taken over by the restless Americans of to-day.

2

The habit of setting apart some hour for putting the inner house in order has prevailed among Christians, too, though our anthropomorphic imagination has usually associated it with prayer or the reading of the Bible, or the ceremonies of the Catholic Church. In the childhood of our parents, little evangelical Christians were taught to retire to their "closets" once a day, and more often when they were unhappy or morally confused, to read their Bibles and meditate and pray. This was but the externalization of what the Hindu achieves by meditation. One turned one's thoughts into words. One achieved a conversation with a listener infinitely wise and sympathetic and good. One read words so ancient, so beautiful, and so removed from the immediate associations of one's life, that they could be shaped into the purely personal language of the heart, like music. In Catholic lands, like Mexico or rural France, one still finds in every household a corner for such meditation. It may be a separate chapel, gaudy with candles and gilt. Or it may be only a rude table in the corner of the peasant's one-room hut, with a vase of flowers on it, and a lace doily, and above it a chromo of Christ or of the Virgin Mary.

That any practical, free-thinking, or Protestant American

should adopt in toto any one of the beautiful old methods of meditation is not to be expected. But we must find our own way to the same end. Surely there is time in the day for inner bathing and setting to rights. Uncontrolled and unattended to, the inner state of many externally well poised moderns is chaotic—a confusion of undigested experiences, a tangle of memories, a cellar full of smothered wishes, noisome and unventilated. There are divided purposes and broken resolutions. There are a hundred half-finished thoughts, unadmitted repugnances, undefined desires. There is a vast collection of moral and intellectual junk—left-overs of childhood teachings, neglected but not definitely discarded, mixed with new attitudes toward life, toward sex, toward economics, vaguely entertained but not really appraised or accepted. Like broken toys, kicking around in all the corners of the consciousness, are childish attitudes and feelings. There is wounded and festering love, disabled ambition, and blind fear. Worry lives in the rafters like a bat, spreading its stench over all; and through the darkness and the dust, fear flies like a ghoul. William Blake imagined the most horrible end of the last Judgment to be a man handed over, not to Satan, not to the fires of Hell, but—to *himself.*

Almost all education and all moral teaching show us only how to put a smooth front on the confusion within. This makes for disappointments in social contacts. How often is a man attracted to one of these pretty girls who is the dream of the fashion sheet, so cool, so poised, so chic. But coming close to her does he find warm sweet rhythms of womanly feeling and sensations, grace of womanly fancy, upspringing wells of girlish joy? Quite the contrary! All is dead, flat, trivial, unfinished. How often the brave he-man, bold, confident, impeccable, turns out to be, on closer view, a petulant, greedy boy, or a crude brute. Plenty of people who are washed, shaved, and de-odorized to within an inch of their lives, nevertheless have emotional halitosis and mental B. O.

To take time to put one's self emotionally and mentally

in order, to orient the little world of ourselves to the vast area which is not ourselves, to enjoy one's memories and perfect one's hopes, to take up now and then one half-baked thought and really finish it—this, too, is an art. It is an art which, faithfully pursued till one gets the way of it leads not only to immediate serenity but to harmony in the day's work and unity in one's purposes. Even in its lowest form, when meditation is no more than that stream of animal reverie which the cow enjoys as she lies in the clover, there is a world of harmless delight in one's own society.

Probably one reason for the decay of meditation is that the former conceptions of the mental life were too narrow, and a mistaken effort to impose the will and the ideas of traditional morality and religion upon the rich efflorescence of fantasy and creature desire led to exhaustion and barrenness. There was a state of mind which the monks used to be much afraid of—the dreaded *accidia*, which might be called the occupational disease of the contemplative life. Accidia seems to have been a state of inertia and emotional depression —a bleak lack of interest in anything around, and a suspension of religious faith verging on despair. It was the extreme of what psychologists call repression. The long periods of meditation and prayer were used too exclusively to kill off sexual reverie and egoistic hankerings. In many this pruning, instead of stimulating the flowerlike opening of thought and feeling heavenward, which all the contemplatives desired and some achieved, only killed the roots. Similarly, among the evangelical Protestants, there was a vulgarization of the experience which has sometimes come with meditation—a secret ecstasy of discovery, a reconciliation of the restless self to all that is not the self. This experience is always special and personal and takes many forms. But among the evangelicals, it was identified with conversion to their particular Gods, and made a public matter. People were hounded to know whether in their closet, alone, they had "found Jesus" —as if this could possibly be any one else's business.

To restore meditation to its proper place in a modern life, one must throw out some of the old religious furniture, and arrange one's inner house in accordance with truer spiritual tastes and wiser ideas of psychic sanitation. Much of the old furniture must be good, and piece by piece one may even set it back, as one repolishes grandfather's clock, and cherishes the old china. That there is a seeking now for some new art of contemplation, some control of the inner life, is evident from the popularity of such books as "The Fountain" and Powys' "Philosophy of Solitude". We are tired of racketing around and living outside of ourselves. We are tired of putting a million dollar front on emotional slums. Many a soul, rushing hither and thither on the new currents of thought, grasping at psycho-analysis, experimenting with sexual relations, picking up new ideas about economics or sociology, running after this new prophet, reading that out-line of the old philosophies, is really seeking something that must be evolved from within. What one really wants is, as Powys says, "a conscious habit of thought by which the soul gathers itself together, cleanses itself, governs itself, steers itself and copes as well as it may with all the pleasant and unpleasant impacts of the vast impinging Not-self."

3

Meditation is so old an art, and has been so widely prac-ticed that there are as many rules for it as for writing poetry. Some of these are rather quaint, and many of them do not suit us now. But there are also, in modern exhortations to the good life, even in such unlikely places as books on sales-manship, a much larger number of suggestions about the renewal of this old art than any one would suppose. Some of these are amusing, some of them are crude; but they show that even business is obscurely aware that man does not live by tooth paste and intestinal emollients alone.

A complete series of rules for the novice in this great art

is offered by the Hindu Yoga. One who has lived in the East may appreciate the good sense and observation represented in the various physiological and dietary conditions of serene thinking, as set forth by the Oriental specialists, without trying to make too heroic a change in one's own habits. The primary rule is that one cannot meditate on an over-loaded stomach; that to eat more than you need is to befoul the mind; and that fruits, whole grains, and vegetables are better for the spirit than meat, pastry, and beer. This is all good sense, and western dietary wisdom approves it. Avoid autointoxication, honor vitamins and the "protective diet," and cultivate moderation in all things; bask in the sunshine, and now and then put your muscles and your breathing apparatus to a little use—what is this but a new lingo for the old wisdom?

It is pleasant to add that some contemplatives of the East appreciate the more airy indulgences of the senses. Tea was discovered by a Buddhist monk. They say that a monk who could not stay awake and think of Nirvana cut off his eyelids, and cast them on the ground. Where they fell, a plant grew up whose leaves, when brewed in hot water, kept meditation from turning into sleep. However this may be, the monasteries received tea as a gift from heaven; and in the tea-ceremony of Japan we find tea-drinking assuming a ritualistic significance. In some places, tobacco has also been admitted as conducive to a mood of peace. I have seen an old Buddhist abbot at Buddha Gaya, one of those good old men whose faces are scribbled over with nice feelings and benevolent reactions to life, seated in the sunshine on the monastery roof wrapped in his yellow robe and smoking his long-stemmed water-pipe, serenely thinking.

A more exotic detail for Americans is the physical attitude of meditation as set forth by the wise men of the East. According to them one must assume an attitude somewhat like that of the seated Buddha, legs folded, spine easily supporting the body, limbs perfectly relaxed, but life coursing full and warm along the backbone. This attitude is obviously a physiological achievement, and gives poise and rhythm to the body in all the motions of life. Such relaxation of muscular activity and tension, combined with the stimulating poise of the spine, might well lead to a superior state of mind. But one can only wonder and admire and despair of training the American combination of bone and muscle and electric nerves to anything like that. Who could tuck legs in trousers under him with that rubbery ease? Nevertheless, there is much to be said for acquiring, through continual practice, the art of conscious physical relaxation. How difficult a discipline this is, is shown in the popular book by a physician, entitled "You Must Relax." Relax! We would rather jump through hoops.

The beauty of these old rituals of bodily position is that they have a kind of poetry. They make an appeal to the imagination that is lacking in the flat utilitarianism of the good doctor's lessons in relaxing. It might be a happy experiment to set an image of the Kamakura Buddha up before one for inspiration, and try, day after day, to discipline our harried bodies to serenity of nerve and muscle, putting to sleep the impulses to do, to run, to jump, and finding instead a mind serenely and gloriously awake.

A third point which is important to the teachers of Yoga is control of breathing. What they say is elaborate and subtle. But who needs convincing? Take the fresh air of heaven into your lungs by all means, but learn to make the most of it. Neither wine nor smoke can do half as much for the nerves or be one hundredth part as precious.

For westerners the physiological conditions of meditation are often found in a lonely walk, especially in the country. Graham Wallis found that thought came most readily "through the slow ascent of wooded hills on a sunny day." Nietzsche believed that all exciting and enlarging ideas came into men's heads in the process of walking. Jastrow remarks that "Thinkers have at all times resorted to the restful inspiration of a walk in the woods or a stroll over hill and dale." Sydney Greenbie, in an editorial in *Leisure* magazine, makes the novel suggestion that, for the American, there is inspiration to meditation in the regular rhythm of his own machinery for getting somewhere, and in the use of those spare moments which our methods of locomotion leave us between one mad dash and the next.

"What can be done with the innumerable hours spent by millions of people in that unavoidable game of waiting? Waiting for some one to keep an appointment. Waiting for a train. Waiting to get there. Long rides on trains, on busses, on street cars, in taxis. . . . We hear much about having an honest dollar. We hear more about not wasting electricity through poor lamps. We hear still more about insulating your home against leakage of heat in bitter winters. But one doesn't hear anything about this leakage of time from out a poor man's short span of three score and ten. . . . Even getting to and fro from the golf course or the concert or the library gnaws half the cheese of good life from you as by some monstrous rodent.

"What then is to be done about it? Don't try to crowd more activity into it. Don't ruin your eyes trying to read on a jogging train. You can't play cards or even solve crossword puzzles with great satisfaction amidst moving crowds. What can be done? Meditate."

But to him as to Walt Whitman and Vachel Lindsay, mechanics are no bar to contemplation. "Don't try to meditate as a religious mystic," he says, "or as an oriental swami. Meditate as an American. Let the rhythm of the train take hold of you. Feel yourself carried on by this great force. Meditate as a bird, when you are in an airplane. You'll get the swing and billowy ease of the air." In the soft, enfolding embrace of our machine civilization, he says, there is also peace—"if we will put ourselves in tune with our own age and with the advancement our own spirit gives us."

4

So much for the conditions of meditation. What of the method? One may disregard esoteric practices such as the contemplation of one's own navel, or the repetition of the all-meaning *Om*, or fixation on abstract ideas like God, infinity, eternity. One may even disregard the kindly practice of Yoga, so appealing to some modern sponsors of New Thought— the practice of letting the sentiment of love flow out to all things, animate and inanimate, caressing each image that comes to one's mind, seeing it as it might be to itself, infinitely important, and, in the great scheme of things, infinitely good. There is something beautiful in this, and healing; for love is the basic human emotion and to release love is to cure much. But for the novice in meditation it is premature. It leads to sugary blandness of feeling, and an uncritical acceptance of much in this world that ought to remain, to an honest soul, quite unacceptable.

But one of the teachers of Yoga does make a suggestion which puts no strain on the unregenerate. He suggests that meditation should begin with a review of all the events and emotions, the personal encounters, the passing moods, of the preceding twenty-four hours, beginning with the last and proceeding backwards, swimming up the stream of memory. In doing this make no effort to pass a moral judgment on your own behavior or on any one else's. Lay aside judgment. And do not ask whether this or that procedure on your part would have been more worldly wise; do not stray off on speculations about money or things or business relations with people, wondering whether you will sell the house, or whether your stock will go up in the market or what Mr. Blank meant by that remark. All these are for some other time. Lay them aside, and just try to remember what happened, looking at it as if it had happened to some one else, gazing down on it as on a street scene from an airplane.

From this point the meditation of Yoga leads home to Brahma. No doubt all roads lead to Brahma, by whatever name one chooses to designate that august Finality. But for the American, untried in these spiritual peregrinations, the road home may be a long way around. So one must, perhaps, take leave of Yoga here, and borrow something from the new psychology which is now known to everybody.

When one has surveyed calmly the stream of one's recent experiences one finds many emotional snags. There will be things you don't like to think about, for no reason at all, inexplicable embarrassments, an unwillingness to proceed in this or that direction, and through it all, like the discomfort of bad weather, threads that general tension and worry which is our modern substitute for the old sense of sin. Apparently no one was ever comfortable with himself till he had got rid of something in his psyche. If we no longer cast our burdens on the Lord, we have to find something else to do with them. It is here that the new psychology steps in with what appears to be a magic.

If you look at anything that bothers you, you soon find that the trouble is something else, probably trivial, often absurd. Once you get it out and look at it, it may even disappear in a laugh. There is no need here to enter into all the Freudian paradoxes such as the fact that when we think we hate some one we really sub-consciously love him, or what we think we desire intensely we really fear. There are simpler difficulties which most of us encounter every day. One is the peculiarly shamed feeling which comes sometimes with trivial disappointments. If we look at them honestly, we find that what happened was all right, even perhaps rather pleasing. But we had allowed ourselves to build up beforehand false and romantic expectations, especially expectations which enhanced our own importance. Once one detaches the feeling of shame or outrage or antagonism from the person or event involved, and puts it on the foolish expectations, everything clears up. Again there is the discomfort of social poses which are contrary to your own real convictions. Sometimes you try to appear better than you are, or sometimes worse, which is what Huck Finn meant when he said you never could suit your conscience. Whatever you did, you were bound to feel "mean" afterwards. Sex has a way of affecting modern consciences like that. And, of course, there are the snarls of feeling which we call "complexes," when a new experience finds a lot of old memories lying around and gets all wound up in them. Then there is "rationalizing," which means finding some "good" reason for doing what you want to do. Since every one is now a psychologist, more or less, and knows all the jargon and has been introduced to all the ideas, one may profitably, in moments of meditation, go over the recent adventures of the ego and, stripping them of exaggerated emotion and social vanity, judge them in the dry light of this teaching. For the most curious fact noted by Freud, and confirmed by nearly every one who experiments with the psyche, even by the veriest amateur, is that a tremendous uproar of emotion, monstrous fears, passionate anger or shame, may be caused by childish memories or ideas which one does not admit to one's self. They are like those specks of dust in the eye, which feel like rocks and blind to agony, and yet seem, when removed, to be nothing at all. When once the psychic speck is located and looked at, there is a great relaxation and sense of peace.

Probably not every one, even after reading the many popular books on psychology, can thus analyze himself in moments of meditation. But to learn to do so offers one method of putting the inner house in order. Some of the virtues which the saints arrived at by fasting and prayer come more easily with really candid appraisal of the gyrations of that pretentious human animal—one's self. We learn to confess meekly our share in the sexual yearnings and egoistic hankerings of all organic life. We perceive that the universe is much larger and much more various than the vale of tears

through which the soul used to travel. All this should lead
to humility and to peace.

5

Yet it must be admitted that modern psychology by itself
is rather bleak. It is an incomparable cathartic, but when it
has done its work, one needs some real nourishment. Then
one must reach out to philosophy or to religion, which is
only philosophy incarnated and made humanly lovable.

There are philosophical attitudes which almost every
thoughtful person rediscovers for himself, such as the attempt
to see through the eyes of the other fellow, which is the
beginning of ethics. After seeing the stream of recent events
in perspective, after stripping yourself as naked as you dare,
it is interesting to go through every personal encounter and
see it as it must have appeared to the other person, another
confused and greedy ego, just like you. Again you might try
to see everything with the long view of time and space.
Suppose you were a spectator on the moon, looking down on
yourself! Imagine yourself a year hence looking back at to-day.
Or suppose, as Kant suggested, that your will were the will
of the universe. What would happen to the universe? Travel
down any road of speculation wherever it leads, provided
only that it takes you away from yourself and the immediate
pin pricks of existence.

In such thinking there is much to be avoided. Don't try
to justify yourself. You may have been right; but how much
does it matter? Don't try to solve immediate personal problems. Leave that for the time when you return to the hurly-
burly of action. Dismiss from your mind every human audience. Suppose that your wife does think this, and your mother
that, and the boss never agrees. Forget it. This is your divorce
and your vacation. One of the greatest sources of personal
confusion and misery in the modern world is that, in casting
out the austere mother and father images of the Gods, we

have taken back into the innermost shrine of the personality images of individual persons. What a blessed refuge from the family the gentle Jesus used to be! Always there, always tender and considerate and infinitely understanding. But where are the arms we can fly to now? At whose feet can we fall, and on whose heart weep out the sinful truth? To ask yourself what God thinks about it is much more illuminating than to ask yourself what Mr. Jones would think. We smile at the saints who used to wrestle with God in prayer. But it was more wholesome exercise than wrestling with the wife in an imaginary argument.

For some, the only escape from the prison of time and space, which the mind has never accepted, and in whose existence it does not really believe, is to see yourself again as something immortal and wholly independent of the restless protoplasm, and so to rediscover the soul. Thus may one escape into consciousness of the whole universe as one's home, and of all eternity as one's portion, as a bird flies from a room into the open air. To avoid the tyranny of individual persons, whose images seem to live in your mind, and with whom you keep up a kind of imaginary converse, it may be necessary to postulate an infinite wisdom, an infinite compassion, and an infinite justice, and so find yourself again in the presence of God.

There are others, like many of the greatest scientists, who do not need to grasp at any substitute for nagging humanity nor claim for themselves a deathless portion. In pursuit of knowledge or of experience, they have come so often into utter self-forgetfulness and awe that they have associated with the simplest facts of existence, contemplated impartially, the ecstasy of the saint's communion with God. Powys, speaking no doubt for himself, tries to define the happiness of one who, day after day, seizes a half hour from work and people, and, meeting neither God nor the angels in his little heaven of meditation, never feels the lack of them. "You look at the clock. Yes, you have a half hour entirely at your disposal be-

fore any living human soul has a claim on you again. This
is your opportunity, and you seize it with avidity. You leave
the house; you walk along the quietest pavement in your
neighborhood. You make your way towards some particular
park railings or toward a churchyard that contains a patch of
grass. Every step of this way is familiar to you, for not a day
passes, wet or fine, but you manage by crafty plotting to steal
this unequalled half hour from the service—or the tyranny—
of your fellow creatures."

As this contemplative walks along, he takes "all the details
of human life in their starkest, barest and most simple form,"
and stripping them of their accessories and fripperies tries
to visualize them against their true background, "which is
not the fashionable room or the squalid house, but the air,
the earth, the sky, and the sea." As one does this, "pain,
anxiety, distress slip away from us like a torn and bleeding
skin. We are alive, and yet on the edge of something else. It is
now nothing to us that in our mortal life we have made no
mark among men. . . . It is now nothing to us that we are but
one solitary consciousness among the uncountable millions
of consciousnesses, dead, living, and yet unborn. Something
has stirred in us that trans-values all our values, transcends
all our personal cravings." "As each individual spirit abdi-
cates its human tenure, retreats into the elements, and shares,
incognito, its fate with the Inanimate," it reaches a threshold
where the most intense exhilaration is at one with the most
intense peace.

What matters how the individual comes to that threshold?
Buddha sought it at the point, where, in the infinite trans-
migrations of individual experience, one relaxes the last
clutch on the self and the changeful forms of things, and
steps forth into the infinity of Nirvana. Dante found it on
the topmost heights of Paradise where the love of a beautiful
woman which had lifted him through Hell, through Purgatory, and from star to star of heaven became one with the love
which moves the sun and every star. It only matters that there

is an experience, so universal that it has been sought in all ages and climes, from the priestess at Delphi to a tired lecturer in America like Powys, turning his back on radio and advertising, and so simple that it is obviously known to the smallest scrap of organic life disporting itself in the summer sun. The Greeks called this feeling *ecstasy*. Is it more than the self-realization of life itself—of life independent of person or purse, of time and place, and whatever has just been happening to you? Who knows? But it is obvious that many who have taken ship with themselves and voyaged "through strange seas of thought alone," have come beyond the sun and the moon, to some far land of the spirit, and the light of that place has been what men call *ecstasy*, a light so beautiful and so precious, that, returning to the noisy marts of men, they are always homesick for it, and think that there is nothing that life can give them which is quite so good as just one quiet moment in which to set sail for it again.

Arts of Social Life

Brothers, attend
How ye shall spend
This fleeting treasure
Of days that pass;
Fill ye your measure
With present pleasure,
The deep sweet glass,
And love and leisure,
And sunny grass.

—HAFIZ

The Difficult Art of
Being Sociable—VI

GOOD society is the flower of leisure. The busy man is seldom good company, except, perhaps, to those who are busy at the same time and in the same way. Even so, to suffer the least interruption of the business in hand, to stop to light a cigarette with a caller or to drink tea in the office as the English sometimes do, or to speak to the wife over the telephone, seems a trifling with the sacredness of work. While one pauses to pluck one of these flowers of human fellowship, another may slip ahead in the race. In the race for what? God knows. All that there can be at the end is more human fellowship. And all that is often found is the splendid mausoleum where love lies buried.

The contact of fellow with fellow is one of the ultimates of human life. Social life, like love, is a magic. If a glamor is not created through which each appears to the other better, handsomer, more charming than most of us feel ourselves to be, it is frustration and ennui. The social gesture clothes ourselves and our possessions with the light of the ideal—simplifying, conventionalizing, ennobling, and making beautiful, as if in a picture or a story. Marise, in satin evening dress sweeping to the floor; Marise, eyes dusky with eyeshadow and lips rosy with something out of a box, hair shimmering from the hands of the hair-dresser, white hands hung with bracelets, is temporarily a work of art. And so, too, in a more modest way is Henry, her husband, expansive in white shirt front and black broad-cloth. They have been lifted out of the humble world of bills to pay, and clients to placate, and children to discipline, and made actress and actor in the great

73

romance of living. Their house, as they welcome other actors and actresses for dinner has all the glamor of the footlights. Gone is the mess of washing, dusting, and eating. The rosy glow of shaded lights falls over all. The silver shines. The damask gleams. "What a beautiful house you have," coo the guests. Beautiful it is. Marise and Henry never knew they had so much. Marise forgets that the sheets came back torn from the washing, and Henry that Junior broke the cellar window with his ball. They expand. They glow. They own an enchanted palace.

This sense of personal enhancement is what social life ought to give. But it can do so only if all enter willingly into the dream, playing their parts with dash and skill, cherishing each the ideal of the other, maintaining with joy the common fiction. Else a harsh word makes Marise know that she is not so young, and down comes her beautiful social self with a crash. A cold look takes the shine off the silver and the taste out of your food, as if a pig had walked through it. The illusion of social contact, like the illusion of all art, is a dream fabric of exquisite delicacy. A soupçon too much of anything, and all is over.

On this account, though most people are afraid to be alone, though they mill around continually in flocks and herds, truly happy social moments are very rare. Many of these gay people in country clubs and ball rooms have probably never known one. For happy social life is the highest product of human culture. It is easier to paint a picture or build a cathedral or write a poem than to focus the wayward currents of human attraction and repulsion for one moment in beauty and in content. Is there anything more inexpressibly dreary than some of these metropolitan parties at which all the machinery of glamor has been assembled and hasn't worked? Liquor flows, but the drinkers are not enchanted—only sad, or noisy, or sick. Women have bared arms and neck and back, and men have kissed them, but desire has retreated mocking.

Every hostess has suffered, in the days of her inexperience, the humiliation of a party that would not "go."

2

Yet social glamor is so simple and so common that almost any unassuming, friendly person, going about his daily business among men, finds a lot of it in the course of the day, lighting his most casual contacts, giving an unexpected excitement to chance meetings with friends or acquaintances, and even casting, at times, its dazzle on the wife. Sometimes you go "whooping" away with friends in a car to find it, and it isn't there. And again you settle down with the family for a quiet evening by the fire, and play a game or read or turn on the radio, and lo! it is there on your own hearth, making beautiful the familiar objects, touching the mate, the children, the dog with the preciousness of intimacy, self-realized and at peace. The young and the inexperienced seek it violently, and sometimes they find it and sometimes they don't; but in any case they pile up a lot of humiliations, heartaches, and disappointments. The experienced learn not to expect too much of it, but to accept it thankfully when it comes, and by delicate avoidances to woo it and keep it, when they want it. But they also learn to want it less and less. For at best the glamor of social life as such is but the promise of something whose fulfilment is elsewhere.

All art is economical. To get the most of a picture with the fewest strokes, the most of music with the fewest notes, the most of a story with the fewest words—this is the goal of technique. So with the glamor of social intercourse. One must learn to make a little social life go a long way. Social happiness, like love, is not to be hurried. There must be time to approach it and time to savor it, and time afterwards to enjoy it in memory. Good pictures spoil each other if they are jammed close together. So do good times. The best part of good decoration is the blank spaces, and of good writing all

that is not said. The best part of human companionship is
the times between when no body is around. So, too, all that
spoils other arts of leisure spoils social life, the most delicate
of these arts. In particular one must preserve one's social
hours from the crowd and all who would boss them for us.
And one must enjoy people for their own sake, and not for
any personal profit to be hoped from them.

The most socially admired people have often been the most
determined rebels against formal social life. Probably there
has not been a woman in Washington within living memories
more glamorous in the eyes of the crowd than Alice Roosevelt
Longworth. Yet she says that Nicholas long ago reconciled
himself to the fact that she was a social liability. If other wives
of other statesmen, pulling wires, giving dinners, were to be
affronted by her failure to carry off the machinery with enthusiasm, he thought the best thing to do was to leave her out
entirely. And she adds that she doesn't think that what the
lady does in this way has really any effect on a political career
—and who should know better than she?

Yet she says that her principal interest in life has been people. Her objection to formal social life is that it has forced
her to see always the same people with the same false fronts
on them. At formal dinners she got tired of the seat to which
rank and precedence entitled her because it forced her to sit
with the same eight or ten ambassadors and officials with
whom she sat at every other dinner. She pleaded with her
hostess to let her sit "below the salt," down among the
nobodies she had not yet met. In a life largely filled with
social affairs, she has gone her way, whimsically malicious,
graciously detached, indifferent to what the world would say,
but always an excited and bright-eyed observer of the social
scene, and adventuring even in these unlikely waters in search
of the social moment, polishing it and refining it afterwards
in memory, even to the point of putting it into a book.
Nothing could be more elfishly just than her picture of the
Hardings whom she offended by keeping herself delicately

outside of the loose gregariousness of whiskey, spittoons and poker that flourished around them; nor more final than her remark. "Harding was not a bad man. He was just a slob."

As some one said, in social life Alice Roosevelt had all the luck—position, wealth, opportunity—but her greatest luck was her own temperament. Yet if one analyzes this luck of temperament it resolves itself into those simple elements which always distinguish the enjoyments of true leisure—the time to perfect and enjoy each experience, decision in removing or avoiding all that interferes with the experience, the absence of any motive of profit, personal or social, and the preservation of individual self from the rushing, harrying, and bossing of organized crowds. In her youth her adventurousness and her indifference to opinion made her copy for the newspapers. She says of herself that she was "greedy" and rushed hither and thither in search of experience with the enthusiasm of a puppy and almost as little sense of direction. But in middle age she has attained to quiet selectiveness and humorous, ruminating enjoyment, like that of an old epicure, who has learned to find in a few simple dishes the slow enjoyment that never belongs to a big banquet board. This is the direction in which our social selves would always evolve, if we would let them.

3

The first necessity for happy social life is other people. There is the rub. The common or garden variety of human being is nothing to make a magic of. A large number of them must be rejected at sight because of some elementary form of social obnoxiousness. If they haven't B. O. or halitosis, their table manners are offensive; they are fat or graceless or ugly. It is true that a genuine flair for social contact may triumph over any physical disadvantage. Doctor Johnson spilled tea on his front; Falstaff was fat, and Socrates looked like a satyr. But they all had two supreme social gifts. They could talk, and they didn't give a damn. Before that beauty, manners, and wealth always yielded, dazzled and willing. Unfortunately most of the people who don't take the trouble to make themselves agreeable to sight and smell and touch have no other compensations. They are an offense.

Next to these, and even more disappointing, are the many who look well enough and move about competently, but they won't play ball socially. They don't answer letters. They neglect to call. They rebuff and humiliate the social-minded by their failure to perform the most obvious offices of human fellowship. They ought to be put away in the cemetery, for, socially, they are dead. A man in the West writes me an earnest letter, begging me to write a whole book on this subject. His burning words describe, better than I could, the way in which at least one half the world affects the other half. "Are there any other headache-giving people in the world," he asks, "to compare with those colorless folk who appear to be possessed of nothing that even approaches responsive life?" After a few illustrations of "cold-water responses" which any one could duplicate from his own experience, he grows philosophical. "At best our dispositions or states of mind are more sensitive than we are willing to admit—so sensitive, in fact, that an ill wind can quickly wither them, while a favorable breeze will as quickly give them heavenly life. . . . The response of the working man to his job, of the student to his school, of the clerk to his customers, of friends to friends, of sweethearts to sweethearts, of husband and wife to each other —in these and in every other human relationship this quality of responsiveness is as much needed to *stimulate* life as oxygen is needed to maintain it. A low degree of responsiveness (I may say the common degree) is as certain to give a drab color to life—and *does*—as a high degree of it makes for all that is worth living for." In conclusion he does not want me to forget that "responsiveness is the crowning joy of a life-giving personality." What can one add to that, except "Hear! Hear!"

Yet it must be admitted that these "headache-giving people" need much more than friendly exhortation. Many of them are quite aware of their effect on other people and miserable in consequence. The deadness goes to the very roots of personality, and will yield only to the most determined change in the whole regimen of life. It is matter of health and physical habit, of psychological repressions, of mental vacuity, of inarticulateness, of wrong social training or lack of it. Above all it is due to social conditions and personal choice which prevent people from living, fully, warmly, completely in themselves and to their own satisfaction. If one wanted to be very pious and drive home the moral of this book, one might say: "That is what you get for having no life of your own and being dragged hither and thither by other people, for not using your hours of leisure to loaf and fill up the reservoirs of vitality; to respond to life around you, and so get the muscles of your face used to moving a little; to experience, and so lay up something to talk about; to make your own the inventions of civilization—music, arts—and so lay up a few social accomplishments. See! You give people a headache."

Yet even more disappointing than the frankly dead are those who have the varnish of life on them and nothing beneath. They are the handsome dumb-shows. To this class too often belong debutantes, and graduates of exclusive schools, and people in society. They look so nice and so charming. They have such a pleasant way of making the preliminary gesture of contact and acquaintanceship. But if you know them twenty years, they are still going through the preliminary gestures. There is no intimacy, no talk, no real co-operation in the excitement of living. They meet each other and move around like pictures. Even as husbands and wives, they are all front. Of course the real trouble is the same as with the dead people. They have no individual life beneath the façade. They lay aside their own desires and tastes, their own hours for rumination, in deference to the common show.

They permit their gestures and their external skills to fill all their hours. When the social strings are pulled, they move as marionettes do. But there is no machinery within for the effective moving of themselves.

Many of these social incompetents are wished on us, willy nilly. They went to the same school with us. They live in the same town. They work in the same office. They may even belong to the same family. They come to our houses, for one reason or another, and before we know it we are weakly going to theirs. The dead ones are frequently so "good" that it is immoral to avoid them. They run the church. They teach in the high school. The dumb-shows are often so rich that it is considered folly to offend them. All community opinion seems to be organized to perpetuate this dullness. If you object, what do you want? "You have to put yourself out for other people some times." The result of this insincerity is a frustration of social happiness which shows itself in a constant underground stream of mutual nagging, criticism, and lying gossip.

For one who wishes really to be happy with his fellow-men, to like them, to respect them, and now and then strike fire with them and spread the magic of mutual enchantment over an hour or a day, there is only one thing to do. Cut out the junk. Outside of the necessary business, don't go anywhere or do anything with people, unless you honestly are having a good time, but try to wake up and have a good time. If, after reasonable effort to find points of contact, you can find none, put the person in question completely out of your mind and your notice until chance brings you together on some plane where you can really meet. It is wonderful how well this works even with people in the same club or the same family circle whom you must see every day or so. People who have been quietly ignored, snubbed, or disregarded have an astonishing way of turning up with a quite new personality, determined to please you and to get your notice. Far from offending or hurting, this procedure will blow like a cleansing wind through a whole social circle, knocking off one false face after another and showing quite agreeable people behind them. The English define a gentleman as one who never unintentionally offends, implying that intentional offense is one of the gentleman's social tools. The Englishman's art of "cutting" may be put to supercilious and unkindly use, but, rightly employed, it is wholesome and its final effect is not uncharitable.

4

So much for the negative side. On the positive side there is one principle too often neglected by the American gregariousness which involves cars all over the map and houses open from porch to bath-room. This principle is: never carry a social relationship beyond the point of mutual idealization. This only means that when acquaintanceship has gone far enough, affection will develop, and affection always idealizes. Until then manners and distance must do the work. Even so, one must learn not to love till one can really trust. All this sounds very formidable, but it resolves itself into very simple choices. In any community, for example, there are a large number of people you can meet with genuine mutual idealization at tea. They look nice. They are set against a beautiful, cozy background. They talk to you a little, but not long enough to show that they have nothing else to say. Well, that is enough for them. Elsewhere, we have objected to formal social affairs, but that is only when a large number are wished on you, and you go without thinking or choosing. But every person who must live long with a limited number of figures and faces, in the town where he is settled for life, or in his business or profession might well choose to meet them formally once in a while, with all the set-up of dress and background and good behavior, just as an artistic recognition of his human kinship with them, and a substitute for closer and less flattering contact.

The same principle applies to other associations. John Smith may be a clumsy and silent guest at dinner, but if you work with him on a committee you find that, under his dull front, he is industrious, reliable, kindly, and just. A certain amount of genuine and active work with other people for some public good allows those who have moral qualities un-cloaked with manners to show them. Here again, one must proceed with caution. One's hours may be easily used up with useless sitting around tables and house-to-house can-vassing. But some community activity, carefully chosen, is a means of genuine human good will. But let your co-workers stay where both they and you are happy. Don't spoil the social dinner for them and for yourself.

Another means of idealizing is to choose only those points of contact which give the other person the advantage. This goes square against the pride, the showing off, the endeavor to belittle and to hurt which are the motives for many social meetings. But it leads to kindness and to social peace. For example, suppose I am a lady from the city, in a country town. I have a hearty, friendly boy of fourteen who chooses to be friends with another bright, healthy boy of fourteen whose mother is the wife of the local preacher. She is prim. She is prudish. She looks askance at my lip-stick, and thinks with horror that I may smoke cigarettes. There is no use wav-ing the lipstick and the cigarette in her face, not because her opinion bothers me, *but because they turn her into a horrid person.* So I do not invite her to tea of an afternoon when some of my gaudy friends might drop in. But suppose I should stop on her porch some evening, and talk about our sons. How warm and nice and motherly she seems. Gone are all the social differences that distort us in each other's eyes. We are just two mothers, and the talk is very nice. But I leave that where it is, also. There is no use spoiling it with tea.

The Chinese, who of all people are the most subtle and the most cultivated in the arts of social life, have a name for this.

They call it saving face. The essence of manners, they think, is saving face, your own and the others. One can have quite a good time in life, if one always seeks the other's best face, and then never moves an inch beyond the point where it might fall off! Always to be putting forth feelers, to be sure that the social path will be safe for all concerned, is only to have what we call *tact*—a proper sense of touch.

The young, the immature of any age, and the egoistic find this hard to learn, and precipitate themselves constantly beyond relationships which begin well and might slowly mature as friendship into mutual irritation and boredom. In the excitement of a happy meeting, they rush into domestic intimacy, sitting around in each other's houses, walking in on each other at all hours, eating together. They wear each other out. They exhaust each other's possibilities. Finally they quarrel, or else they settle down to mutual boredom and contacts maintained through habit, alleviated by talking about each other behind each other's backs.

Some, having themselves suffered from snubbing or isolation, have a really good-hearted objection to "exclusiveness." They forget that exclusiveness is mutual. You may not want to invite the cook to your dance, but neither does she want to invite you to hers. Socially you make her quite as uncomfortable as she makes you. To take advantage of wealth or position to impose yourself on another is no kindness. Expansive, well-to-do people who come into New England communities as summer residents often have a pretty picture of themselves making friends with the "local people," inviting the minister and the doctor and the high school principal to dinner and expecting them to be grateful and impressed. Instead they find themselves against a cold, clannish exclusiveness, rendered bitter by the economic dependence of the town on the rich visitors. The lower one goes in the social scale, the more determined is the exclusiveness. A failure to recognize this and to respect it without resentment is often not kindness. It is vanity. Manners, education, and wide experience break down exclusiveness, but only when they subdue the crude, individual self to something impersonal and common to all. They teach one to cherish and polish the social contact, but not to ask too much of it.

The Fine Art of
Manners—VII

ALL human contacts,
even the closest, have in them an element of illusion. It is
the privilege of art to choose its illusion and to heighten it by
emphasis and exclusion. There are those who think that the
conventions and manners of social life are not "natural."
When they seem artificial it is only because they have not
fitted the occasion or have not been carried off with beauty
and ease. The essence of this art, as of others, is to conceal art.

Nature herself has manners, and never objects to throwing
a party, or putting on a little superfluous front. Making its
seeds, the plant blossoms out in petals and perfume as if in
a ball-dress. The sun, coming back to his job of lighting the
earth, stages ever and anon a big show of rose and orange and
moving clouds at sunrise. The growing year comes in with a
party some fine day in spring, when everything from the apple
bough to the bee is out in its best; and it goes out in a long
parade of autumnal magnificence, graciously dropping gifts.
Manners are the same kind of beautiful and unnecessary
flourishes added to the prescribed movements of life. Most
people have far more good will and interest in their fellows
than they show. The special occasion, the dressing up, the
conventions of greeting and congratulation give them a
chance to show it. To be sure, the social minded are constantly baffled by the dullness with which their advances are
received, the inability of others to join them in making life
agreeable. But even so manners are worth while to him who
cultivates them. Even in the heart of the jungle the orchid
blooms for no eye to see. Even on desert mountain tops the

moon comes up in splendor just the same. And a man who is mannerly is better company even for himself.

The social illusion is not the less potent for being somewhat intermittent and changeful. It is an emanation of life itself and is most intense where life is most intense. It is one with the transfiguration of sex and the enduring enchantment of love. Once the character of the illusion is recognized, one can learn to produce it by the simplest means, and to spread it over most of the necessary contacts of the day. My correspondent in the West, who writes so feelingly about social responsiveness, says quite rightly that we must learn to be actors and actresses on the stage of life, if we are both to receive and to give happiness.

Every social moment is a drama which involves setting the stage, dressing up, and playing the part. But, as on the stage, the atmosphere may be produced by the simplest means. The means to glamor have altered little from age to age and from place to place. Firelight and lamp-light, flowers, wine, food, dress, music, singing, and dancing—all the parties of the world have depended on some combination of these things. Yet because the symbols of social glamor are so universal, the barest gesture in their direction creates the mood as surely as the piling up of vast social machinery. If you shade the lights and draw the chairs into a circle, and brighten the fire, have you not already a social centre? When the coffee steams fragrantly, or the cigarette smoke makes a little social halo around you and shuts you in together, or the drink sparkles in the glass, is there not already a feast? If you turn on the radio or tune up the fiddle or strum on the banjo, have you not an orchestra? If you shave or wield the powder puff in expectation of meeting another, have you not dressed up?

A little nicety in touching up the environment and one's self, constantly and almost automatically, will give everything from toast at breakfast to the last "good night" the grace of a party. A person of social culture, in his casual little adjustments of things to make others and himself comfortable, to please the senses and to protect the pride, carries about with him and uses all day the concentrated essence of all that the vast machinery of balls and feasts has to offer.

The fine art of manners was probably never carried to such perfection as in that gorgeous and most cultivated social life of the Fujiwara family, rulers of Japan in the early middle ages, as described in the "Tale of Genji" by Lady Murasaki, herself a member of the family and lady-in-waiting to the Empress. Yet, after her own alluring description of dances, flower festivals, letter-writing, social contests in poetry, music, art, the making of perfumes, gorgeous dress, beautiful palaces, exquisite gardens, and the soft, sweet, delicate ways of people who lived to be beautiful and make life beautiful, this high born and cultivated lady observes in her diary: "The truth is, I now find, that I have not the slightest interest in the society of any but a few indispensable friends. They must be people who really interest me, with whom I can talk seriously on serious subjects, and with whom I am brought into contact without effort on my own side, in the natural course of daily existence." This is exactly the conclusion reached by Edith Wharton, who, in talent and social position, singularly resembles this lady of ancient Japan. All good society, she says, is and always has been the intimate intercourse of a few friends, brought together by natural congeniality, who give grace and fun to the inevitable business of common living. The ultimate purpose of manners is, in Wordsworth's beautiful phrase, just to add sunshine to daylight.

2

There are those who purport to believe that there can be no manners in a democracy. They are hypnotized by the old titles of prince, knight, and court, and not familiar enough with the actual remains of these things to realize that, in a ruder world, they meant only what any moderately educated man has and takes for granted in our lucky age. They think that the conscious formation of standards in a petty mediaeval castle was very much different from the same process in a western college fraternity house or an eastern boarding school. They will have to be dead and look back across three or four hundred years before they see the charm of our country clubs, and the jollity of our daily customs. They say: "But aristocratic civilizations had people who looked beautiful, and so served as a standard to the masses; people who talked well, and so set a pattern for common speech." Well, we have movie heroes and heroines. They do just as well. They are even as wealthy, and probably no more foolish. We have the radio, which is already moderating the flat, slovenly speech of twenty years ago, despite the female falsettos that come over it, and the musical howl of the crooners.

But where is our Sir Philip Sidney and our Madame Recamier? Where? Look around. We have one aristocratic family which would have been a treasure to old courtly societies, with sycophants and poets to celebrate its ways. Almost every member of the numerous Roosevelt family has the happy, neighborly manner which sets a real standard for the American social scene. They give to the frank and kindly customs of American family and village life—the getting together of the family for Sunday dinner, the picnics, the excursions, the walking out on the porch to greet the visitor and to say good-bye, the exchange of little gifts over the back fence, the practical jokes, the "joshing," even the going into the kitchen to help the hostess who has no maid wipe the dishes—to all the simple American ways of home and village they give a kind of public grace and noble universality. They show that the final achievement of a democracy should be to make every democrat an aristocrat.

To give the typical Rooseveltian impression that we are all good simple people and understand each other—though of course we have our faults, and I know yours as well as you know mine—is to put on a social face no less than to give the impression that we are all very rich, and have no end of servants in the background, and are, in fact, first cousins to the gods. As social faces go it is probably a more subtle and artistic creation than the old social face of aristocracy, and is what aristocracy itself, if it keeps on evolving, finally comes to. But when one meets such a family or such a group as the Roosevelts, one finds underneath a social discipline rigorously imposed. They answer letters promptly and graciously. They make calls where kindness, gratitude, or respect demand it. They omit dress suits, cards, or formal announcements where common sense makes them superfluous, but with infinite time and trouble they create a new custom or social duty, if kindness seems to call for it. With all the appearance of ease, they preserve their own dignity and that of others, as deftly as a courtier, and in cutting out social nuisances, their strokes are just as sharp and unerring. A skilful simplicity and economy both in our social backgrounds and in all our personal arrangements is more really native to the American scene than the crazy pretense of keeping up with the Joneses.

Our own social customs are as charming as any that were ever devised. We have only to realize their charm, and perfect it—to look around and choose what pleases us in our own manners and social customs and then to polish them by imitation of whatever seems the best, omitting all that seems unpleasing or superfluous. A miscellany of the special American social creations and graces which would bear comparison with any of the graces of old-time social life might include: the lovely table an American hostess can set, without a maid; the things she can dish up from her ice-box, with the help of everybody, in a kitchen as pretty as a boudoir; the American country club; the place to dance where the combination of colored light and shade and syncopated music makes such enchantment as the more social and romping round dances and the formal dance patterns of the past could not equal; the various pretty rituals and appurtenances which have grown up around the game of bridge; and, in sophisticated metropolitan circles, the cocktail hour. The electric exhilaration

of our atmosphere, the abundance of sunlight, the ease and
generosity of natural wealth are all friendly to the social illusion. Ours is a bright, beautiful, and romantic land, and our
own impulses are leading us to a bright, beautiful, and romantic life and behavior, if only we trust ourselves and go
ahead, and use our increasing leisure to perfect our own
happiness.

3

Though I have called the charm of social life an illusion,
there is a difference, wide as the gulf from heaven to hell,
between the artistic acceptance and perfection of this social
illusion, and the crude seeing of things as they aren't, through
a mist of egoism, which is the untrained person's response to
human contact. The illusion of art has been defined as the
"willing suspension of disbelief." The illusions of daily life
consist in being fooled by what isn't so.

Where manners and social custom fall short of a true art of
living, the social illusion makes fools of us. There is, for example, the illusion of wealth. Obviously possessions play a
part in arranging a handsome stage for the social drama. But
slavishness to wealth is largely an archaism. Time was when
the rich man in a community controlled all the means of
livelihood. Time was when to be invited to his house for
dinner was to enjoy the feast of a life-time; to go anywhere
with him was to ride in a carriage or a car, when ordinarily
you would walk. The general diffusion of social comfort now
means that you have one car while your rich neighbor has
three. But what difference does it make? You can only ride
in one car at a time, yours or one of his. What you eat at his
board is very likely to be the twin of what you can have very
comfortably at your own. There is, of course, a cook and
an extra maid in the kitchen, but you don't see the kitchen.
Now and then rich people have enormous houses. But one
may have as large a house and as many servants by staying

over night at a hotel. Whatever reality there may once have been behind the illusion of wealth, now-a-days the individual's possession of riches can seldom be of interest or use to his neighbors.

Yet there is still a confusion of social glamor with wealth which often leads even the poor into a fierce competition to get and show off possessions. Such competition is often keenest where culture should outrun wealth, as in college communities where salaries are fixed, and every one knows what they are. Yet when Professor Jones gets a car and flaunts it, Professor Brown's wife immediately wants him to get one. Teachers and preachers sometimes talk as if each were trying to persuade the other that he has a million. This is just a crazy misuse of the impulse to put on face and create a glamor.

Another way in which people are fooled by the social illusion is in social climbing, and the belief in the magic of social contacts. When the glamor of the social scene begins to act on them, it goes to their heads. They think they are in fairyland, and that Santa Claus is just around the corner. All sorts of things—big contracts, fancy jobs, fortunes to marry, tips on Wall Street, political opportunity—are supposed to come through social contacts. It is true that pleasant, capable people find opportunities in life by moving around and making themselves known. But about the only people who are really "put over" by pulling social wires are those who would put themselves over, without special social effort, in the ordinary course of their work or of interested living. The sum total of a long course of social contacts is about what one would get by working as hard in any other way. But this is only for the gifted and the fortunate. For the many, the chase of the social Santa Claus is just a way of doping themselves against their own ignorance and incompetence. It appeases the ambition which should drive them to really learning and doing something. Social log-rolling is often just a device by which the unsuccessful keep themselves that way. They mistake the general social illusion for a special magic to be worked from on high for their exclusive benefit.

If we realize that it is the function of manners and social machinery to create an effect similar to that of music or art or the drama, we are saved from much disappointment. Some pleasant and popular people suffer from an inferiority complex which is only the failure to realize that they are behind the footlights, and not in the orchestra seats. Other people seem to have parties that go. *Theirs* are long struggles with guests who don't turn up and programs that break down. Other people are admired, loved, well spoken of. And so are *they*—to other people.

There are some who distress themselves trying to compare the struggle behind the footlights with the concentrated essence of the glamor as it comes to them from reading and hearsay, from the social columns, or from novels about beautiful and popular people, or from casual and jealous observation of the neighbor's house when there happens to be a party, and the lights are all lit, and people whirling up to it in cars. They forget that the events compressed into a page of print may be the social cream of days and years. Neither journalism nor literature have to mention the humdrum getting up and going to bed between the airy good times, or the long hours of earning the wherewithal or otherwise preparing for fun. Jealous neighbors don't remember the many times they didn't even notice the other house because nothing was going on there.

Often the failure to enjoy the social illusion is just tiredness. The remedy is not to pile one excitement on another, but to stop and turn gratefully back to rest and to loneliness. What we often mistake for the disappointments of social life, the cold shoulders of friends, the rudeness of strangers, the talk that falls flat, the cruel indifference of the world to one's important self, is just the outcry of rasped nerves and overworked endocrine glands. Like the peevish child who wants sleep but will not go to bed, the spirit is crying out for the dark and the rest of being alone.

And withal we want too much. If we put ourselves out sufficiently for other people, if we acquire beauty and charm and social skills, if we choose lovely stage sets and costumes, and have sufficient vitality to throw off the social glamor, which is as beautifully evanescent as the flower of the plant and as dependent on the slow storing of life through the winter of discontent—if we do all this, there are moments when we stand atop the world, and everything seems to exist to feed us with infinite admiration, infinite praise, and infinite love. It is a grand moment, but only a moment. The play will end. The music will stop. This feeling that we are the universe, and that this moment will become eternity is only an illusion. Why believe that it will last? Nothing does.

4

One of the functions of manners is to keep on the plane of artistic enjoyment those artificial means of heightening the glamor which have been employed in all societies. Rightly used, the offer of tea or coffee, wine or cigarettes, becomes a ritual, a symbol of unity in the social mood. But to go beyond the point of social stimulus is to substitute physical doping for imaginative self-forgetfulness. Such physical doping has resulted from the Puritan substitution of food for these more airy ways of titillating the senses. The more wine, cigarettes, and the like have been cut out, the more food has taken their place. People have met only to gorge.

There are few checks to social life more serious than the overuse of food. It involves a lot of preparation and uses up the time together in a mere physical function. People are seldom at their best after a heavy meal. They just sit and look fatuous and bore each other. And when, as often happens now-a-days, the guest, instead of settling down for the evening, looks at his watch and says he has another engagement, the hostess gets nothing for her pains. She might as well run a restaurant.

Food attractively set forth is, of course, a social ritual, a gesture of sharing all you have, a community in well being and vital security. In every family the sitting down together at table should induce the social magic. But in these cases, the fodder should always be subordinated to the other effects, beauty in serving, graceful manners, attractive dress, and the sense of all time before you in which to enjoy each other's company. Americans often are told that in Paris life is leisurely. People take "time to enjoy life." This is mainly nonsense, but what they do take time in Paris to enjoy is their meals. The office lunch hour there is not one hour but two. A good deal of social life at other times consists in sitting around in cafés, making a bit of wine or pastry spread over hours of talk or observation of other people.

There is something to be said, too, for the old notion that to ask another to sit down with you at the family board is the ultimate gesture of friendship, implying a mutual obligation thereafter to help and to stand with each other against the outer world. Every older civilization has learned to guard the intimacy of the family, and to make entrance into that intimacy an honor. We Americans give our food and the inner sanctuary of our houses too cheaply. This makes our personal life shallow, and our friendship unimportant.

It would be well if we could have less exchange of food and more ceremony. The dearest parts of family life are the ceremonies—the birthdays, the anniversaries, the celebrations of the comings and goings of one member or another. There ought to be ceremonies for the family, and ceremonies for the intimate friends, involving common memories of past good times together, common jokes, common symbols. Something of this sort grows up naturally in groups where there is youth and imagination, as among school friends. But there are gregarious masses of people in small towns, always piling into each other's houses, always herding together here and there, who seem to have nothing of the sort. Ceremony is the craftsmanship of social life, and all craftsmanship takes time and patience. Waste and carelessness are its enemies.

5

At a certain point, what we have called the social illusion materializes in affection, and, married to all the solid moralities of human intercourse, it becomes household warmth and light, making beautiful the humdrum repetition of the days, investing even the old furniture and the cat with a sense of comfort, secured in memory and resting fast on hope. Wherever, in our social adventures, we find friendship and love, and, finding them, know how to keep and to enhance them, we come to rest. The illusion is then only simple reality. What people are really seeking in all their social gyrations can only be perfected in domestic intimacy, and completely realized in the enduring love of one man for one woman. This is perfectly obvious to youth, which, in all its fury of social life, is frankly seeking the mate.

Where there is restlessness and hankering and no satisfaction among older people milling around gregariously, it is because they do not realize that what they are seeking they already have. If we just blow on it, the permanent warmth of affection will throw off all the rainbow lights of the social magic, and the blessing of it is that when the color fades, the comfortable fire will still be there. When one simply comes to rest in friend or lover or child, savoring their charm for us, bringing out all in them that we most enjoy, expressing our pleasure and receiving it back manifold in words and looks and kindly offices, we have what the hasty, greedy, and empty-hearted are seeking with the fury of frustration in drink, noise, and promiscuous kissing. Among friends one needs neither music nor dress nor the great banquet board; for with them one may always talk, and talk is the greatest of the social magics.

The Spirited Art of
Conversation—VIII

THE greatest of the social magics is fortunately the least expensive. All that it requires is a little muscular instrument three or four inches long which every one possesses. But there have been few arts more momentous in human history than talk.

There used to be in Athens a chunky, homely, idle fellow with a shrew of a wife who, not being comfortable at home, hung around the marketplace and engaged in conversation. These conversations soon became the rage. Wherever Socrates was, there was a party. Plays and banquets could not compete with him, and indeed to make a banquet a success, some one had to bring Socrates along. When he was finally condemned to death, for no good reason one can now discover, he made even his sojourn in prison a continuous social reception, and went to his death with some of his best remarks on his lips. Thus he became the father of European philosophy, and grandfather of the modern university.

A few hundred years later there was a charming young man in Palestine who gathered people around Him to talk, on mountain slopes, and by lake shores, in public inns, and in friends' houses. He was of a hospitable disposition and often saw that there were refreshments on these occasions—loaves and fishes, bread and wine, whatever He had. His span of life was short, but in three years He talked the Christian religion into existence.

Centuries after this there were some idle ladies in castles and drawing rooms in France, who, being denied a formal education, manufactured a substitute for it in talk. For nearly a century they made the salons of France the intellectual centre of the world. From first to last they were just simple women. They wished to be amused. They did not wish to be bored. Whatever was not plain to a woman's common sense was, in their eyes, probably not true. They hated long harangues and big words and the quarrels the learned men got into. They sometimes treated the most distinguished men like boys. If they would quarrel and be bores and talk so that no one could understand them, they could just go elsewhere. And so they talked dogmas and superstition and the whole clumsy structure of mediaeval thought right out of existence, and talked into existence modern science, modern languages, modern social attitudes, and the whole idea of political democracy.

The curious thing is that the women who thus gave to the life of the mind a romance and excitement never known before nor since, who launched upon the world the ideas which made the American Revolution and the French Revolution, these undeniably charming ladies, were on the whole neither young, nor beautiful, nor rich, nor even well educated.

2

There have been many efforts to create salons since those merry old days in France, but they have been mainly unsuccessful because the people who tried it were either too wealthy or too beautiful or too socially distinguished. Many conversation groups figure in history because the members were individually famous. But the group was not originally formed out of distinguished people. People who set up a fine house, give grand dinners, invite all the well known names, make copy for the social columns. But down in a shabby old restaurant in a back street or out in a country cottage where young artists and writers pool their scanty resources and talk and smoke all night, there is the group which will make copy in history. Such a group were the young people who gathered around Jig Cook at Provincetown and elsewhere—a company which included at various times Eugene O'Neill, Throckmorton, Frank Shay, Edna St. Vincent Millay, and Susan Glaspell. But that was before they were famous.

Great conversation is usually an accident. But one may, on looking over the various samples of it in the past and even in the near present, find certain common characteristics which ought to serve as a guide to any one who wishes to cultivate anew this most absorbing of the social arts.

The first rule is to begin as simply as possible. If you have lost your money or your job or are stuck in the country or can't afford a theatre ticket or a ball gown, so much the better. Most people, around whom brilliant conversation has grown up, have been people in similar situations. Beginning with nothing in particular, one must get the habit of assembling two or three people for talk under comfortable circumstances. By comfortable we mean purely elementary comfort. One wants just enough to set the ball rolling and nothing more—either a cup of tea, or some cigarettes, or a good fire, or something to drink, or a simple meal. (Good talk has always flourished in taverns, but it dies in the hotel de luxe. It springs up naturally around camp fires. It is the result of conditions which strip off the social veneer and bring people together on some plane of elementary humanity.)

Together with the sense of primitive comfort, there must be plenty of time. The guest who looks at his watch and must be going is a dead loss. Genuine laziness and even some irresponsibility are a great help. The talk goes best when one ought to go to bed but doesn't, when one ought to wash the dishes but just lets them stand. Among women the good housekeepers and worriers about the material comfort of their guests are no salonières. One reason why English and American women have not succeeded in this art is that they are too active and efficient. Food, dress, and the success of the party are more to them than just sitting around and talking.

Having created the right atmosphere, some one must lead

right out into the deep waters. No talk is interesting till it gets a little dangerous. People used to be warned not to talk about religion, sex, or politics. They are about the only things worth talking about. For talk is much more than a way of getting rid of a few more hours. To be worth anything it must make a head-on attack on that world of hidden opinions, prejudices, concealed experiences, confused feelings which keep a man lonely and often make him miserable. It must cleanse and it must exhilarate. The reason why most parties are so dull is that each person is too busy guarding his own private collection of emotional and intellectual junk. People are all pretending to each other. They are afraid to take their real feelings and opinions out and air them, and so to admit humbly their common humanity. If people would only open their mouths and talk honestly, they would find themselves much cleverer than they supposed. And they would also find that there isn't half as much in the world to be afraid of as they had imagined.

If the party is well-to-do and respectable, talk is likely to be smothered behind the professional and social front. One is afraid of saying something not worthy of a doctor or a lawyer or a prominent business man. The women are afraid that some one might "gossip" or "repeat it" or misunderstand. Talk cannot flourish except in an atmosphere of tolerance and of trust. To create such an atmosphere, to make people stop cowering lest their political party or their church or "morality" or the economic system or anything they choose to stand for be endangered by a word—this is very difficult. It requires that behind the party there should be a stage manager with poise and sympathy and humor. And it takes time.

If the more admirable part of the population is gagged by its respectability, the so-called "Bohemians" are not really much better. They have got rid of respectability and the effect for the moment is exhilarating. But all the good results of this gesture are soon lost to two other great enemies of conversation—drink and flirtation. A little drink and a little play of wit and sentiment between men and women may set the conversation off in high style—but a little goes a long way. When there is a bottle before you, the passage from wit to idiocy is very short. And being interested in talk for its own sake, and the whole company for its own sake, is impossible if you are too much interested in one person. Yet purely impersonal discussion is also dull, and in really good company one should be safe in making just a little bit of a fool of one's self. One may be foolish—but not too foolish; personal—but not too personal. It is as simple as that!

3

Groups who manage to avoid these more elementary pitfalls are likely in America to pitch headfirst into another pitfall. The peculiarly American vice in conversation is running in one track. We like results. We like to get somewhere in talk as in everything else. So when we get a subject between our teeth, we run it to death. We are too tense, too determined. The result is one or two exciting sessions, and then we fall apart. This tendency to run in one track is increased by our respect for the specialist. Nearly everyone is a specialist in something. He wishes to assert himself. He wishes the facts to be known. He doesn't want any nonsense about what he knows. If we are to talk well, we must learn to be easy. We don't need to be the advertising agent or publicity expert for our own specialty. We don't really have to get anywhere in talk. Why get anywhere if it is pleasant to be where one is?

If there is the tendency on the part of American groups to run in one track, there is the worse tendency on the part of hostesses who have received a little of the usual social training, to keep the conversation hopping from one subject to another. They do not permit their guests to stimulate each other freely. They waste too much time trying to draw out the dull and the silent. They ward off "personalities" but ask too much about your recent illness or your motor trip. The sum total of this is likely to be that lots of everything is suggested and nothing digested. It is as if one were to remove the soup before the guests have tasted it, and rush on the entree after they had merely picked off a mouthful of the fish.

Another tendency of the lady who makes a business of being a hostess is the tendency to lionize. The man or woman who must have the center of the stage at all times, must be the talker to be listened to from end to end, the one whom the Five-foot Shelf experts picture as the focus of every one's surprised attention—that one is a studied and artificial bore.

But the hostess is not the only one to blame. The very essence of social life is restfulness, and American social groups don't know much about that. One lady complained that she couldn't create any conversation because her guests were too restless. They interrupted each other. They were afraid to be serious. They cut off every serious subject with smart Alec remarks. Humor is the salt of conversation when it is the play of a genuine mind over the genuine surface of life. But it is not to be cribbed from funny sheets. Let us look for wit if we can find it, but let us give the old jokes a rest.

Yet one who has heard much conversation among many peoples may well admit that Americans have many conversational gifts of their own. There is a natural and electric vivacity, of a different quality from that of the French, the greatest of conversationalists, but just as effective in creating an atmosphere of mutual excitement. Americans are frank and realistic, and so keep well out of those marsh mists of mysticism and long winded philosophy in which the German talkers get lost and which the frank and realistic ladies of the French salons considered the bane of intellectual discussion. Though on such subjects as morality and politics, Americans are the greatest of living rationalizers, they are nevertheless rather open-minded and kindly about the general material of life and manners. You can open your mouth before an American without fear of revealing that you don't live on what he considers the right street or belong to what he thinks is the right club, and so of getting snubbed—which is much more than one can say about many English people.

Above all, the Americans have the gift of fresh and pungent phrase. For real picturesqueness and inventiveness in the use of their own language they are probably without modern peers. English slang consists in using the same dumb words over and over—"I say, old chap," and "I mean to say," "Cheerio"—"if you know what I mean." The American school boy considers a slang word as a challenge to himself to think up a synonym. Being told to "scram," he finally concedes that he will just "amble along," whereupon his friend thinks they had better "toddle." Unfortunately this precious gift of speech is spoiled by the teaching of English, and overlaid with words and images out of a literature which, to our experience and landscape, is essentially foreign. All of which was illustrated by a cultivated gentleman and an American dough-boy whom I heard years ago, remarking in succession on the appearance of one of those gimcrack arches of white plaster which in war-days towns put up to welcome the returning heroes. They looked, for all the world, like something beaten up by the cook out of whites of eggs or whipped cream. The gentleman, passing under the arch, looked up and murmured, "What an atrocity." The dough-boy cocked one eye at it and observed, "Some weddin' cake." This realistic effectiveness of our common speech is the sign of something native to Americans which should make for good conversation. To which one may add, for good measure of social gifts, that the average American is good-natured, and he is no fool.

With these assets, all we probably need for a flourishing art of conversation is that we should all be shut up for long periods in country houses, or lose all our cars, our movies, and our telephones, or, at any rate, keep on being poor.

The Sophisticated Art of
the Salon—IX

THE salon makes a perennial appeal to the imagination because, of all the historic centres of social glamor, it was most the product of wit and talent, and the least dependent on wealth. Again and again a clever lady in a college town or a big city sets up a regular Sunday evening hour or a five o'clock cocktail hour, and thinks to see herself another Mademoiselle de Lespinasse. But her dream soon fades in the pre-occupations, irregular attendance, and general lack of social cohesion of her guests. Suddenly to reproduce the salon in our midst, full grown and sparkling, is impossible. Yet it answers a social need that is very keen among us. On this account it is worth while to review the history of the salon and its tricks, in the hope that something may be suggested which could gradually be worked out in our own social life.

While the arts of the salon began in the Middle Ages, among small groups of people shut up in castles and forced to find self-amusement, we must not be too much dazzled by such words as "palace" or "duchess" or "countess" or "court." Almost any American of moderate means and the usual education, living for a while in one of the more backward sections of Europe, will find himself associating with the local "nobility" as the only persons around who have any education or freedom from continuous manual toil. And he will take it as a matter of course that social affairs should centre in the near-by "castle" or "villa" or whatever they call it, as the only house above the level of a hovel. While we may speak of the salons as beginning at first in castles or palaces, these were nothing like the great chateaux of the Loire district or the later palaces of genuine royalty by which tourists in Europe may be really impressed. Conversation no more flourished at the great courts than it flourishes now in the homes of great wealth. It was always a free lance business, and the solace of people with more wits than possessions. By the time the salon reached its perfection in Paris, it had come down out of the castle to very simple drawing rooms, or even to boudoirs and bed-rooms.

As far back as we have social records, there seems to have been in Italy and France a form of social "game", as it was called, which depended on organized but impromptu talk. The mediaeval court of love was an elaborate form of such a game. In it such nice questions were discussed as whether a lady could have her own husband as a "lover", it being solemnly decided by the judge that she could not. In the "Decameron", written in the fourteenth century, Boccaccio takes what was probably a not unfamiliar form of social amusement as a frame-work for his stories. He tells of seven ladies and three gentlemen, all close friends or relatives, who took refuge from the plague in Florence in a country house owned by one of them. There they proceeded to elect one of their number as "queen" or "king" of the day's program, each holding the crown in turn for a day. The monarch for the day was to choose their diversions and to direct their talk. After this fashion it was decided that their principal amusement should be telling stories, and so they did, sitting in a circle, the "queen" directing the performance, commenting on the stories, and calling on each in turn to perform. This kind of amusement was the beginning of the salon.

More than a century after this, another Italian wrote a book with the popular game of talk for a frame-work. This is called "The Courtier" and sets forth the virtues of a well-bred person fit to share in the ruling of a state. By state was meant not a great political unit, but one of the small principalities, hardly larger than an American county, into which

Italy was divided. From "The Courtier" it might be gathered that the great-grandsons and great-granddaughters of Boccaccio's noble folk, entertaining themselves in a country house, had advanced beyond their ancestors in democracy of social organization and in flexibility in conversation. De Castiglione, the author of this book, tells us that in a beautiful country villa, presided over by a gracious duchess, it was the custom for the whole company of guests to repair to my lady's private sitting room after supper. There the duchess appointed some lady to govern the games for the evening.

But here autocracy ends and democracy begins; for after this potentate had suggested her games, every one in the company was called on to express his ideas, and a vote was taken on the best plan. Most of these proposed games were just talk. One cavalier proposed that each should tell what virtue he would prefer to have the person he loved best adorned with. Another thought it would be more interesting if each should tell how and when he had made the biggest fool of himself. A buffoon here interrupted and suggested that each try to tell why ladies hate rats and love snakes. He said he had a story to illustrate this and started to tell it. But he was promptly suppressed by the presiding lady who "bade him be silent."

Finally, by due process of social law, they arrived at the decision to spend the rest of their evenings together in trying to define the virtues of a "courtier." So every evening they gathered to discuss first one phase and then another of manners and behavior in the court circles to which they all belonged, arguing back and forth, rallying each other, telling stories to illustrate various points, but all under the rule of the elected mistress. At a certain point the queen would say that was enough for this evening, and call for dancing or other amusements.

Cut short at an exciting point, like a serial yarn, the conversation would go on informally all next day in the gardens and galleries of the villa, and the whole company would

arrive primed next evening for a new chapter in this group-
created drama of talk.

2

So for centuries these games went on, young daughters
sitting in with their mothers and learning how to preside,
sons improving on their fathers, till they culminated in the
polished and easy brilliance of talk for its own sake in the
salons of Paris, in the late eighteenth century. By this time
the social sceptre which had wavered back and forth in the
earlier days between masters and mistresses of ceremonies,
with preference always for the mistress, was exclusively confined to the distaff side. If one may judge from contemporary
memoirs, no two men, however brilliant and distinguished,
could talk to each other without a lady between them as
umpire. To start a salon a lady did not need to have beauty,
wealth, or position. All she needed was the friendship of four
or five brilliant men, prominent in the literary, intellectual,
or political affairs of the day, who liked to have her the queen
of their conversation. This group was called her *fondation*.

The intimate group which composed the *fondation* of the
salon used to meet for supper, gaily rehashing events and
talk of the previous evening, gossiping without scruple, and
arriving by informal agreement at the program for the current night. After supper, the doors were opened and *toute le
monde* admitted. This was like the arrangement now common, especially in small city apartments, of having a few
guests for dinner and asking more to come in "for coffee."
It must be remembered that while some leaders of salons,
like Madame Geoffrin, had large houses, some of the most
popular had hardly any roof they could call their own.
Madame Recamier held her salon for a time in a rented
bed-room. Mademoiselle de Lespinasse was just the poor
young paid "companion" of the famous Madame du Deffand.
Her salon began when some of Madame's guests, suspecting

that the young companion was interesting, began to come early and tip-toe down to her little room to talk to her before presenting themselves to the great lady above. There was a dreadful quarrel when Madame found it out, but the young companion's friends stuck by her and helped her to set up on her own.

Toute le monde, admitted after the intimate supper or other meeting of the social cabinet, was not, of course, literally all the world. It consisted of a changing group of friends of the *fondation,* aspirants for association with the group who had got an introduction, as to a club, and interesting strangers. From it were recruited those who were interesting enough to become stand-bys of the salon, and finally part of the *fondation.* Ladies who thus ran salons practically never went anywhere themselves. They were always at home. And the gentlemen of the *fondation* were in honor bound to be present every time or have a good substitute.

Among people who thus met week after week, year after year, there developed an extraordinary team work. At the same time the old formalities were constantly simplified. Refreshments were reduced. Songs and dances and set programs were dispensed with. Talk just carried itself easily, wittily, gracefully. Every one was now on the lookout for the *bon mot,* the brief sentence which summed up brilliantly or beautifully some general truth. These were caught up and repeated from salon to salon, till the authors of bon mots became as famous as if they had written a popular book. One of these famous sentences was the remark of Ninon de Lenclos: *La joie de l'esprit en marque la force.* The force of a soul is to be measured by its capacity for joy.

3

Yet the sense of government in talk was never lost. To the end some groups still kept the custom of sitting in a circle, a lady alternating with a gentleman all around the ring, with the mistress of the salon leading and calling on each in turn. There was also the general rule that no one should be allowed to talk more than five minutes at a time. When necessary, criticism was direct and explicit. Dull or offensive talk was simply silenced. When people failed to come up to the necessary standard of manners and intelligence, the mistress of the salon said they were not to come again, and they didn't. It is a pity that the decision and the publicity in dealing with offenders common in the salons, and in modern European drawing rooms where the salon standards still prevail, is not imitated by our casual and easy American hostesses. One day a young man who was a guest at Paderewski's country place said, in conversation with him, "Is not Madame Paderewski older than you?" Paderewski immediately turned away from him, and said loudly enough for the offender and all who were near-by to hear, "That young man is not to enter this house again." Any mistress of a salon would have done the same to a young man crude enough to imply, in conversation with her husband, that his hostess looked old.

While talk was allowed which we should consider risqué, hostesses applied without mercy the good old rule of the salons which has never been improved on, that the "wit must be greater than the dirt." The sharpest personal criticism was allowed and repeated with a laugh, if it was clever and if it was deserved. There was also the rule that any technical or philosophical discussion must be in words which every one could understand. People were allowed to talk about their own specialties only so long as they could make them interesting to everyone. No one would have been allowed to tell a long story about how he got stuck in a motor car. In the earlier days the rule common among provincial gentle-folk everywhere, that certain subjects like God, the church, the clergy, and the king were to be spoken of with respect was applied in the castles. In the later days in Paris, nothing was respected. That was one of the reasons why there was a French Revolution. Yet the principle of social self-govern-

ment, and social authority willingly delegated, and social
laws made by willing agreement and enforced by those to
whom it was agreed to leave the enforcement, was so general
in the salons that I wonder if the ideal of political democracy, at least in the form in which it was held by the pre-
cursors of the French Revolution, was not really an out-
growth of this old social tradition.

While wit and brevity were cultivated, and there was much
sparkling persiflage, amusing anecdotes, and merciless gossip,
the vitality of the conversation was due to the fact that it
kept close to fundamental questions of conduct and the whole
management of life. Big general subjects, like the policy of
Japan in China, so dear to our open forums and discussion
groups, were of small interest. What these people were interested in was how to live, to live beautifully and entertain-
ingly, with as much pleasure as possible and as little pain,
right there in Paris. Every general question was brought
down out of the clouds and related to the immediate business
of living. Anything that prevented immediate happy living
was, at first cautiously and then fearlessly, turned over to the
wrecking machine.

Parlor Bolshevists were nothing to these drawing-room
democrats. The dogmas of the church were demolished; new
ideals of social well-being were formulated; manners were
simplified; the divine right of kings died in the airy impu-
dence of ladies; it was gradually agreed that nothing need
be believed unless when you all talked about it together it
sounded sensible; nothing need be done, if after a good evening saying what you pleased, it seemed foolish. As old beliefs,
old codes, old rights and privileges were torn to shreds and
swept into the fire, along with the other debris of last night's
party, new fields of interest and of human inquiry opened up.
Any one who had anything interesting to tell was eagerly
welcomed and listened to—whether it was something new
about chemicals or plants or minerals, or whether it was the
strange customs of people in far-away lands. So new intel-

lectual highways were opened, and courage was gained to go forward in them, without fear of God or the devil, and with applauding ladies and gentlemen behind.

4

Where conversation is still good, on the continent of Europe, the old customs of the salon still hold. I have attended weekly conversation parties in Rome where they still sat in a circle around the lady, who, in this case, was the wife of a distinguished savant, and ruled the conversation of his friends for him. She used to sit by the fireplace in his study, with her husband at her left. The salon was held every Friday afternoon. Armed with a card of introduction one was admitted to the simple city apartment and directed to a little side room where refreshments were set out. The lady and her husband were not present to greet one, but some of the gentlemen who constituted the *fondation* of the group were usually present. They would approach the stranger without introduction, quietly bring a cup of tea, and start in immediately, in any convenient language, French, English, Italian, or German, talking about almost anything, avoiding small talk and getting down quickly to some general proposition about living.

At five the various chatting groups converged on the study, and took their places in the circle. The lady proposed the question for discussion and asked some one to start it off. After that it was a free for all. The meeting broke up promptly. The lady retired. But groups stood around in the rooms chatting or strayed off together.

While it may not be possible to imitate these old customs of the salon in our social life, they may well suggest methods of developing in one's own social group the habit and the continuity of conversation. We talk well and often brilliantly, in spots. But we lack social government, and our social customs are too chaotic and too crude to provide a working machinery for talk. Here and there for a time one of the old customs is hit upon and something happy develops, but lacking a mistress for dictator, and a *fondation* as a cabinet, it falls to pieces again. One group of professional story writers in Provincetown did fall into the way of telling stories—often just old tales refurbished—and calling on each other for tales. It was astonishing how amusing something familiar cribbed out of Boccaccio or the "Arabian Nights" sounded when re-told by a good American in the American language and with something of the American technique of the short story. The custom seemed to have arisen spontaneously through a shop talk about plots.

Last winter a group of people in a New England country town got together twice a month in one home or another to read modern plays. The reading was to be confined to plays on the boards within the last two or three years. Hence they had to lean heavily on such collections as those of Burns Mantle. Different groups would be elected by informal vote to put on the play next time, and three or four of them would read the text together, with such action and costume as their time and enterprise allowed. This performance blossomed out naturally into those discussions of living which are the staple of all really good conversation. How earnest they were on the whole subject of fathers in families suggested by the "Barretts of Wimpole Street," and how real the play was in a town when such a father and such a daughter might live on any one of the old streets in any one of the old square white mansions. To get good talk it may be necessary to start with some such program, and just let it fall away, as the talk gains strength to stand alone.

But of course the main difficulty is that we are over-programmed. These old salon groups had nothing to do but talk. The nightly or weekly or bi-weekly meeting was their only amusement. We need sufficient misfortune to hem us in somewhere and make us stay put. Or else, as I said with regard to social life in general, we need of our own accord to cut out the junk.

The Kindly Art of
Letter Writing—X

THE oldest and most gracious of the literary arts requires no publisher. Though its rewards are in love and honor, in the enthusiasm of friends and the good will of readers rather than in money, this has also been true of much of the writing of books. To write a good letter does not always bring you a check—unless you write to a debtor or a sales' prospect, and luck is with you. But it may get you a job, a friend, or a wife.

Modern business daily demonstrates the importance of letter writing. But while business letter writing is brought to an ever-higher degree of finish, social letter writing has correspondingly declined. A bright stenographer, with a little special training and experience, can take brief notes of what her employer wishes to say, and turn out a letter, easy, well phrased, and courteous. But graduates of finishing schools and of the five or six great women's colleges which have the pick of the bright and well-to-do girls of the country, girls often from families of background and culture, dash off semi-illiterate scrawls. Nor is this confined to the graduates of to-day. I once had to correspond pretty constantly with the alumnae of a great woman's college. The graduates of twenty-five and thirty years ago were even worse than the young ones. The only ones who ever sent a letter above the level of a twelve year old's scrawl, in hand writing, diction, or manners, were those who had business or professional experience, and they often wrote frankly and charmingly. A young man who came to Traversity, the Travelling University, with eight years of private schooling behind him, but scarcely able to put a sentence on paper, after two years in business sends long, entertaining, and well phrased letters about some enterprise he is interested in, dictated of course, but bearing every imprint of his own style and personality. No doubt the lady stenographer has intervened to help him out. But where is all this feminine talent in social correspondence?

Not only is style, and the decent use of English, now the monopoly of business, but manners as well. It is now the florist who remembers your birthday and tells your husband about it; the telegraph company which thoughtfully provides you with Christmas, New Year, Easter, and Mother's Day greetings which you can send by merely putting a check after the "canned" sentiment. The kindly, the considerate, the interested letter writers are now the persons who want to sell you something.

Yet "service" and "the creation of good will"—slogans of modern business correspondence—are just as important for the whole conduct of living as for salesmanship. To widen one's personal influence, to tie people to you in comradeship and sympathy and gratitude, to make others feel your sincere concern for them, even when you don't want them to buy anything: are not these things of some importance? Though most people dread writing letters, and put off the job as long as possible, almost every one thoroughly enjoys it when he gets at it. It combines the pleasure of literary creation with the joy of comradeship. One's own personal life is twice enhanced: once when one sees how interesting all the small doings of one's world look when set down in a letter to a friend, and again when the reflection of one's interesting life comes back in the friend's answer. The writing and the reading of a letter make articulate a warm current of mutual good will like something caught out of the air by the radio. Besides, the habit of letter writing heightens and makes dramatic that moment which, even in our times, is for many the high spot of the day—the coming of the postman. To get good letters, one must first write good letters.

2

Though Uncle Sam's mails are still, no doubt, weighted
with letters which would put old literature to shame—full,
bright, affectionate letters—modern life has put real difficulties in the way of the social practice of this ancient and
beautiful art. The telephone, the telegraph, and the automobile have done away with those small social notes which
were once indispensable to the friendly conduct of life, and
encouraged the art of writing letters. In India, where tele-
phoning is still arduous, and messengers are cheap, you are
always being handed a "chit." A chit is a small social note,
asking you to tea, bringing you a message or a compliment,
reminding you of something. There is always excitement in
unfolding the small bit of paper and thinking of an answer.
Harassed teachers know how readily children still take to
note-writing. Such notes have, at various times, been brought
to a high degree of social charm. The old Japanese used to
send notes in beautiful hand writing on all sorts of colored
paper, tied to appropriate sprays of flowers. The *billet doux*
of the French lady, sweet with her own special perfume, still
smells of romance. Emily Dickinson, a little mothlike recluse
in a formal old house in Amherst, was always sending little
notes in verse to her neighbors and friends and relatives next
door, or sometimes only from one room in her own house
to the next. She tied them to flowers or to cookies for the
children or to funny little gifts made with her own hands.
So, only, her shy genius became known and in this simple
way she got a recognition most poets never get through
publishing.

The passing of the need for social notes has left wreckage
in all personal letter writing. Even in the most carefully
appointed homes there is often no place in which to write
a letter. The desk is littered with bills and advertising circu-
lars. There isn't the right sort of paper. The fountain pen

leaks. The correspondent's address is lost. It is the failure to allow time or space for letter-writing which makes it a chore. It was once the delight of lovely ladies, and the equipment for it was cherished no less than the powder pot and the eyebrow pencil. In the eighteenth century in France and England, the close, friendly groups of the cultivated and well-to-do kept up a constant communication by letters which the authors tried to make amusing, friendly, and skilful examples of the reporter's art. Advertised by the recipient, they were admired and passed around, and sometimes reputations grew out of them no less effectively than from publishing. One of the most charming features of this letter writing was the way in which it flourished between members of the same family, and the warmth with which affection for a sister or daughter or wife was expressed. That even this expression of family kindness was considered an art, and subject to critical discussion, is shown in a note written in 1740 by Mary Granville, a high-born English lady, to her sister.

"I am just come from the tea-table," she writes, "where we have had a warm dispute occasioned by Madame de Sevigné's letters, which one of the company said, were very fulsome and wanted variety of expression to make them agreeable, and that a very sincere affectionate person could never be at a loss for a new thought on such a subject as friendship. If they were, it was a mark that their affection was not very warm. The lady that started that dispute would not yield that point, but maintained the heart might be very warm though the imagination was not very bright. Another lady in the company said *that* was her opinion, too, and that *words may be wanting where love is not*; upon which says a wise philosopher in the company, 'What need have you to be in a fuss about sweet words, cannot you say *My Syrup of Violets* or *My Syrup of Cowslips?*' This turned the disputant spirit into a loud laugh, dispersed the company, and gives me an opportunity of flying to her for whom no expressions can be too kind to do justice to her merit, and my love."

No doubt conversations as good as this are heard every day around tea-tables, and letters as whole-heartedly sharing a bit of social experience sent off by every post. Yet it is with letter writing as with conversation, of which letter writing is but the written twin, developing with it and decaying with it. One cannot read these old records of social life without a certain wistfulness. We are really just as clever to-day and just as charming, but we don't take time to set the social moments in these little frames, or to isolate and make the most of our social skills. The lady does not usually fly from her tea-table to her writing table to dash off to the dear sister who wasn't present a full report of what she said and what he said and all about it. More likely she gets into a motor car and goes somewhere else. Yet if any woman would cut out half of her social affairs, and make up the rest of the time in just such performances as this, following her own fancy and impulses in brief communications with her friends between times, the impression would soon get about that she was a very charming person, and when she did appear at a social function the pleasant or amusing atmosphere thus engendered would cling about her and glorify her with more than the glamour of a new dress.

There is here and there now-a-days a friendly person who, though he does not write letters, often thinks of cutting out bits from newspapers or magazines and sending them to a friend who has some reason to be interested. How we all like such persons, and how the attention flatters us!

3

The passing of the need for social notes is not the only difficulty. There is a very real difficulty with hand-writing. Many people now handle a typewriter more easily than a pen, and hand-writing therefore suffers the decay that comes to all things which have ceased to be really useful. The penmanship taught in the schools is a relic of the old business hand, fitted for the filling of ledgers and the rapid taking of notes in the days before shorthand. As such it was, at best, fluent and clear, but never beautiful. Superseded for business purposes by type-writing and stenography, its ruins are seen in the ungainly, scrawling, slanting, crammed-to-the-margin penmanship of social letters, which lacks the first quality of all social intercourse—*charm*.

There are two solutions of this problem. The first is frankly to accept the typewriter for personal letter writing, and to try to restore to the communications of friends the valuable elements taken out of social intercourse by business. Any one who has a large personal correspondence now is likely to find, on looking over his letters, that most of the good ones—the amusing, well phrased, friendly ones that really bring the personality of the other close—are written on the typewriter. He may also find typewritten letters which are especially distinguished and charming in both appearance and language. Mary Pickford writes such a letter—prompt, considerate, and delicately flattering. Theodore Roosevelt, Junior, writes an equally charming letter. In the briefest sentence or two, worded with the graceful colloquialism of his family, he compresses all the warmth of a bright smile and handshake.

The reasons why the type-written letters seem the best are several. In the first place the ease of reading gives a sense of warmth and directness. Not so much seems to intervene between yourself and the other person. In the second place, probably most of the articulate people—those who in any time or country would write the good letters—now use the typewriter professionally or have secretaries. In the third place, the typewriter encourages to finish, because it keeps before you the standard of the printed page. An unpunctuated sentence, or misspelled word, or even a crude phrase looks much worse when type-written than when scrawled by hand. One is not so likely to allow for slovenliness. Nor does it now detract from intimacy or warmth that the writer keeps a carbon of his letter to you along with yours to him. Time was when to keep copies of one's letters had the look of vanity. It was as if one expected them to be published for posterity. But now the carbon seems a kind of courtesy and gives dignity and continuity even to intimate correspondence.

Probably, then, one must accept the typewriter as part of the machinery of social life, like the telephone and the car— and with the typewriter, the filing cabinet. True, neither the typewriters nor filing cabinets now used in offices are household ornaments; but as more and more women graduate from business into the management of the home, they may assert the taste which has put color into dish-mop handles and made dust-pans really convenient. Typewriters may become graceful, colorful, light, compact, and filing cabinets take on all the more recent graces of radio cabinets.

Then the modern Madame de Sevigné will turn to her writing desk as to the telephone. Whenever the name of a friend comes into her mind, she may jot down whatever she has to say, a kindly word of concern, an amusing incident, discussion, argument, anything. She may even write what, on second thought, it would be foolish to send, but it will be off her chest. And doing this, she may even achieve Madame de Sevigné's style, which many think is the most beautiful informal prose in the world, and make language do anything she wants it to. It will be gay, dignified, tender, sober, mischievous, reckless, slangy, poetical, and dignified by turns —just like that of the incomparable Madame herself. Her carbons, neatly put away, in what will probably, in these future times, be a beautiful filing cabinet, will be the record of her life, with all the interest of a diary plus the warmth of friendship. She may even keep copies of the letters she did not send. It is worth while having one's say sometimes, even in the privacy of a filing cabinet, and amusing, tragic, or ironical afterwards to know what one thought at the time.

A college girl to whom this suggestion was made said, "Oh, but I could not bear to keep copies of my letters. They would look so foolish afterwards." Better is the attitude of a gay little girl of thirteen who sat in her father's study, reading with shrieks of laughter, the file of her scrawls to her father which he had kept since she was four years old. "What a nut I was!" she kept saying, and, when she came out, there was a new comprehension in her eyes of herself as a continuing and developing person. A smile at one's own expense does no harm, and the people who are interesting to themselves are also, within limits of kindness and courtesy, interesting to other people.

Much of the budding desire to write, now expended on fruitlessly imitating the standard pulp magazine story or spinning movie scenarios, might better be spent in genuinely writing to friends. The friend is the best audience in the world. If the desire really to interest a definite person cannot make you write well, nothing will. Out of the constant digesting and communicating of the experience of life, this reaching out to other people in love and interest, this adaptation to many hearts and many minds, may finally come the true literary skill. You may learn at last what every real writer must learn—to write to the whole world as your friend. Even if the aspirant does not become an author, he or she will have passed many happy hours writing, unharassed by the trivial restrictions of current fashions in literature; and will have so spread the influence of heart and mind that life will be infinitely richer in friends and interests.

4

The second solution of the modern difficulty with letter writing is to make hand-writing again an art. What has ceased to be useful in hours of work, people often keep for ornament and relaxation in the hours of play. Thus hunting and fishing which were once the means of getting a meal are now the pleasure of those who wish to escape from too many and too elaborate meals. So it may be with hand-writing. In many times and places it has been a work of art. The exquisite

flourishes of Chinese letters, the delicate lacelike strokes of
Arabic writing, the fine, clear, open lettering of the mediaeval
Christian manuscripts—all these have been perfected in love;
and have yielded as much pleasure as drawing or painting.

In the tenth century in Japan beautiful handwriting on
beautiful paper for social purposes was brought to such a
point of individuality and grace that it outranked wealth and
beauty as the asset of a cultivated lady or gentleman.
Attracted by a lovely girl, a gentleman would lose interest
in her at once, if her reply to his first note was written in a
"crude unformed hand" or on badly chosen paper, or was not
charmingly phrased. A lovely missive, coming into a palace,
would make all the ladies' hearts beat wildly. When Princess
Murasaki saw the handwriting of the Lady of Akashi, her
rival, she "knew what to expect." An affair with a lady who
could write with such "masterly handling of the brush" would
be no ephemeral matter.

In the tale of Genji which tells about the court life of this
period we hear with approval of a lady writing "in faint,
sinuous ink strokes on the blue gray paper which her mourning dictated", of a letter on purple paper in a bold script,
attached to a spray of wistaria, of one on "greenish paper,
very thin and fine, laid down on a stout backing."

We also hear of an antiquated court lady writing in stiff
awkward strokes on dingy purple paper, heavily perfumed,
and of a pretentious bounder who thought he was master of
all the fashionable arts and wrote in "a clean bold hand on
thick Chinese paper, heavily scented", but whose style was
"tortuous and affected". We learn of a letter which looked
like "an uncommonly fashionable missive", because it was
written on a single sheet of blue poetry paper, and attached
to a carnation, but, when it was opened, every one laughed
at the handwriting which was in a "very cursive style, adorned
with hooks and flourishes which seemed to wander about at
their own will and stand for nothing at all." And we learn

of a princess whose handwriting was "vague and purposeless," and so a great disappointment to her guardians and lovers.

So much for the letters that did not come up to standard. But we hear also of a letter written in sharply contrasted light and heavy strokes on a deep brown paper "in a masterly style which would not have disgraced a lady of the court"; of a long letter on four or five sheets of Chinese paper, in which the handling of the ink was "quite masterly"; of a letter on light blue paper tinged with gray, designed to dazzle a young girl; of a letter written by Gengi on soft thin paper with such care that "a young girl who did not admire it would be rustic, nay brutish". We learn that Princess Murasaki, who did all things beautifully, sent a letter on "sandal-wood paper of Michinoku", written "informally but with great elegance", her style like that of Prince Genji, her guardian and teacher, "with added touches of girlish delicacy and grace". We also hear of a mature suitor who sends a letter on white paper, "in a competent hand," attached to the largest and handsomest iris flower his lady had ever seen. When she opens the letter, she finds that the style is "spirited and apposite." Who would not know that this was a man to marry?

Since there is nothing so individual as handwriting, who can tell whether the projection of personality through ink and paper, may not come into its own again, in the days of beautiful living which we all hope lie before us? People may again learn to add to clear and beautiful calligraphy some touches of art and fantasy such as the little pictures the old monks, copying manuscripts in the quiet of the convent, used to put in the spaces of the capital letters. So gradually we may again evolve letters which are not only literary but artistic creations. Even in these rushing times, some people find interest in penmanship for its own sake. In his autobiography, Arnold Bennett tells how he perfected a beautiful handwriting and wrote in it 150,000 words—the whole manuscript of *An Old Wives' Tale*.

Some progress has already been made in this direction in the new "manuscript writing" which progressive schools are substituting for the old business hand. And Marjorie Wilson, the beautiful lady who advertises in the magazines to make you charming, even dares to suggest a revival of the old Japanese interest in beautiful paper. She says we should as soon think of sticking to white linen paper as to the old fashioned white muslin for our dresses. Why not many papers for many different occasions? She suggests that you choose your paper as you choose your clothes, collecting various colors and styles, for various moods and occasions. Then, whenever the heart prompts, when you are lonely and want some one to talk to, when a friend is sick or has special good luck or celebrates a birthday or an anniversary, or on any of the other innumerable occasions a kind heart can discover, you pick out just the right paper, and make a letter thoroughly individual, pleasant to look at, but even pleasanter to read. This may seem at first an affectation. But it is certainly better than putting an *x* after one of those sickly sentiments the telegraph company offers to send for you. The charming development of our Christmas cards, which grow more ingenious and beautiful every year, show what might be done in making social correspondence also a graphic art.

The Whimsical Art of
Playing with Children—XI

A LITTLE girl of ten sat on a mat in an old Japanese palace—a pretty little girl, in a robe of purple silk faced and lined with green, who had been so washed and powdered and perfumed and brushed by many ladies in waiting that she looked like a porcelain toy. But her heavy black hair stood out fan-wise from her vivid little face, irrepressibly alive and childlike. This was the little Princess Murasaki, whose name meant, "The Purple Lady." The first syllable of her name—*mur*—meant "purple," and this, as Kipling would say, is the point of the story, "O Best Beloved."

Over the purple lady bent the greatest prince of the Empire, Genji, the "shining one", a man so handsome that tears came into the eyes of young ladies when they saw him, breathing forth from his gorgeous robes the rich perfume which only the Imperial Family could wear. Murasaki looked up at him in distress. She was trying to write, with her brush dipped in ink—and that is very hard for any ten year old fingers, as any mother, father, aunt, or uncle knows. She dared not let Genji see what she had written, for did she not already know that a lady who had a poor handwriting could never find a husband?

Genji laughed at her distress. Taking from the pile of many-colored writing paper one stained with *purple*—for you are not to forget, O Best Beloved, that the first syllable of Murasaki's name meant *purple*—he wrote in large, bold strokes part of a poem called the *Murashi-no* poem, which described the Murashi moor where, if you are bright, you may already know that "the grasses are purple-dyed." Then he wrote some verses which he had made up on the spur of the moment, while Murasaki's eyes followed eagerly from stroke to stroke. The poem said that Genji loved, oh so dearly, "the dewy plant that grows on Murashi moor," by which, if you are still bright, you may guess that he meant Murasaki herself. Then Prince Genji told her that she needed a writing lesson, and forthwith sat down and gave her one himself, guiding the little hand and the wayward brush over sheet after sheet of paper which he took good care should always be purple. But all the while the poem about the purple moor, and the purple plants that grew there ran in the little purple lady's head, until suddenly it dawned on her that even a little girl could make verses, too. When Genji at last told her to write something alone, she bent to the task with a great look of importance and mystery, and would not let him see what she wrote till she finished. Then he laughed. For Murasaki had written a neat little poem asking what plant it was that he said was her relative.

But it happened that Genji had serious matters on his mind. He had been making love to a lady hidden, as etiquette required, behind her screens of state, and when he had hopelessly committed himself, he saw her for the first time and—she had a long red nose! So Genji tells Murasaki that he will now draw her a picture of a lady. He draws a fine lady, and just as Murasaki begins to admire it, he lengthens the nose and puts a bright red tip on it! Murasaki protests. Gengi asks with surprise, What! doesn't she like red noses? Of course red noses are all right! And forthwith he dabs the red paint on the end of his own handsome feature. Murasaki is horrified. Catching a glimpse of himself in the mirror, Genji reflects that maybe the poor lady wasn't so bad. A red nose will spoil any beauty, even his! So he turns to comfort Murasaki by assuring her that now the red will never come off. She will have to get used to him like this, for there is the red nose, and what can she do about it? Murasaki in a great fright runs and calls the ladies in waiting, and they bring a basin. While one lady in waiting holds the basin and another the towel, she stands on a stool and scrubs and scrubs at Genji's nose. But whether the red came off or not is another story, O Best Beloved—and you will find it all in one of the seven beautiful large volumes of the Japanese *Tale of Genji*.

It was always fairyland to Genji—the room where little Murasaki dwelt. Whatever trouble was on his mind—intrigues of great councillors against him, the memory of his mistress who had died in his arms, the terrible wrong which from boyhood had been always on his conscience—all these things he laid down at the door when he entered the little girl's presence. He possessed thousands of estates and dozens of palaces, but the doll house he and Murasaki made together, and the little kitchen he fitted out for the dolls with real little pots and pans, were more fun than any of them. Beautiful ladies often played on their zithers to him until all his small discretion, where ladies were concerned, melted away, and Genji was in another scrape. But there was no zither he loved so well as the big thirteen stringed instrument from China over which he used to guide Murasaki's little hand. From which it may be gathered that one lovely child to play with is worth all the thrones and palaces in the world.

2

Genji is not the only great state personage who found fairyland always waiting for him whenever he crossed the borders of the children's country. There was a great president of the United States whose children have made famous the way they used to play with him. When he came home, he always had a toy animal or two somewhere in his pockets. Heating a hairpin in a candle flame, he would carefully brand them with one or another of the names of the various imagi-

nary cattle ranches owned by the younger generation. Teddy
Roosevelt's were the Elkhorn brand, Kermit's The Maltese
Cross, and Alice's The Triangle. On rainy days or towards
dusk, when work was done, he would hide in the gun-room
or some other room on the third floor, and when, in their
wild career, the children approached, he would growl or
howl like one of the beasts of the jungle, and so scare them,
shrieking, away. He said that these hours, alone in his jungle
lair, were among the most peaceful he ever enjoyed.

There were also those wild chases in the wake of father
over hill and dale, through swamps and mud, of which the
one rule was that they should proceed in a straight line
through anything that came their way—water, dung piles,
briar bushes, anything. He once took Monsieur Jusserand,
the French Ambassador, on such a chase, making the rule
that, when they came to water, every one should drop his
clothes completely and come right on through in perfect
nudist style. The French gentleman emerged from the water
clothed only in a pair of gloves: "But that isn't fair," shouted
Roosevelt. "You have your gloves on." "But," said Monsieur
Jusserand, "I was afraid I might meet ladies!"

Any place is wonderland where children are, and rich in
vast and strange adventures. But no better point of departure
for wonderland has ever been found than an English country
house. There was always leisure, and plenty of it. Nothing
to do, for the servants did everything; nobody coming, for
it was too far for anyone to come; nowhere to go, for it
was probably raining. In such a great grass-bound, tree-
walled, solemn, lonely, and ancient seat of the great art of
doing nothing, a young Oxford don found a little girl named
Alice, and set off with her on the trail of the White Rabbit,
and what they didn't see and what they didn't do before they
came back! They walked through looking glasses and skipped
over squares in a land that looked like a chess-board. They
conversed with a cat, and when they looked again, they

were talking no longer with the cat, but only with the cat's smile, which he had left behind.

In another English country house, "where children and mirth abounded," a young landscape painter, named Edward Lear, embarked on scientific study and community enterprise in Wonderland. They found and classified all the plants of the Nonsense Botany—*Manypeoplia Upsidedownia,* and *Small Toothcombia Domestica,* and *Knutmigrata Simplice,* and *Blue Bottlia Buzztilentia*—and preserved their pictures for posterity. They invented the limerick, and wrote reams of society notes about the young lady from Crete, whose costume was far from complete; and the young lady from Parma, whose conduct grew calmer and calmer; not to mention the old person from Ems, who casually fell into the Thames. They had a cook book, and made Gosky patties out of a pig three or four years of age, which they tied by the "off hind leg to a post." They were to "visit the pig and beat the paste alternately for several days." We are glad to record that this barbarous advice was followed only by a laugh. They made Crumbobblious Cutlets and Ambloongus Pie, which they served up "in a clean dish" after which they were to "throw it out of the window as fast as possible". Tiring at last of these domestic pursuits, they set sail with the owl and the pussy cat in a beautiful pea-green boat, and met up with the Jumblies who had gone to sea in a sieve.

Their heads were green and their hands were blue
And their brains were perfectly dead.

But no, they were somebody else again—somebody seen by children on Cayuga Lake in New York state, half a century afterwards, no doubt collateral descendants of the Jumbly family.

One of the quaint things about wonderland is the way the kindly beasts live about in the most interesting houses, and have the most interesting social life, and talk to man and play tricks and wear clothes, just as they used to do in the old twilight of man's history. The beasts that were painted on the walls of Dordogne, and those that stare, vast and solemn and profoundly divine, out of Egyptian sculpture, have gay little descendants among the teddy bears and white rabbits of every well provisioned household of children. One does not even have to go back to Uncle Remus for accounts of "de animals." A. A. Milne has given us the latest news of them, in the record of the immortal Pooh Bear and his friends. Probably there are scores of households now, in which an enterprising parent finds as much fun as Milne among the creatures with which the baby has littered the house. There is a distinguished literary man who can never come across "Louis So So" or Pink Bear or any of the bear tribe without setting them up to mischief among the dolls. What havoc he makes them work with the wardrobe of Rosemary, and how they steal the food out of Marjorie's dishes! Once the young mistress of Pink Bear, distressed at the fading of her darling's fur-coat, dipped him in tintex and hung him on the line. He was stolen from the line by Father who solemnly averred that, when last seen, he had been standing on the edge of the wine barrel in the attic of the barn, where some cherry liquor was brewing, and no doubt he leaned over too far and fell in and was drowned. The young mistress said nothing but went on a still hunt, and soon re-appeared with Pinky, pinker than ever. "What!" said Father, "I heard for a fact that he fell into the barrel and was drowned." "Oh," said the bright daughter, "he did, but he drank his way out!"

Surely it is the dearest and tenderest of all the idle pursuits of man—this adventuring with the children in wonderland. It more than compensates for the times when one must wash their little faces and wipe their little noses and spank their little—but that is another story. It even makes up for the endless nagging about elbows on the table, and rubbers on the living room rug, and squabbles just outside the study door. It takes two to play at the game of wonderland—a child and a man. The child needs someone to give form and continuity and articulateness to what he senses through all those wonderful channels of perception which are overlaid in mature man with solemn prejudice. He needs to make articulate and gaily dominant that humor and detachment which are the expression of his own dawning intelligence, making sport with the dream-world of babyhood.

For the grown-up to follow the child back into fairyland, sensing from his bright eyes and delighted gurgle when you are on the right track, saying things and doing things you never dreamed of till this minute, seeing the quaintest things emerge like an emanation from the magnetic company of the child, and feeling all the time an immense exhilaration and release—who that has tried this does not know what a cathartic it is for the unconscious? We have never escaped from fairyland ourselves; we have just laid it by. Or we have made the mistake a bright child never makes, and treated it as reality. The less of the child's play and imagination he has in him, the more fatally does the man believe in fairies, and, what is worse, act on that belief—the fairy who gives him the tip in Wall Street, the fairy who will somehow pay his mounting bills, the fairy who will let him drink all this stuff and not have a headache tomorrow. To play rightly with children is to release a whole flock of incredible beasts, fairies, and ogres from our own unconscious, and after gambolling with them in the sunshine of the intelligence send them back to fairyland, where they belong. The more conscious and articulate the fairy world is, for child or man, the less harm does it do.

There was a lady who made the dreary suggestion that instead of Mother Goose, we should teach our darlings facts. This is a sample of her nursery rhymes:

> *In my little head so round*
> *Twenty-eight small bones are found!*

As if strictly speaking, the statement that the head is round is not as metaphorical as the statement about the old woman who lived in a shoe, and as if the twenty-eight bones weren't for practical purposes a fiction, too, being something that the average person cannot know from his own experience, but must take on faith in the laboratory. The difficulty with these dull fictions of the mature is that there is no gambolling of the free intelligence among them. If we could play with some of our fictions of religion, politics, economics, and morality, as the child sports with Bre'r Rabbit, willingly suspending disbelief, and then gaily recapturing it when the game is done, how wholesome would knowledge and learning become!

3

As the child begins to grow up and get an education, new worlds open to the parent. There is, or may be, the family reading hour, which should be, if possible, after supper before the fire. One should start in babyhood with verse, accenting it heavily and singing it in a chant. Mother Goose has a fine rocking horse rhythm, and Milne's verses are beautifully sonorous. What a fine mouthful is

> *James, James, Morrison, Morrison*
> *Weatherby J. Dupree*
> *Took good care of his mother*
> *Although he was only three.*

There are fine passages in standard poetry which the child will love to hear intoned almost before he can talk.

> *And I will make my kitchen*
> *And you shall keep your room*
> *Where white flows the river,*
> *And bright blows the broom.*
>
> or
>
> *That orbéd maiden with white fire laden,*
> *Whom mortals call the moon,*
> *Glides glimmering o'er my fleecelike floor*
> *By the midnight breezes strewn.*

Many a conscientious mother, beginning the child's education, wades hopelessly through dull little one syllable stories, spanking restless fingers between times, and making restless readers "sit down again and be still". The only things that are worth doing with a child are things which are thoroughly entertaining for the grown up. And chanting verse, finding beautiful, sonorous, if sometimes senseless verse, with beautiful long words such as every child loves, and chanting it with all necessary exaggeration is fun. And doing this, you just naturally recite all of Edward Lear, and the verses in "Alice in Wonderland," and graduate into "When We Were Very Young," and de la Mare's "Peacock Pie" and on into Longfellow's "Hiawatha," and Tennyson's "May Queen," and Vachel Lindsay's "Santa Fe Trail" and the "Ghosts of the Buffaloes." And if you think you knew anything about poetry before, or learned anything about it when you parsed it and scanned it and looked up references to mythology in school, you don't deserve the fun you will be getting out of making a noise for the young with it.

From poetry one graduates into the beautiful inconsequence of "Alice in Wonderland" or "Pooh Bear" or "Br'er Rabbit." There comes a time when poetry is done with for a space. They won't listen to it. They even take to facts, and books about birds, beasts, and insects, and wood-lore and machinery are all the rage. There comes a time when the fairy tales drop into the background, and "Little Women" and "Huck Finn" and "Tom Sawyer" take their place, with which should be included a less well known book, "Sube Cane," by Bellamy Partridge. And then one moves forward to "Uncle Tom's Cabin", which every child should hear at the time when it will be to him what it was to us in our childhood, or at least to our mothers and fathers. And there is "Ramona," too, whose excellence the school teachers seem to have forgotten. And so one advances to Dickens and Maggie Tulliver and "Lorna Doone." An elder, of moderate education and intelligence, who does not enjoy the course in adult education offered by slowly inducting the changing imaginations and tastes of his own children into literature, in the fireside reading, has missed something.

Music is equally illuminating to the parent. Remembering his dreary hours of scales and his wondering what it was all about, he finds this new way of teaching children to transpose from one key to another and make up their own melodies and chords from the beginning very exhilarating. Music and drawing both, as taught to the children now-a-days in their progressive schools and brought home to parents, may become not an artificial accomplishment but a genuine language, and means of understanding and communication between members of the household. Nor need a parent be ashamed to learn from a child or with him at any age. Bruce Bliven came into a friend's house one evening all "het up" with a new way of using his spare time. He had got so interested in watching his young son take music lessons that he was now taking the same lessons himself, a year behind his son, and having the time of his mature and busy life.

A lot of the child's materials for crafts infect the parents with an itch to get at them. Who can watch a child manipulating a finger-painting outfit, and not long to plunge into that green, blue, yellow, and red mud with all ten fingers? The latest leisure pursuit for parents seems to be those small kits of materials for making toy boats and airplanes which are sold by the chain stores, and which include everything from keels to paint in microscopic forms and quantities. It takes two to make one of these fairy boats—a man and a child—for little fingers and patience are seldom adequate; but let no parent touch them unless he has nothing else to do for the day.

And then there are "houses". They begin with getting all the chairs in a corner and borrowing the couch cover for a roof. But they ought to go on to maturity and culminate in setting up a real house for the bride on a corner of father's acreage. That is the way houses were made in the good old

days when land was used for what it is good for, and it may be
the way in which they will be made again when the subsistence plans of the government come to domestic flowering
all over our empty land. One of the many great advantages
enjoyed by the child in the country is making "houses." It is
too bad when the stones are stolen from the wall for them, or
when the tenants keep moving out and leaving the wreckage,
like the nomad tribes who, whenever their houses get dirty,
leave them and build new ones elsewhere. But they are fine
when made from driftwood on the beach or set up in a natural
cave, and still better when they are elaborated into a little
log cabin somewhere that becomes a week-end playhouse and
picnic center for the family. Thoreau said that he never came
on "a man engaged in so simple and natural an occupation
as building his own house." House-building would be common if the children had their way. We have seen a professor at Dartmouth high in a tree building a tree house with
the small son, and when we climbed up there, how still it was
in the green tree tops, and how caressingly the sky came
down to meet us, and how the squirrel paused, chattering on
a limb, to cock his eye and his tail at us, and how the tree
swallow flew down and said he had a mortgage on this piece
of sky. Lacking a piece of land to build a house on, there is
always a house to be constructed within the house, a game
room or a playroom in the attic or an outdoor livingroom
in the backyard with outdoor fireplace and furniture made
by the bright disciple of the school-teacher of sloyd.

And there is the outdoors. For a few years between our own
childhood and the youth of our children it usually becomes
just a place to play golf in or drive a car through. But how
new and populous it is to children, and to *us* when we see it
again through their eyes! There is a squirrel in a tree, and
the birds come down and eat the crumbs, and a spider lives
in the attic rafters, but we didn't know these things till
Frankie found them. If there were no children, we should

never see the first flowers of spring, nor taste the last nuts of autumn.

If there were no children, there would be no holidays, no jack-o-lanterns at Hallowe'en, and no stockings hung for Santa Claus at Christmas. And if children didn't grow up, and burst into the period of dancing, and of bringing all their friends home for after-the-party raids on the ice-box, and of frilling out in evening dresses and blushing with lip-stick, we should miss the Indian summer sociability of the time when daughter makes mother get a permanent, and father has to learn to dance again, and the house must have everything from a new radio to a new screened porch; and we don't run a home any more—we run a club. But this also is reviving for parents, and if they are wise, they will receive back their youth from the hands of their now vanishing young, and say, "Thank you. I'll keep it."

At present children are too much worry, expense, and trouble. But that is because we are too solemn about them, and cling too greedily to our own grown-up fairy tales and toys. Walter Pitkin says that parents should end at forty, and probably he is right. Our children ought to be allowed to go on more quickly to the grown-up plays they hanker for— earning a living, building a house, and getting a spouse. They ought to go on to it more quickly and get it over sooner, leaving the forties for their parents, and later for themselves, as the high noon playground of life. When the golden age comes, if it ever does, children will take less of our working hours, but we will more and more gladly receive at their hands the dearest and most glamorous pursuits of leisure.

The Delicate Art of
Courtship—XII

THEY used to call it courtship, but now they call it petting. Petting is the great new equalizer between man and maid, the last glorious achievement of the profit era in the way of getting nothing for something.

There is no need of taking Mrs. Grundy's word for it. Most of us who haven't lost our teeth and eye-lashes with age have had plenty of it. The kind of courtship which was put out of style by petting was awkward, embarrassing, inarticulate, expensive, and ineffective. The new method is quick and easy. Young people pet themselves earlier into less ignorant and more tolerant marriage. Then they join the circles of expert married petters, and quite seriously, and often with a subconscious righteousness of intent, endeavor to substitute for divorce a kind of inter-familial courtship, which is already stereotyped and banal and as bound by some strange law of its own as marriage. You know how it is. Madge, dear old Madge, whom you went to college with, comes to you and offers you her husband on a silver platter, while she makes off with your beloved. And then you look at George—good old George, you probably went to college with him, too— and you just have to take him on for the duration of the evening or the house-party or whatever it is. You wouldn't want Madge to think that you didn't appreciate her property. Isn't that better than jealousy, and getting excited about Reno? It has even a kind of sanitary effect on the conjugal emotions. After a session with some one else's mistake in matrimony, how gladly do you come home to your own major error! How you notice the forgotten curl on the forehead and the nice smile—and then the dear cozy closeness and the feeling of "this is what I wanted all the time!"

This is all to the good, but even in maintaining diplomatic courtesies across the borders of matrimony, is petting any substitute for the grand old idiocies of courtship? Wouldn't you really like it, beautiful lady with the skin men love to touch, if you sat like a queen, shedding glamour on all and sundry, and a gentleman came and bowed down before you, and—it was only your hand that was kissed? A distinguished sociologist, who expounds the glories of the golden age to come from lecture platforms and in print, and who was once so respectable that he was on the faculty of one of the greatest women's colleges, sent to the wife of a friend, after a session in which the lady had proved a little reluctant, a post card bearing a picture in the best Micky Mouse tradition. Under the picture was written, "Don't monkey around me unless you mean business." Wouldn't it have been nice if that had been a sonnet?

As we sit in the midst of all our great mass production of cheap sexual excitement, and feel just a little bored with it, suppose we took a little of our spare time to turn this new easiness between the sexes into a new art of courtship? Suppose, by taking a little thought, we could transform these crude, unleashed desires into a new art of manners, and into means of self-adornment and self-display? Suppose we developed the little social dramas of approach and retreat, such as the social dance, which allows any two participants a conventional equivalent of the embrace of lovers under the tolerant eye of the whole room in the beguiling enchantment of light and music? Suppose that into the formless, jelly-fish mauling and mushing, which we have in many quarters, we were to put again the backbone of a genuine social code, and so start the beast on an upward evolution which might ultimately end in the development of heart and brain and nerves enough to be fastidious? Suppose we could even put gaiety and swagger and humor and social play into such mooning and crooning as bursts from the maudlin heart of the whole love-sick world every time we turn on the radio? "I lo-o-o-ve yo-o-o-u. I am so lo-o-onely-e-e," wails the radio crooner. So you do, you poor soul. So you are! It is an old story. But it ought to be retold now—in different words.

2

The art of courtship has already done so much for the world that we might trust it to do a little more. There is, for example, the transformation of youth. The romance of our late teens and early twenties, the fraternity house-parties, the free roaming off of youths and maidens in pairs into the moonlight, is something unknown to most older civilizations. There never was a greater social experiment than turning over the dangerous pastime of courtship to the young, and making it the basis of the gravest of life's choices.

Before the northern European peoples, but especially the Americans, did this reckless thing, courtship was not used by any civilized people as a prelude to permanent mating. Even in nature, nothing so momentous depends on it. It is there the prelude to each individual sexual culmination—a very different matter indeed. Though the art of courtship had often been beautifully developed, it had been as a social luxury, a means of taking up and turning to art or ornament or personal pleasure, the free surplus of desire beyond the uses of the family. In the Orient it was usually the means of acquiring a mistress in addition to the wife, and this was its use, too, in Greece and Rome. In many societies it has been a means of persuading a married lady to look with interest on some man other than her husband. In the Middle Ages it was even considered desirable for a man to court all his life a beautiful married lady. So Petrarch courted Laura. So Dante courted Beatrice, who remained his guiding star, to the topmost heights of Heaven, long after he had married another woman and became the father of more than half a dozen children. In those days it was believed that courtship need not necessarily lead to mating. It might lead to poetry or an heroic death or to the love of God. The work of the beloved lady was done when she had turned the man into the *gentleman*.

But even so, in the countries where the mediaeval ideal of courtship was most beautifully developed, in France and Italy, no one thought of trusting it to the young or making it the basis of such a bread-and-butter affair as marriage; and among old families in those lands, who value their ladies and the continuity of domestic life, nothing of the sort is considered now. Marriages are arranged by the parents, as they are and always have been in the Orient, and in all countries outside of northern Europe and America in very recent times.

Yet we in America have actually taken the great romantic ideal, developed, as it was, by mature people under social conditions which, strictly scrutinized, Mrs. Grundy would find immoral, and have given it to youth as a guide through the mists of immature sexuality and social inexperience. We even believe that the process of courtship brings such illumination that people not old enough to choose anything else in life may, under its benign tuition, choose a mate. And what American, with his youth fresh in his memory, is ready to admit that this is wrong?

Where American youth is happy—and it is probably, on the whole, the happiest youth in the world—it is because it is frankly provided with the machinery of courtship—the dances, the parties, the dressing up, the arts, the graces, the awareness which education and literature and art and music can give to the whole beautiful illusion. Where the machinery and background, the traditions and manners, and general tolerance of courtship are not provided, there is nothing to do but pet. Sex is not always an end in itself in marriage or out of it. It is, for the crude, an approach to general human intimacy. "I am so lonely," sings the radio crooner. So he is. So are we all. But there are none more lonely than those whose bodies meet, but not their hearts and minds and their two worlds of dreams. To bridge this loneliness, even between girls and lads, there must be all the more complex and subtle approaches which only a common culture makes possible,—conversation and ceremony, manners and games, enterprises developed in common, and finally and, most important of all, that participation of each in the other's world of dreams which is the culmination of romantic union and which is possible only when there is some poetry or music or religious faith held in common. Much of the beauty of mediaeval courtly love had its source in that great store of poetic imagery and practice which belonged to any man or woman brought accidentally together, by reason of their common membership in the universal church.

The charm of all social life is mutual idealization. But the idealization is far more intense, exciting, and potentially rapturous between members of the opposite sex than between those of the same sex. One of the perversities of man, as a social being, has been the attempt to separate sex from that enchantment which human beings naturally exercise on each other, and so make it either a thing apart from polite social recognition and unclean, or a subject of coarse humor, or a matter-of-fact physical appeasement. A certain amount of humor is no doubt wholesome. It is the natural protest of man's intelligence against the grotesque physical machinery to which Nature has tied his most glorious emotions. The mechanism of sex is not really worthy of the heights and depths of man's capacity for love or even for desire, just as the mess and physical degradation of child-bearing is not and never can be worthy of the heroism and high consecration of motherhood. Nature was no artist here—we have to admit it. All the more reason then for invoking and never letting go the enchantment which veils the great organic mistake in a mystical intensification of the human magnetism. Personal happiness depends on courtship as a personal and social art, with all that manners and culture can give to enhance it, learned in the process of getting a mate, and perfected by continual practice till old age in the more various excitement of keeping her—or him. And general social pleasure depends on an imitation of the mutual flattery and endearing gestures of courtship in manners and dancing and social play, as a means of discharging harmlessly, in social fire-works, those general currents of attraction between men and women, which allure us and make fools of us, but which, in most cases, would even in casual mating bring no satisfaction. The amorous readiness of man is just part of the beautiful superfluity of nature, which hangs the melon vine all over with large yellow blossoms and calls all the bees to "make whoopee" over their honey, without ever expecting more than a small fraction of them to turn into melons. So in all polished societies the lucky leisure class has filled its idle moments with imitation love-making, which might be anything from the consecration of a great mind to the woman who could meet and respond to him in his world of dreams, as with Dante or Michelangelo, to the irresponsible twitter of the cocktail hour. The difficulty with some modern experiments in this direction is not that they are not morals, but they are not art.

3

So far as the younger generation is concerned, the new doctors of leisure are already busy providing the stage for the development of a new art of courtship, and with it more glamorous social contact in general. John A. Piquet, under the title "Love and Leisure" in the August, 1934, number of Leisure magazine tells rather beguilingly of the means which some communities are taking to destroy loneliness. He tells of dances organized by the American Legion, "with elegant furniture and carpets" lent by friendly merchants. He tells of community plays in which people may "appear before their home-folks as they had long wanted to appear—fascinating girls, dashing men, heroic happenings." He even tells of a "Romance Survey" made by a group of citizens in Los Angeles! The Survey finds the state of "Romance" in that great city, gilded all around the edges with the footlight glamour of Hollywood, "deplorable." "Young people do not know where to go to meet each other and make friends. Frequent divorces were arising because young wives had insufficient recreation. Their husbands, tired from the day's work, did not know where to take them at moderate cost. Hence in the very place where our movie romances are made, romance in real life has a hard time of it."

He says that "these are the reasons, in large and small towns alike, why matrimonial journals and marriage 'agents' flourish, despite the law's rather puzzling crusade against them; why we have two million old maids and bachelors, and a million divorces and countless unhappy couples; why people marry second choices because their circle of acquaintances is so narrow; why immorality stalks rampant among the legion of unsatisfied or mismated souls; and why loneliness and lack of friends makes leisure time a period of suffering rather than of joy and usefulness." He serves notice that "civilization is waking up. The millions want something more than happiness in fiction and movies. . . . They want these things in real life itself!"

In a similar vein Mary J. Breen, in a book entitled "Partners in Play," which is by far the most stimulating and thoughtful of the various paper-covered pamphlets which have been rushed out from all sources to meet the new desire for something to fill "leisure," discusses means of bringing young men and women together and the social conduct of such affairs. Her book is full of the most alluring recipes for dances, parties, stunts, and picnics, and of kindly, tolerant, and knowing comment. Compared with the socio-moral teaching that used to be handed out to the young a few years ago, how joyous and generally inspiring is the new attitude, even of the Y.W.C.A., which with the National Recreation Association, sponsors and publishes this book. It indicates a profound change in the whole moral and social outlook of those who make themselves keepers of their brothers' and especially of their sisters' souls. Gone is the terror of the unwanted child and the ruined maiden, which used to be camouflaged under the solemn euphuisms of lectures about the "facts of life" to the young, and furtive, panicky watching of enamored couples. The knowledge of an adequate, though still bootleg, technique of birth control in the background makes the new elders wonderfully cheerful and easy. They sit smiling on the chaperon's seat at the dances, with a copy of Judge Lindsay's "Companionate Marriage" at home on their book shelves, twenty years younger than the chaperons of our day, and one hundred years wiser.

But more potent even than the passing of the social terror of sex, with the slowly spreading knowledge of birth control, is the universal recognition of the danger of the transference of social glamour and romantic adventure from members of the opposite sex to those of one's own. The homo-sexual fixation of the social illusion developed naturally from the terrified taboo of parents on anything that might lead young lovers "into trouble," but it had the curious result of neither restraining nor disciplining the physical impulses, but only of taking the charm out of the general social contact of men and women. The evil spreads far beyond the circles of the "fairies" and is pretty general among the older graduates of the "best" schools and colleges. Here is, for example, a fine, public spirited, upright, and honorable man of forty, a graduate of good schools and always a popular man with other men. He has a good, well-knit physique, kept to the top of fitness, by the social games on the golf course with his masculine cronies. Observe him among other men at the club. How free, joyous, and amusing he is, always something to say, always a story, always a sympathetic word or inquiry, always standing with his hand on the other fellow's shoulder, or giving playful punches and nudges here and there. A good fellow, and among men very charming. He is released with men. He swaggers before them and invites affectionate and friendly attentions from them. He glows. He shines. He is himself in this dear familiar company. Not an effeminate type at all, but rather a man's man. But see him with women, with his pretty and fetching little wife. He is kindly, but dumb, flat, and dead. He has nothing to say. Before even a casual, friendly smile from a woman he retreats in secret panic. Her words he answers in monosyllables. No woman, even his wife, ever sees that sly, warm, humorous smile that creeps over his face at the first jibes that greet him when he sticks his head in at the the club door. He is dull and embarrassed.

His wife cries herself to sleep night after night, and has headaches, and tells her woman friends she is going to leave him. Why, she can't explain, but a terrible embarrassment fell between them from the day that they were married. He breaks through it periodically in swift flashes of man's desire, which go and leave him deader than ever, and make her tense, hysterical, miserable. She runs hither and thither asking her woman friends what is the matter, oh what is the matter? He is so good to her. He gives her everything. He never really says a cross word. But he is dull and miserable at home. He hastens away to his dear friends and business in the morning, and comes back reluctantly at night. And always they are so constrained before each other. At the sight of her a blank, impassive mask falls over him. She starts when he speaks to her, and pales with dread when she hears his step on the porch. Why doesn't she talk it over with him? "My dear, we can't *talk*."

His mother says she can't understand it. He was always such a good boy, a true "one-woman" man. He never fooled around with girls, till he met this pretty little thing, and he was so foolish over her before they were married, giving her a gold watch, and pearls, and a piano, and things he couldn't afford. And since then he has just *slaved* for her, and never looked at another woman. He was just as pure as she was when they married. Had not his mother taught him herself to keep himself for the one woman he would love. What more is necessary for a happy marriage?

There are thousands of such cases and some of them go much further than this in intimate human agony. The source of the trouble lies deep in the social mores and in the deficiencies of our common culture. A text book on psychology in use among the students in a back country normal school tackles the question fairly, and tells the young misses of nineteen and twenty who are going out next year to carry the torch of learning into the villages, that the most important thing in adolescence is to achieve "successful hetero-sexuality!" It is a long word, and a grand one. May we take it to mean that even pedagogues think that there should be more and better courting? If so, perhaps something will be infused into education which will give emotional and imaginative coherence to those quaint odds-and-ends of literature and music and art which form the staple of school-taught culture, and which are so absurd because no one has yet seen the practical usefulness of culture. But if it were understood that personal happiness and, above all, happiness in love, depends on social patterns, and emotions, and imaginative pleasure held in common and of a nature to shed glamour on the common social life, perhaps we should see that culture is practical and so find a "background" which isn't quite out of key with the present American foreground.

The new forms of community recreation—the plays, the musical festivals, the dances, the agreeable social centers—promise something long needed. Suppose that we could add something to them, something like those old conversation games, and courtly exercises in which the creators of modern occidental manners, in castle and villa, once formulated, in jest that covered deadly earnest, the manners of the "courtier" and "what a gentleman may expect from a lady", and "in what manner a knight is expected to obey his lady's commands", and what is a "very parfit gentle knight". We don't need to pretend to be knights or copy the habits of "courts". But there must be new words and images in which to express our own ideals of ourselves and of each other. Used as we are to political self-government, we might find new forms of social government to order and increase that mutual glamor which belongs to all human contact but is most instinctive and most beautiful when what used to be a "lady" meets what used to be her "knight".

4

But, after all, the young take care of themselves. They are even growing decorous and graceful. The elders always worry too much about the young people. It is a means of diverting their own attention from the mess they are making of their own chaotic middle age. For the American ideal of "romance" puts an intolerable strain on us as we grow older and fatter, and are engulfed in houses, business, and children. In America one is not only expected to be in love, after the fashion of the old poets and knights and romance makers, when one marries, but one is to stay in that sort of love all one's life. If one does not, it is quite all right to be as idiotically enamored of some one else and, breaking the news to one's partner in the great enterprise of creating a home that one no longer loves him "in that way," to marry some one else, and start a new home and children. No other people except the Americans ever tried to make the most important of the social institutions out of any such dream-stuff.

Yet the men on whom the shining mantle of the old knights has thus come to rest are, by common consent, the most inadequate lovers in the world, and the dumbest in the intimate business of marriage. So at least the French, German, Italian, Polish gentleman likes to tell you, bowing to kiss your white hand. But after a little adventuring in international society, the American woman discovers a strange thing. What all these polished gentlemen are professing, with their lovely manners, and their courtly flattery, and their beautiful articulateness, and what they don't mean at all, the poor dumb swain from home really feels and isn't saying, or doing anything about it either. This is, by now, a platitude, but it is rediscovered by every feminine adventurer in European social waters with amazement. Don Quixote and all his knightly ancestors do still live, back in the inmost hearts of the dumb husbands at home. It is about the only place in this world where they are to be found in the flesh.

And, strangely enough, there is something about this absurd ideal of romantic love kept at a high rosy pitch till death do us part which is entirely congenial with the American temperament, and would be congenial to our social mores, too, if we ever took time to work them out. The life-long hypnotism of romantic love is constantly achieved by the plainest Americans, especially in those parts of the South and the West where life is most quaintly native. I know a business man nearing sixty who after a long and unhappy marriage with one lady, whom he had endured in the most quixotic spirit of chivalry, fell in love with a young woman in his office. He is normally a rather silent dry man, hailing from some of those sun-bitten great open spaces of the West, and looking for all the world like Uncle Sam. In the old days whenever he spoke of the young woman in his office, a beautiful light used to come over his hard features, such a look as one might paint on the face of a knight kneeling in a chapel before the image of the Virgin Mary. Later being released from his first marriage he married this young woman. They have been living in the West for fifteen years, raising a family of children whom he calls the "buddies." Meeting him recently in New York on a business visit, a friend said, "And how is Ellen?" referring to the young woman in his office, long his wife. Exactly the same look of worship for the Virgin Mary came over his face, and his voice softened. "She's fine," he said, "getting a little gray, but just as easy to look at." He went off for a moment in a lovely dream. "Just got a letter from her," he said, patting his breast pocket. "I write her every day, and she writes to me." He was just as beautifully and completely hypnotized as he had been fifteen years before when the lovely young lady was but a hope and a vision.

Such men need to know nothing about the art of courtship. They follow their own simple instincts to words and behavior on occasion, which no knight could better. But this Don Quixote came out of a rather simple primitive American background, and so could be the kind of person the American naturally is.

In many cases our immense capacity for romantic feeling is overlaid by community habits and city customs that are quite alien to it. If Americans were the kind of people who could settle down to making only a social and business partnership of marriage, all this living outside ourselves, this perpetual intrusion of Tom, Dick, and Harry in our houses, this ringing of the telephone, this buzzing back and forth of cars, this loud preparation of the children and all their friends to get into the car and go somewhere—all of this might do very well on the domestic stage. But we rest the whole stability of marriage on the continuance of what we call "romance." And we mean *romance*—we mean the whole glorious, ruddy, high pitched illusion, the mutual hypnotism of two souls shut off from the world in a common dream. It is as necessary to the American as food, and a great deal more necessary than sex. His sore heart wails for it over the radio. He spends his money on anything that appeases for one moment his perpetual hankering for it. And he finds it with astonishing frequency in a mere wife. But how can he possibly keep it, in the kind of domestic and social circumstances he lets himself be involved in—never any rest, never any privacy, husband and wife separated from each other by a perfect barrage of inconsequentialities? This dead front which American husbands and wives so often present to each other, this state of mutual tension and discomfort, is not really sexual repression, as the psycho-analysts say it is. It is a repression of all that leads up naturally to the sexual union, and all the rest and peace and intimacy of comradeship that should come after it.

If "soul-mates" and "dreams come true" and going with the loved one down that "long, long trail a winding into the land of my dreams" is what we really want—and all real expressions of the popular heart and soul show that it is what we want a great deal more than any one wants sex in the raw—we shall have to set ourselves to the long slow discipline of making it for ourselves through customs and manners and domestic arrangements which allow time and space for the slow and delicate growth of the mutual dream.

Already instruction in the use of leisure for the perfection of courtship is coming from an unexpected quarter. Physicians and neurologists are trying to teach shy and hasty husbands that wooing is the indispensable preliminary to every individual act of mating, if the woman's nerves and organs are not to be wrecked. Women are learning more slowly, and with less outside help, that coyness and coquetry are not means of alluring the lover and making him spend money on her, but indispensable stages in the slow awakening of those deeply hidden feminine centres of sensation, and of the carefully guarded womanly impulse of self-surrender, which turns cheap and easy appeasement into something of cosmic dignity. The art of courtship is more than a plaything for children. It is one with the art which makes music out of the chaos of noise that assails the human ear. To the impulses of human desire it does what the artist can do with the colors, which when the child splashes them together in his paint box, all run into one another and make mud.

Suppose one even faces the possibility which still seems so shocking to some, but which is probably inevitable—the spread of such knowledge of safe and unobnoxious contraceptives among young and old alike, and even such control of disease, that the fear of undesirable social consequences would be taken out of all love-making. Love will then cease to be a matter of "morals" at all, and will be controlled only by taste and expediency and, among the best men and women by the artist's desire to make one whole, round, beautiful thing of life. But would this do away with courtship? It would only increase the need of it, and the consciousness of a longing that cannot be met by sex but only by what the American rightly calls "romance." For, in the past, the idealization of the relations of men and women was not increased, but only rendered sterile and finally burdensome and embarrassing, by an attempt to make it a substitute for the simple mechanics of birth control. And everywhere there has been a sexual starvation which, like other starvation, knows neither taste nor decency. But it is only the hungry man that will put up with any kind of food. Where hunger no longer rules, choice begins and pleasure in all the fine manners and beautiful settings of the art of dining. So even on its lowest level of physical need and appeasement there might be for sex the social skills and decorations by which such public ladies as the Japanese geisha have raised themselves above the degradation of the profession in which they started.

However amusingly, swaggeringly, and prettily, the men and the gay ladies of some civilizations have managed to limit love to one compartment of their lives alone, I don't think this is possible for Americans in general. Foreigners laugh at us as "romantic." So we are. Romance is our favorite word. But why not? Listen to the outcry from our collective heart in the crooning on the radio. It is painful. It is pathetic. It is maudlin. But it is characteristic of us, as the stout bawdy singing one hears in some European villages is characteristic of other lands. One woman for one man, and he Don Quixote and she the Helen of man's unrealizable desire; all one's life long, in the kitchen and by the hearth, to find the blue heaven of "dreams come true"—that is what we want. We want it to the softest depths of our silly hearts. People so deluded as to want anything like that can, by following their dream, really find it. But if we are to find it, we must take time to be beautiful and to make beauty; we must cherish the common dream with all the skill of manners; and, regarding the illusion as the most precious of our household possessions, give it not only our secret worship but our best time and thought as well.

5

So much for courtship in marriage. But what of all this extra-marital excitement? Adultery is, of course, a very old leisure time pursuit. But, as Judge Lindsay points out, there is something singular in the present attitude. He says that people of the type who would have turned from it in genuine and instinctive moral horror in the past are disposed to stop and question, if not to condone adultery and practice it. A charming lady, a graduate of Vassar, and long and happily married to one husband, a lady of the type who has always been the final standard of womanly goodness and arbiter of social manners, said, with a tolerant little smile, of some of her brother's friends, "Oh, they are one of those crowds that practice *noble adultery*."

There is much more law and good feeling and much more of an impulse to some new and better code of social manners in such groups than Mrs. Grundy would admit. Partly the modern experiments are due to an obscure consciousness that, where secure and unobnoxious forms of birth control are understood, and the family is built from the beginning on a plan, with children "spaced" and prepared for and given each its proper chance of nurture, there can be no adultery; for the very means by which the family is spaced and planned can be used to prevent any adulteration of the inheritance through any other relationship. Partly, these inter-marital courtships are a release from the universal domestic frustration. Partly they are, strangely enough, a way of finding new approaches to the beloved at home—of getting knowledge and practice missed in youth. One does not need to have Judge Lindsay assure us, with his "cases", that the "way to a more perfect monogamy may be by way of a triangle." Anyone with open eyes can see couples who carry on "affairs" by mutual agreement because of something that seems to be contributed thereby to the intense and absorbing drama of their pursuit of each other. This is no doubt morbid, and, among intelligent people, it seldom lasts long. It is, however, a drastic remedy for a more morbid deficiency in their own education and social heritage. Partly also the unlovely attempt at release through drink, jazz, and "petting" is a blind reaching for something that has been achieved in the past by giving imitation love-making a place in social life, if only it is carried off with grace, sprightliness, imagination, and wit. Having only simple, domestic patterns to go by, we make a mess of it. But one can imagine that in the far distant and civilized future, it might become a rather charming game of "Let's pretend."

GOD is Love, says the Bible. But so is man. Love is the only human emotion. All other emotions are phases or disorders of it. Is not the energy of anger, the energy of an actual or potential outrage to love? Are not jealousy and envy forms of sick love? The relation of fear and anxiety to love is not so obvious, but what the psychoanalysts tell us is easily proved by experience—that they rise in the consciousness when there is undue suppression of sex, and to most people sex is love. As for all more generous emotions—pity, affection, hope, faith, admiration, awe—are they not only colors of the spectrum into which the white light of love is broken?

In dealing with any bright child, one quickly learns that there is a wonderful release of energy and joy in tricks which call out a child's interest. Suppose Mother tells Annie to set the table. Annie frets and leaves her game unwillingly. She drags her feet. She pouts. The task looms like a mountain. Then Mother says, "Annie, open the tissue paper on the table. See! They are three roses for the table. And you may get down the blue plates." Annie's burst of interest in the flowers communicates itself to the dreadful table setting. She runs. She flies. She gets down the blue plates. No need to tell her this time not to forget the tumblers. She remembers everything she ever was told. She turns out the task like a veteran butler, twittering with interest.

This release which comes from seeing familiar or unbeloved things in a light which suddenly attracts one has been much studied by the psychologists. Jung and his school call this mysterious stream of underground energy, whose release and concentration make us happy, and whose repression makes us miserable, the *libido*. This is the Latin word for desire, understood as organic hankering or need. It is a larger word than *appetite* or *sex* or *love*, but it includes all of them, at least when the psychologists employ it. But it is far from a satisfactory term. To find a word which means love in both its organic and its cosmic force, and in all the intimate human relations of affection and tenderness also, is very difficult. When Freud was criticized for referring all the emotional experience of man to sex, he said he would gladly have used such a word as "love" but he did not do so because that word had been so refined and made pretty that it allowed man to evade the facts about his own psychic habits and the mechanism in which his "higher feelings" were rooted. Yet sex was too narrow a word for what Freud meant; since it is to man not only an experience but a symbol, and the sexual imagery that runs through man's thinking and dreaming is partly a way of representing to the imagination something else that man wants—appreciation, admiration, intimacy, help, security—all the goods which a lover might bring. So some psychologists use the word *libido*, as being larger than sex, and a little nearer the ground than love. Yet now that Freud has taught us where to look for the roots of it, why not use the word *love*? It is, after all, the word people really use, and in enough different senses to cover almost everything. Annie, properly stimulated by the roses, loves to set the table. The lover loves his mistress, but the mother loves her child, and the saint his God.

But, whatever we call it, we know how it works, and its generally miraculous character. Annie's experience in setting the table can be duplicated by any of us with almost anything we are accustomed to do. When you turn to a familiar task or experience perfunctorily, you are not really neutral to it. There is a positive sensation of dread, inertia, dislike. But suppose you throw just a little more energy into it. You put your mind on it. You take a little more time over it. You try to do it well. Suddenly you find yourself borne along on a warm current of energy. You like it. You are having a wonderful time with it. You don't want to stop. And when you do stop, there is an afterglow of exhilaration and satisfaction. This applies to everything one does from hoeing the garden to taking the wife out to dinner. The old legends make it a miracle that when Saint Francis, from a sense of duty, began to wash the leper's feet, he was suddenly overwhelmed with a love for the leper, and kissed him gladly. It is a miracle that any one can repeat. Show a kindness to one who you do not like. Do it thoroughly, taking plenty of time, adding all that can make your action pleasant to the other. Do you not find yourself warming to something like love?

This is the secret of the great saints and the great artists. They learn to put just that extra psychic force into their contact with man or with the wonders of the world. So they are lifted up and borne along on a mysterious current of energy. The saints felt it as the love of God, dwelling in them and flowing out from them. When they lost it, they were miserable, and thought that God had turned His face away. Artists have sometimes called it inspiration, which means literally, breathing in—breathing in a little more life than other people, and giving it out. Probably this energy was what Buddha meant when he said that those who would be released from the evils of this world must, among other things, learn "right rapture."

Most of the religions which have really made men happy have emphasized this simple miracle of loving. Its effects are so immediate that, presented in the most banal form, as in some of the Pollyanna exhortations of New Thought, or wrapped up in any sort of theological hocus pocus, the exhortation to love, when it is obeyed whole-heartedly, brings to the individual something that seems like a revelation from God. This accounts for the shining faces among the new disciples of creeds that seem absurd to the critical intellect. It

accounts for the joy with which saints have gone to martyrdom and heroes to death.

There is a point up to which the release of psychic energy
through love brings no weariness but rather a general increase in available force. Like the oil in the widow's cruse,
the energy of love seems to be miraculously renewed. The
typical exhaustion of the neurotic person, the sense of fatigue
and inertia, is due not to over-using this current of energy,
but to blocking it or repressing it instead. Much of the weariness of daily living is not the use but the frustration of energy.
Though there is probably a limit to the individual's capacity
for loving, most people are stopped by circumstance or training far short of that limit.

However exhaustless love seems to be, there are boundaries
set to it by time and space. We cannot do everything and be
everywhere and give our attention to all that comes under our
noses. One source of unhappiness in a complex civilization
is the constant stimulus to our interest, and hence to potential love, without opportunity to go further in effort or experience. Social and urban life teases us like the girl who
invites and flirts and gives nothing. To find peace and happiness one must exchange the unsatisfactory philandering with
many interests or people for an honest loving of a few.

Often this is achieved through an experience which at once
concentrates and releases the great energy of love. For most
it comes with the simple process of falling in love with an
individual, permanently and irrevocably and accepting with
joy the discipline of building on one absorbing emotion a
family and all other social relations. For some it has come
with the discovery of a life's vocation. For a few it has come
with religious conversion, in which a vision of the whole
meaning of life has taken the form of falling in love with a
Universal Person, and submitting the psychic energy to Him
for evermore. Often the opening of the one channel through
which the psychic energy can run happily to the end of life
has been unexpected and instantaneous. But in these cases

there has usually been a long period of experimentation and painful seeking. Most people have to make a mess of one or two love-affairs before they can carry one through to rapture, and from rapture to peace. The inspiration of those who in a moment, by an accident, have discovered the opportunity for a life of happy work, the conversion of those who, in a flash, have known God, have come, like the visions of dawn to saints and seers—after all night vigils. For those who long and honestly try to find a way out from the marsh of emotional frustration into which most of us plunge at adolescence out of the sunny and open fields of childhood, there usually opens an exit into happiness. But unless we do struggle and try, and keep on trying, we may get stuck in the mud for the rest of our lives.

Hence some portion of those hours in which industry and trade permit us to live, instead of working to get something to live on, may well be devoted to the great business which Saint Francis called "setting love in order." This involves many different activities. There must be some thinking, and much experiment. There must be choice and steady use of such emotional nourishment as comes from books or art or music or religious ritual. There must be deliberate seeking out of people, and equally deliberate avoidance of them. There must be self-training in social skills and emotional attitudes. In each life there are three great departments in which love must be separately set in order. One must set in order the love for one's self, the love for one's fellow, and the love for that something beyond, which is neither one's self nor another, and which has been personified as God. Not every modern mind can be happy in the old simple imagery which made of the mystery of the universe, conceived as a whole, an infinite and loving Person, with a special interest in one's self. But the need for a personal approach to that mystery remains. Those to whom God has become just a name for a dim ghost in an empty heaven must seek some other way of visualizing that great whole which is not the self and the contemplation of which brings ecstasy and self-forgetful-ness. It has sometimes been found through science, and some-times through art, and sometimes by very simple people, in a wordless secret of self adjustment to things as they are. The three-fold setting in order of love was once said to be the sum of the law and the prophets. The Christian was to love his neighbor as himself, which meant adequately loving himself first. And he was to love God—or some ultimate, selfless goal of human endeavor—with all his heart and his soul and his mind and his body. This is the whole of the high art of lov-ing, and very much easier to say than to do.

2

Despite our immense waste of romantic love on ourselves, most people have a larger surplus for their fellows than they are somehow able to show. Much of the criticism, unkind-ness, or even positive cruelty in social groups is a frustration of good will. When there is some real excuse for showing kindness,—a great illness, an automobile accident, a fire— how gladly do even the unamiable hasten to help and to share! At the beginning of a great disaster, such as the Mis-sissippi Flood, or the World War, there is great exhilaration and happiness because the barriers to mutual good will are broken. Between friends, between parents and children, be-tween husband and wife, the same holds true. In moments of death or threatened danger, they know how much they love each other, and draw near, and even dare to say it or at least to show it. But when the special stimulus is withdrawn, they fall apart. Each begins to put on a false front to the other, saying irritably what the heart knows as false, keeping silent when love cries to speak, withholding the caress and the kindness —for God knows what reason.

It is with love, as with poetry. The amateur has his inspira-tions, but he has not knowledge and practice that enables the experienced poet to fill in between inspirations with beauty deliberately created. So the amateur musician of talent often comes upon a lovely musical theme or phrase, but he does not know how to build up from it the finished piece. So love, which is the poetry and music of life, needs craftsmanship. There are words and gestures, caresses, and acts of homage or of service or of comfort which come naturally in the high moments of feeling. When the feeling recedes, one must manufacture their equivalent to carry over to the next fine moment. These are the traditional graces of all civilized intercourse in families or among friends. Many intimate groups suffer intensely, needlessly hurting and irritating each other in every contact, because they lack the external forms of love. Many suffer, too, for lack of any common ground of social or cultural activity on which to meet. And many because, having that common ground, they let the intimacy which they secretly long for be frustrated by the external commotion and intrusion of everything and everybody upon every one which is characteristic of the American family.

So when one sets love in order, there should be time to realize the blessedness of whatever love is ours, to fondle it in the imagination and let the enchantment which is in all love shine out, and then to find ways and means of expressing it. Kind words and endearments hurt no one. If you love, it does no harm to say so. Where the physical ties are close and conscious, as between husband and wife and parents and young children, caresses are the natural language of affection. They make poetry of that close contact in all the physical functions which is otherwise an offense to human dignity. Without them in close family life there can hardly be emotional health. On the other hand, where there can be no physical union, or where the physical ties should begin to weaken as in the case of parents and older children, undue caresses lead to perversion. Many who are too reserved in their relations to mates and families rush too easily into intimacy with strangers. Making unconsciously an emotional demand which the other cannot meet, they are for ever getting their feelings hurt and being inexplicably disappointed or humiliated. The psycho-analysts have dwelt almost exclusively on the repression of sex. But an equally common repression is the repression of every manifestation of love except sex. It is the only intimacy that some husbands and wives know. The remedy is not more sex but more of its by-products. As an experienced playwright once said of the drama, the effectiveness of the last act is entirely determined by the preparation scenes.

Instead of physical closeness ritualized and made beautiful in caresses and words of love, there is an unnecessary bossing and nagging and using each other's property and walking in on each other at all times. If one were truly to set intimate love in order, one would do away with all communism which had nothing to do with the comfort of each other's presence, and, conceding more separateness in non-essentials, would make a more leisurely and lovely drama of the moment when hearts and minds and bodies can really meet.

As one moves from the centre of intimate love to the outermost circumference of neighbors and acquaintances, manners and conventional gestures of good will progressively take the place of caresses and endearments. But they are just as necessary. Much ill feeling is engendered by carelessly neglecting the points of contact with others. To make a due exchange for favors received, social and otherwise, to answer letters, to make calls, to take part in a reasonable amount of communal enterprise—this sort of thing is the grammar of human intercourse. But how many people can honestly say that neither love nor friendship nor neighborly and general human kindness are being scanted and given a shabby second best of their attention?

Of course the difficulty is partly that our lives are cluttered with people with whom we have no normal points of contact. Many people sacrifice the various relations of love and friendship to an unthinking gregariousness. They are never happy except when they are being stirred around in a featureless human stew—and they are not happy then, only reduced to a bland but tepidly warm neutrality of feeling which dopes their craving for intimacy. Some people flee from the difficulties of the most complex and beautiful of all the human relations—that of man and woman in permanent union—to herd thus with their own sex. Most people who live in this way are secretly unsatisfied. It is for them and of them that the radio wails, "I am so lonely."

3

To the ancient Chinese the most interesting employment in the world was to make a kind of chart of their human relationships—to say, "So much and Such and Such I owe my father and mother"; "So much and Such and Such I owe my benefactor." "So much and Such and Such I owe my servant." This is the teaching of Confucius, and by the teachings of Confucius the Chinese have lived for 2300 years, and have created the most enduring society and the most polished social life the world has ever known. Once the exact degree or quality of the attention you owe to father or friend or servant is determined, according to Confucius, it is to be translated into what he called "ceremony." Ceremony meant finding exactly the right words, gestures, actions, and gifts to express this carefully defined relationship of yourself to another. Each relation was to be worked out like a poem or a picture until you found exactly the behavior which expressed your feeling.

The result of practice of this sort in any art is that at first the results are formal and labored. But with continual practice there comes an apparent ease and spontaneity which can never be equalled by the untrained, however gifted. So Chinese social life has, at times, seemed over-formal and decorative. But when one knows intimately a social personality created by this great tradition of China, one must give it the wondering homage aroused by any other art. This fluency and adroitness in meeting and handling people, this inspired brilliance both in showing courtesy and in giving insult, and this strong basis of genuine integrity and kindness in all personal dealings—it seems like the gaiety and ebullient good will of a nice child. But it isn't. It is only the spontaneity of knowledge and of practice.

Crude and sentimental as we still are, in all relations to people, we find something obnoxious in the idea of submitting love to definition and to practice. We are like those amateur poets who think they will lose their precious "inspiration" if they learn to scan; like these gifted players by ear on the piano who think their genius will evaporate if they practice to the metronome. But one can imagine rather charming forms of self-amusement which might increase the beauty of friendship and love and even lead to that knowledge of people which makes for leadership. Consider, for example, what Confucius might have done with that malicious game which Alice Roosevelt and her mother-in-law devised. They had to deal with a large family of the Longworth relatives and be more polite to some of them than they felt. So they revenged themselves by drawing a chart of the tribe, showing all the ramifications of relationship, and indicating in colors the psychosis from which each individual suffered—a different color for each psychosis. If Confucius had been playing a game like this, he probably would have produced a very beautiful piece of decorative art, showing in symbolical colors the quality of the love he owed to all with whom he came in contact. Blue might have stood for all the loves which are natural, and as it were from Heaven, the love of parent, of child, of brother and sister. Yellow, which in old China, was the color dedicated to the Emperor might have stood for all general and communal obligations. Red, which was the color of religion and ceremony, but also the favorite color in social life, as being, as a Chinese once told me, "the most glorious color", would have stood for all the social relations which make the joy of social life—intimate friendship, personal love.

Probably a similar chart was the basis of Dante's great

poem, "The Divine Comedy," which is the drama of setting love in order, played out on the whole great stage of the universe, with Hell, and Purgatory, and Heaven as scenes. One can imagine that Dante, as a disillusioned and embittered man of thirty-five, took all the people he knew, and some he had read of in books, and said to himself, "What do they really look like in the long view of Eternity?" So he sorted them out and put some in this and some in that circle of Hell, and some here and some there in Purgatory, and some in the ascending series of Heavens which lead through bliss to the heart of God. Crude people, who have not really read this great and curious human document, have said that Dante put in Hell all those whom he disliked and wished to revenge himself on. He did nothing of the sort. Two of the most touching and heart-broken meetings with those whom he had loved or admired or pitied are in Hell, and there is more than one to whom he is personally luke-warm in the higher reaches of paradise. He makes it quite clear that in his mind, personal love and the judgment of God were two different things. He could love and pity and admire individuals while recognizing unflinchingly the social evil of what they had done. If Dante did not draw on paper a chart of Heaven, Purgatory, and Hell, with all their several circles and inhabitants, he must have had one in his mind. And one can imagine that this sorting out and labelling of all his multifarious human contacts must have been potent to release the one great love of his life—his love for Beatrice—which, he says, had been long frozen in his heart.

Those who are confused and miserable in their personal relationships might find help in trying to represent graphically to themselves their troubles and their desires and all the ideal possibilities of love. Such effort would stimulate sub-conscious thinking which might lead automatically to adjustment, and it would sharpen their observation and give them perspective on themselves as well as on other people. Business cannot move to-day without carrying charts and graphs of all its relationships. Why should the business of selling be more orderly than the business of living?

Love needs not only definition; it needs practice. A delightful lady, who was stimulated by one of Marjorie Wilson's talks on charm, and who probably is delightful because she takes an interest in such subjects, told me that her happiest hours recently were spent in a way she was very shy to confess. After some persuasion, she said that she had decided to take the busiest hour of the day, which happened to be between ten and eleven in the morning, and try to make every human contact that came her way as charming as possible. In her case, the hour she chose offered her a great variety of experience. Some days she was home. and the person who called between ten and eleven was the fish-man. Some days she was in an office, and had to fill the hour with conferences. Some days she had to go on an errand. Some days she had guests. On Saturdays the children were home, and a crew of their friends descended about this time. On Sundays the husband was home, and at ten they were just getting through breakfast and reading the paper. She said she never realized how dramatic and exciting her life was till she took just one hour of it each day to play the drama of human relationship through with art and beauty. There were never two days alike, and if she really put her mind on any one who came her way in the given hour, the most delightful vistas seemed to open. Every one was like a character in a story, and she so filled up her cup of good will in this hour that there was enough to give flavor and excitement to all the rest of the day.

And this brings to the final requirement of the art of loving. Love needs not only definition and practice. It needs realization. We do not realize our happiness in those who are dear to us. We go through the most precious experience with half our minds somewhere else. We let trivial externals nag us and distract our attention. The husband comes in, after hours when you have been missing him. Do you let yourself feel or say how glad you are that he is back? No, you say,

"Did you run out of gas in the car?" You drive a long distance
to take the son at school out to lunch. Do you give yourself
a chance to shine inwardly with the pride you feel in him—
the dear sturdy chap? No, you say, "John, take your elbows
off the table." It is true that it is often necessary to notice
these things. But it is even more necessary to give love its
place and its time—to savor it, to relax in it and let it flow
through you, warming every nerve, to say to yourself, "This
is happiness and I have it." That footlight glamor of the
imagination which we call "romance" is inherent in all love.
In the highest moments of happiness we are always in a
dream. So when we pause to realize and to make our own
whatever love has been given us, something emerges which
insensibly transforms this place and this moment into fairyland. We don't have to wail with the radio crooner our longing for the "land where dreams come true." We *live* in it,
and have built our house on its Main Street.

4

As for that Immensity beyond, which is not the self—
neither one's self nor another—no one is really happy till he
has found his own adjustment to it in love. The traditional
method of finding such adjustment has been through religious
faith. But there is a modern difficulty with traditional faith
which is quite different from that of our own fathers. The
trouble with it now is not that its teachings offend the intellect, but that its symbols have become foreign to the imagination. A generation ago, people had a touching faith that
the only real things were things they could see and touch
and eat. Since they couldn't see or touch or eat God or the
devil, they were agreed that they did not exist. But, in our
generation, we have awakened to a doubt of material reality
as profound as our father's doubt of the immaterial. We know
that in giving up theology for science, we have simply changed
one hocus pocus for another. One by one the thoughtful

people begin to see that the only reality man knows is the reality of his own experience, and that experience itself is only one kaleidoscopic stream of fictions. What are light waves and sound waves, really? They are not light and sound to us till they strike us. It is the mechanism of our own ears that makes sound, and of our own eyes that makes light. It is the mechanism of our own heart that makes love, and out of our own great need we make our own God.

In every place where men are not, in the silent streets of the sleeping city, in the moonlit sky of midnight, in the white blaze of the desert, in the green shade of the forest and the gray width of the sea, there is something to which the heart of man goes out. In his highest moments of creative activity or even of personal love, that which he serves is nothing human. There is a rapture of recognition and of love for something that cannot be seen or handled or touched. Saints have known it, but so, too, have poets and artists and men of science, and simple nobodies alone on a long walk, and children by themselves in the sunshine, and even, I think, the beasts and the bees.

The discovery of this is as personal and individual as falling in love. Sometimes the discovery is made at the altar of some long established church. Sometimes it comes through lonely meditation. Any activity in which self is really forgotten brings one within sight of it. When you do anything, however trivial or simple, whole-heartedly, letting your interest flow out to it, forgetting yourself and all future profit in delight in the thing itself, in work well done, you touch the hem of Him whom men have called God. There is a margin of love which is neither for one's self nor for any other person. The greatness and goodness of any man is to be measured by the width of that margin. He who lacks it has no security against change and circumstance, against the weakness, the weariness, the monstrous cravings, and dreamlike delusions of all flesh. No personal love is strong to endure unless it is anchored in something that is not personal.

Our cold-blooded fathers, propounders of the great heresy of utilitarianism which has driven us all into the ground, would have said, "That is very well. All you mean is that in every life there should be a large number of impersonal interests—art, literature, the public good." But I mean much more than this. I mean that there is a surplus of desire, of hankering, of longing which must find its satisfaction in the impersonal—and not a bland satisfaction either, but that dramatic climax of love and interest which is the saint's and the poet's ecstasy—but also the child's shriek of delight in something perceived and something done, alone by himself, in some adventure on his own among the wonders of the world. For interest and desire, like physical passion to which they are in some obscure way related, must have their climax; for only in the climax can they be resolved, like passion, into peace. The universal restlessness of modern life is the restlessness of desire—stimulated continually, but not satisfied. There is a climax in any creative work brought to a complete finish, in any action successfully carried to the end. But there is also some necessary climax of pure feeling in which a man finds and makes his own in love some vision of life as a whole.

No man is so low that he is not dimly seeking his own salvation. Neither the doubt nor the sarcasms of the critical intellect can abolish the inherent necessity of the heart. But to point any individual soul to its ultimate home in the universal and the impersonal is beyond the wisdom of a layman. One can only take refuge in the grand old promise: "Seek and ye shall find. Knock, and it shall be opened unto you."

Arts of Civilization

I think it is the part of good sense to provide every fine soul with such culture, that it shall not, at thirty or forty years, have to say, "This which I might do is made hopeless through my want of weapons."—EMERSON

The Necessary Art of
Self-Improvement—XIV

SUPPOSE some one
had left you a large estate—house, barns, meadows, woodland, water; and suppose at the same time you had been left
a great store of money, furniture, and working equipment,
on the condition that it could be used only for the improvement of this particular estate. Who is such a fool that he
would not get to work on the property at once?

Something like this has happened to man. He has been
given one wonderful property in himself. Some one else has
started it and looked after it for years before he took it over,
and has spent a lot of time and money on it. And for its
improvement he has an unlimited store of things gathered
and created by all the fathers of our race—arts and skills,
knowledge and materials, the whole vast heritage of civilization. Of this any man may have as much as he can take and
put into himself—and no more.

We have such a hankering for expansion, for getting and
improving some property, that if we don't turn this energy
on ourselves—and most of us don't—it shows as a perpetual
effort to get something else in life—to get money, to get
amusement, to get excitement, to pile on ourselves and show
off any kind of thing. For a while during the great profit era
the world went mad, getting external property, piling up
buildings, stocks and bonds and machinery. But financial
disaster is now teaching us that no man may safely hold
external property beyond his own capacity for really using it.
If he tries to do so, it simply evaporates. The world is actually so rich in materials and even in skills that every one

might live like a millionaire. The reason we don't do this is only that we aren't big enough to use a million apiece. So since our passion to get and improve property when applied to external things has landed us in an impasse, many believe that we should approach the problem from the opposite direction, and put our energy into improving ourselves.

The beauty of this for the individual is that what you *are*, you really have. No man can take it away from you. When those who have had money and high social position lose it in a financial depression the best part of their wealth is still theirs. This is the training, the experience, the manners, and the accomplishments which they have bought in the past with their money. In so far as they have used wealth to improve themselves, they are still rich. In so far as they have spent it on anything else they are poor.

While most forms of self-improvement were once only the possession of the rich (and some forms can still be bought only with money), modern civilization makes most of the working wisdom of the world available to every one. Indeed the curriculum of the average "best" school or college is puerile, antiquated, and absurd compared with the curriculum any intelligent person can make for himself by walking around any large city and really using its museums, its parks, its libraries, its free concerts, its public life for his own education. And even in the more sparsely settled country districts, the equivalent of a college is offered free to any one who will make use of the farm bureau and the university extension services, the activities of clubs, the county organizations of one sort or another, and supplement them with reading, music over the radio and the like. When Ezra Cornell founded Cornell, he said he was going to create a school where anybody might come to learn anything. That was his idea of a university—a place of universal knowledge. Now-a-days the world is that kind of university. In it any person may learn anything. He has just to decide what he wants to know and look around. If he can't find it in the library, he will find it in a museum or at the county fair. If the public school teacher doesn't know, the farm bureau agent or the Y.M.C.A. secretary will. If he can't find it in a magazine, it will come to him over the radio.

The education offered in the schools and colleges has the value of continual practice in a limited number of intellectual and social gymnastics. But that is all. Whether you went to college or not, your real education is something you have to get for yourself, and much of it must be got in the years that follow the time when it is decent to graduate. For a man of forty to go back to school is ridiculous. But there is some schooling that can only begin at forty.

The largest room in the world is the room for improvement. There is not one of us who, when he looks over that property he calls himself, cannot discover a great deal that ought to be done with it.

2

Suppose we begin with the physical plant. You would think from the way most of us pamper our bodies that we really loved them and wanted them to be good specimens of their kind. But human beings in general are still pretty poor samples of organic life. A crowd of people on the street is worse to look at than a herd of scrub cattle. If you sit in a parked car, on a city street, and watch the passersby, how many do you see with lithe, slender, upright bodies, how many who are not too fat, how many that can walk, how many with good complexions, how many past youth whose faces are not setting into ugly lines—scowls, pursed lips, absurd fixations of the features which mean neither age nor wrinkles but just lack of attention.

Youth is often lovely to look at, and so should age be also. Most of the physical decay which we think is the result of aging is only the result of gluttony, laziness, slovenliness, or stupidity. There is not the slightest reason why, as people grow older, they should grow fatter. And the only reason why they grow fat is that they eat too much. It is true that many people who eat too much do not get fat. Instead they get colds or sinus trouble or indigestion or appendicitis. The fat ones are those healthy and cheerful souls who are able to keep too much food from poisoning them by storing it away as fat for future use. But now-a-days no one needs to be a human storage plant. A man might as well be a Chinese coolie as to go around with from five to fifty pounds of concentrated food he isn't using strapped to his innards—better be a coolie, in fact, for the coolie, now and then, can put his burden down. Any one who weighs, at any age, one pound more than he weighed when he was twenty and champion of the country club tennis court or the school basket ball team can do very much worse with his lunch hour than to omit it. No one needs advice about this. The life insurance companies and the food specialists assail us with information about how to do it. All one needs is grit.

Other forms of physical aging are as unnecessary as fat. Stiff muscles need not come with the years. They are a sign not of age but of laziness. Muscles that are used often improve with age—at least in some respects, as old dancers, acrobats, and stage performers in general often demonstrate. Wrinkles are no sign of age. Three fourths of the wrinkles, even on a very old face, are signs of temper, nerves, or just careless mannerisms. The wrinkles which are really the writing of experience into the face are often very beautiful. Lack of general up-to-dateness, grooming, and grace of manner and of motion are no signs of age. They are merely a sign that one is beginning to be dead before one's time.

If we did not all shamefully neglect and abuse our bodies, even those who start with a poor endowment of looks or health ought to grow handsome and healthy with the years. This is what the frail, spectacled boy that was Theodore Roosevelt did. This is what Annette Kellerman did. As some one said, if a woman is not beautiful at twenty it is God's fault. If she is not beautiful at forty, it is her own. So one is dependent neither on God nor the doctor for health and physical fitness. One is only dependent on one's self.

3

Another way of improving our personal property—which means ourselves—is to practice the great art of interior decoration on the inside of our own heads. This means filling the memory with a few ornaments, in the way of literature, and music, and making some attempt, through reading and learning continually, to put order and beauty into the musty junk most of us collected in school and the new intellectual contraptions we have picked up outside of it. Learning of some sort we do all the time. We are assailed with information, tormented with instructions. We have a thousand teachers, shouting at us from the press, from the newspapers, from the printed matter on the outside of the canned beans. We don't sit down in peace at the banquet board of knowledge, and relax afterwards and digest what has been served up to us. We nibble all the time. There's always some wonderful dish of knowledge on the sideboard, and some one crying it up and thrusting bits of it at us, "Taste this, just a bite. See how good it is."

Since no one lets us remain in a state of ignorance, we must, if we are to escape mental indigestion, take hours in which to order and to carry to something like completion, these various spurts of interest in this and that. And against what we can't digest at the moment, we ought to have the protection of some large substantial interest of our own which is temporarily using up our curiosity and time. There has been much talk lately of the value of hobbies. The hobby has a two-fold effect in creating peace of mind. It concentrates the interest in one direction and lets it come to something like satisfaction, and it shuts out teasing odds and ends of other interests.

But while hobbies are amusing, they are often trivial. They don't help one to reach that fundamental disorder in the mind, that maladjustment between all the odds and ends of knowledge which have been thrust at us from our kinder-garten days, and our own real impulses and desires and ex-perience of life. Only a sustained interest in the arts that really enter into our own dream world, literature, music, the drama, and really answer our questions about life can help us to serenity and assurance in all our real living.

While most institutions for adult education still hand out knowledge as if it were a kind of *hors d'oeuvre*, there is an immense general wealth of literature and art available to any one who really wishes to make it his own. You don't have to have another make out a course of study for you, or hear your lessons, or guide you. It is really more interesting to be your own teacher. Some day the real function of the public school may not be to teach anything beyond reading and writing and arithmetic, and after that to guide persons of all ages to the innumerable institutions and people within their own communities that can help them to anything they want to know. Already the Girl Scouts and the Boy Scouts, in the work for the various badges, are teaching young people how to go ahead on their own, finding their own school in the institutions and materials of their own communities, and their own teachers among their friends. The list of requirements for the various badges in the Girl Scout and Boy Scout manuals offers a wider, more really exacting, and far more socially valuable curriculum than the advanced grades of the schools. And any bright scout, boy or girl, proceeding on his own, will win ten badges and find fun and adventure in doing so, while he is aching through four or five "required sub-jects" in school under a load of "home-work."

Any person can study as the scouts work for badges, map-ping out a certain amount of ground to be covered ahead of time, seeking out help and companionship, and going ahead at his own rate. It is fun. There is no greater entertainment for idle hours. And if one does not stick too closely to books, but roams around in search of living material, and tries to make friends among those who are similarly interested, life opens out on all sides.

4

Another way of improving one's personal property has been brought home as a necessity by the depression. The collapse of industry precipitated on the world millions of poor souls who could only do one thing, and there was no more of that thing to do. As Walter Pitkin says, the breadlines are full of printers who cannot run lawn-mowers, and chauffeurs who cannot hoe gardens, and teachers who cannot hit typewriters, and Ph.Ds who cannot write English. This narrowing of skill to one specialty cuts off the whole organism from experience and leaves it on the level of the senses, helpless and hungering—an addict of cheap, bought amusement and dependent on cheap, bought goods. When the one skill can no longer be bought and paid for by industry, money stops, and with it many comforts and satisfactions.

On the other hand, the various skills of a Jack-of-all-trades are equal to so much money in the pocket, and equal, too, to an increase in life and happiness that cannot be measured. The family of a successful superintendent of schools was wondering why this able gentleman was always in debt, and was not able to keep up the appearance of well-being and wealth maintained by one of the young teachers working under him on half the salary. The young teacher had a pretty little house and garden, a beautiful young wife, charmingly dressed, and was rolling around in a new but inexpensive little car, with a nest egg ahead for the long looked for and desired baby. Why could he do this, and not his betters?

The answer was in the combined skills of the young man and his wife, with which they joyously filled all the time out of school. They had bought on small payments a run-down house in a poor section of the town where, as happens in many New England sea-coast towns, the slums were on the water-front, had rebuilt it with their own hands, had screened their bit of shore from the neighbors with cedars brought in from the woods, and carried dirt and stones to make a garden. The wife made all her pretty dresses and knit all her pretty sweaters, and ravelled them out when she was tired of them and redyed them and made others. They had a garden in a vacant lot. They picked wild berries and made jelly. About all they ever spent money on was the car and the payments on the house, and raw materials to do something with.

They were joyous. They were amusing. Friends gathered into their little house because something interesting was always going on there, and lent a hand with everything from painting the house to cooking the meal. Yet they seemed always to have lots of time and a great fund of energy, for their skills released time and energy. The superintendent's salary could not be stretched to cover payments to others for all the things his young teachers did for themselves. And the energy they spent having a good time doing something, he spent worrying.

The government is so disturbed over the disaster in which the poor Jacks-of-one-trade, in business and industry, have been landed that it is financing subsistence homesteads which will enable workers of all kinds to do for themselves what the young teachers are doing. But more is involved than social security and a better standard of living. For nothing that wealth can give will compensate for the loss of those nameless and unnoticed satisfactions which come with actively creating one's own environment. Happiness consists in the number and variety of pleasant sensations and small releases of energy. There are bound to be more units of pleasure in growing and picking one's own peas in one's own garden and bringing them in and cooking them than in seeing them come on a restaurant table in a dish. There are all sorts of associated sensations, the pleasant smell of the garden, the crisp feel of the pods, the surreptitious taste while they are cooking, the nourishing, steamy fragrance as they are lifted from the pot into the dish. There are various small prides, the pride of achievement, the pride of possession, the pride of abundance.

It is in the recovery of all these little pleasures and prides and climaxes that the fun of camping consists, or of hunting and fishing. Oftentimes at sunset, the camper wonders where his day has gone to. The hours have raced along. A minute ago it was morning and now it is night. He washed the breakfast dishes and rowed for the milk, and then it was lunch time. He ate lunch and had a swim and got water from the spring, and by that time it was night. But he has the exhilaration of having lived much and found many adventures in this simple day. This was because every activity really involved a series of little dramas, little obstacles overcome, little efforts rewarded, and all the time new areas of sensation were awake and functioning. He was seeing, hearing, smelling, touching—a great deal of which he did unconsciously, but which nevertheless fed the hungering nerves with something for which they are starved in the city.

So, when one is improving one's self, one may well acquire as many as possible of those skills by which one shapes one's own environment—camping and all its associated techniques, building, cooking, sewing, knitting, every form of decorative craftsmanship. Walter Pitkin says that an intelligent person can learn a new skill every six months. In the new centres for leisure-time activities, people turn to the manual crafts now with a kind of hunger. Balked in their efforts to improve their environment through buying things, their hands itch to make something, to grasp what they want in life with hands of skill. For men, especially, the various crafts bring a great release. Women have never wholly surrendered their crafts. Ten women can ply a needle for one man who can wield a hammer. In consequence, their daily experience, moment by moment, even under modern conditions, in cities and flats, has been more really diversified and interesting. There is no one so high in the economic scale that he can afford to give up the use of his hands. Even the Prince of Wales, they say, finds diversion in knitting.

5

In all this improving, what about the moral life? If one is to be healthy, handsome, intelligent, artistically skilled, and manually competent, is not one also to be good? But moral exhortations have been so overdone that we are as dead to them as to the traditional church images of God and the devil. A good deal of moral preaching is just a way of distracting attention from the real trouble—poor health, physical slackness, emotional suppressions, or generally bad social and economic conditions. There is nothing more deceiving than a good moral glow. It has as little effect in improving one's subsequent behavior as the "kick" of a cocktail.

To be honest, kindly, and courageous, to keep one's word and pay one's bills, and hurt nobody, seems such an obviously necessary and useful way of proceeding that one wonders why the preachers make so much fuss about it. Anything else so quickly lands you in trouble that one would think any one who is not a fool would be good. But the great main highway of morality, like the great main highway of religion, has been so trampled by the crowds, and so littered with paper bags and peanut shells and collapsed balloons that one has to make a detour now, and seek the good life by some private path— something that leads through the woods and by fresh fields, and by springs which are not yet walled in concrete and piped into every house.

So we are not saying anything here about being good. The trouble with most of us is not that we are bad; it is that we are slack and disorderly, undisciplined and confused. We can't do any good to our neighbors—even when our service club tries to ballyhoo us into it—because we don't know how to do good for ourselves. So we might as well leave "service" and "helping the other fellow" to the business convention, and experiment with some simple way of making life tolerable to ourselves. By the time each one of us has built up his own particular property of flesh and blood into a cleanly, habitable, beautiful, and efficient plant for the person who has to live in it and run it—which is himself—it may possibly be of use to some one else, too.

The Wholesome Art of
Exercise—XV

THE thriftiest of all leisure time pursuits is the making of a fine body. Not only need one spend no money on it. If one follows the Physical Culture pundits, one will soon have twice as much money in one's pocket—and nothing to do with it.

For there never was a more practically effective way of transforming the clogged and rusted human machine into a dynamo of energy and a sculptor's dream of beauty than the way of Bernarr Macfadden, in his palmy days, before he succumbed to money, advertising, and hooey. Macfadden was effective because he was a miser and a fanatic. He did not tell you that, if you wanted to be slender, and also healthier, you were to reduce your quantity of food. He said, "Eat nothing for a month." He did not suggest that to do without a pillow and sleep on a mattress that is not too soft is good for the spine. He said, "Sleep on the floor." He did not say, "Open your windows and ventilate your room." He said "Go out doors, and then stay there." He did not say, "Moderate your use of white bread and pastry." He said, "Cut it out." He did not tell you to take some exercise. He said, "Fall into the pond and swim. Then stand on your head ten times. Then run thirty miles barefoot." By the time you had taken Macfadden's advice, you had saved all your room rent, three fourths of your food bill, and half your expense for clothing. No wonder Macfadden himself got rich.

Despite its incidental charlatanism and its intolerable hot air, the Macfadden system is the best one can find just because it is so violent. The human frame is keyed to a spareness of

diet and an intensity of sustained physical energy which seems
incredible to the modern product of the machine age. For
a hundred thousand years human beings probably had no
houses to sleep in, no clothes to wear, and food only when
they happened to find it. When one is precipitated out of
civilization into such conditions as most human beings have
lived in from time immemorial, in an exploring expedition
or some of the more adventurous forms of travel, one's psyche
turns a somersault, and recovering the attitude of primitive
man finds it good. I have climbed a mountain in the Philip-
pines barefoot through unbroken brush. I remember that it
was fun, and that my feet weren't even sore afterwards. But
I couldn't run across the lawn barefoot here without discomfort. In the interior of China I have gone along for days
without food. I don't remember that I was even hungry,
though I do remember how good the chicken tasted when we
finally begged one and ate it without salt. Every one who
has stepped out of the vicious enchantment of civilized comfort knows this. And he knows a generally high, excited,
fearless, and happy state of mind that goes with it. We suffer
in civilization because we never call out our real physical
forces, and with them the true glory of the soul. And much
of the energy which might carry us over the landscape, lithe
and fleet-footed as the deer, we spend in the untidy process
of eating, digesting, and getting rid of food.

Theodore Roosevelt made himself into the remarkable
man he was by discovering and releasing in an originally
feeble body this tremendous undercurrent of vitality which
is our heritage from primitive man and which, unused by
civilization, helps to make us uneasy. Going west from
Harvard and New York, he threw himself head-first into the
wilderness. Almost the first thing we hear from the West is
that he has been forty-eight hours in the saddle, with nothing
to eat, and only the water in mud-puddles to drink. Let any
man walk out of Wall Street and try that! As one reads of
Roosevelt's activities, in his periodic plunges out of urban or

political life into the wilds, one's bones ache for him, and one's muscles cry out in sympathy. But it was just by this determined leap into primitive circumstance that he called forth those deeper levels of energy which he, of all men, knew best how to experience. His use of them was somewhat limited by the fact that he had, fundamentally, a commonplace mind. But they gave him that zest in action, that hilarity of enjoyment, and that moral fibre which made him a unique and attractive public figure. If his life was not prolonged by this method, it was made supremely good while it lasted.

The fact that real exercise of the body (and with it real exercise of unused and joy-giving levels of the consciousness) is dependent not on things bought and paid for, but on conditions which, if they were not made an art and an amusement, would represent the starkest poverty, needs emphasizing because of the rather curious conditions disclosed by the "Study of Leisure Time Activities and Desires" recently made by the National Recreation Association. The Association undertook to list the leisure time activities of 5000 people chosen at random from the industrial cities of the East, such as Boston, Worcester, and Newark, and to compare what people were actually doing with what they would like to do if they only had a chance. The five activities which were most generally indulged in were, in the order of their popularity: reading newspapers and magazines, listening to radio, attending the movies, visiting or entertaining others, and reading fiction. The five activities which, in contrast, they would like to indulge in if they had the opportunity were: playing tennis, swimming, boating, playing golf, and camping. The reason they amused themselves with the first set of activities when they desired the second was that the first involved little expense and could be pursued alone. The second required the participation of other people, and considerable effort and equipment.

This is a situation as strange as it is deplorable. If there is any justification in urban life, it is that thereby people are able to enjoy in groups activities and common equipment which they could not enjoy alone. But here are our big cities filled with people sitting passively in rooms, fingering over newspapers and magazines, wandering out to the movies, milling around in that formless gregariousness which is not society and which is inimical to all social arts. Theirs is a loneliness compared with which the life of the solitary hunter in the wilderness is social excitement. For the hunter has at least the birds and the insects and that contact with Nature which, to man, is generally companionable. And he may relax into that dreamy content which is the natural state of organic life when it is undisturbed from without. But the city dweller is stimulated continually, and furnished in the magazines and the radio and the motion pictures with means of visualizing all that he does not have. And then he is completely frustrated by the fact that he cannot walk up to what he wants and reach out his hand and take it, or even fight physically for it, but must pay for it money which he does not have. This list of desires noted among the 5000 people indicates not so much the free impulses of men as the physical activities most often and most alluringly set forth in print, and in motion pictures, or in the displays of shop-windows. They also represent the hunger for sharp physical activity either under circumstances naturally adventurous, as in water sports and camping, or in activities which give form and tense drama to contact with other people.

2

Of the two forms of activity most desired—the contest with nature or the organized contest with man—probably the first is more generally alluring. The Editor of *Leisure* magazine is often amazed by the perpetual call for more material on fishing and hunting. To the poor victims of the profit era it seems necessary that even when they go into the woods or out on the water, it must be to get something—if only some meat that they do not need. All men think in symbols. Hunting and fishing are symbols of all those delights of effort and sensation which belonged to man when the sky was his ceiling and the ground his bed, and his dinner ran wild on four legs. Yet there are some who, even in hunting, do not know what it is that they really desire. They think they are hunting when they ride up to the water in a car and mow down hundreds of ducks with machine guns. They might just as well get a job in a slaughter house.

No one need deny the primitive need to renew himself by struggle with his mother nature. This country is still a wilderness. Within walking distances of many of the great industrial cities there are still places where a man may go for the night, and lying down under the stars, say with the old French Jesuit in Canada, "My bed had not been made up since the creation of the world." Swimming pools cost money, but ponds, creeks, rivers, and sea are still to be got for the asking. A walk around a golf course costs money, but a walk on a country road costs nothing. There are other things to chase over the landscape than a ball—birds, and insects, fossils, Indian arrow heads, the spring flowers in the woods, the berries in the pasture. Incredible as it seems on the face of it, a few people in this country do not own cars. But they all have feet. And, thank God! rain and snow, night and sunshine still belong to every body.

Little of the equipment alluringly set forth for campers by advertisers is really necessary. One can still make a good camp stove with stones and a good fire with wood. You don't really need one of these gadgets that burn gasoline from the car. There is no better camp-bed than one of boughs well made. And though the tent is the oldest of habitations made by man and has got into its fibres through the long centuries the smell of the wild, one can make a lean-to almost as fast as one can unstrap a tent and set it up. The government periodically tries to remind us of our great property, belonging to each man equally, in our national parks, where for a small fee for

upkeep, a man has a home all summer and as much longer
as he can keep warm there. Some day the voice of the government may be as loud as that of the realtor, and we may begin
to understand what we possess in our great wilderness, and
how to use it.

So with such equipment as boats. Men had boats long
before there were yacht races. Any child can make a raft, and
so, too, can any man. Nor should it be beyond a degenerate
son of modern man even to make a boat. The rudest savages
somehow do it.

One who is really in earnest about coming to grips with
nature need only do this: Let him walk out of his office
in the evening and just keep on walking right ahead in a
straight line. Soon he will be out in the open country. Then
let him simply do the next thing that looks interesting, and
the next. If he does not come back till morning, what difference does it make? Men slept well long before there were bed-
rooms. In eastern Europe after the war many people discovered this simple fact. They had no houses; they had no
food; and they had no jobs. But they had heels and they
took to them. Out of the epidemic of youth-wandering soon
arose new forms of organization, new companionship, new
health and strength and self-help. When wandering among
the young broke out in this country, people stood aghast. But
it was better than standing in bread-lines at that, better than
herding supinely in rooms and cellars and waiting for some
one to do something. It was best for those who really kept
to their feet, instead of trying to pick up rides in cars or
hop on freight trains.

Whatever else one lacks in the way of exercise, one can
always walk. Of course it wears out shoe-leather, but men
walked before there were shoes. The new doctors of leisure
are collecting a great deal of lore about hikes. How various
the art of walking becomes when all its possibilities are listed
in such a book as Mary Breen's "Partners in Play." Among
the kinds of walk she enumerates are: The Companionate

Walk, the Walk Contemplative, the Walk for Relaxation, the Questing Walk, the Winter Walk, the Moonlight Stroll. Among the hikes which may be turned into games for a group of walkers are: The Gypsy Patter Run, the Progressive Supper Hike, the Exploring Hike, the Circuit Hike, the Social Evening and Hike, the In-the-City Hike, the Know Your Neighbors Hike, and the Penny Hike, which is made by flipping a penny at every corner to see which way to turn next. There are also over-night hikes, with breakfast at sun-rise, and long hikes over such routes as the Appalachian mountain trail which is studded with over-night shelters.

Next to walking, the best exercise is swimming. Swimming pools are charming things, and there ought to be more of them. But many a child learned in the old swimming hole, and if a child can find some water to get wet in, so can an adult. Good places to skate are hard to find, even in a northern winter. No sooner does the ice freeze over than the snow comes and covers it, or a rain makes slush of it, and it freezes again in lumps. When we are civilized, every town will maintain a clear space for skating as rigorously as the dairy farmer maintains his ice-pond. But there is still the snow. A good resolution for New Year would be to let no beautiful, deep, white fall of snow come from now till lilac time without leaving house, office, or flat and falling right into it. And there is always bad weather. There is almost no bad weather which is not good if you go right out into it. To souze along in the rain with your boots making a sudzing sound and a river running off your nose or down your back is fun. To beat against the wind is fun, and it is fun to go creaking over a winter road with the temperature twenty below zero.

When I began to write this book, I asked some of my friends to tell me about the most delightful hours they had spent recently. I have already told about the lady who cultivated charm between ten and eleven A.M. There was a middle aged man who said that he got caught alone in his summer home during the bitter winter of 1934. Though he was in good training and knew all about vitamins, he could not keep well, and awoke one morning to find to his horror that he was very near pneumonia, and a blizzard was steadily snowing him in to the roof. So he decided to fall back on some of the more fanatic health nostrums and to see if he couldn't get rid of his cold by fasting. He ate nothing for thirty hours which brought him around to the evening of the second day, and the weather was still howling like hell let loose. No one, not even the postman, had been along the road for two days. Feeling a little better and thinking he ought to eat something, he found that he was without milk. Suddenly he decided that he might as well die struggling. So, shivering and gasping, with his throat still feverish, he bundled himself up and stepped out into the blizzard, with the intention of getting through to a farmer, a mile away, and getting some milk. Floundering through drifts, up and down Alps of snow, he reflected what an idiot he was. He was no longer young. He was ill. He had eaten nothing for thirty hours. Of course he would die of exhaustion in a few minutes. But instead a wonderful exhilaration began to take hold of him. His breathing cleared. He felt energetic and warm. He got the hang of the snow drifts and began to go over and around them quite easily. Glowing and merry, he arrived at the farmer's, drank a glass of warm milk right out of the milking pail, chatted and found the farmer's kitchen as glamorous as a ball room. He came cheerfully back and, falling into bed, slept the sleep of the dead. Next morning his cold was gone; he felt twenty years younger, and hungry enough to eat a walrus. This he remembers as the most glowing experience of the winter. He says he often wonders, as he passes the farm house, where the magic has gone which that evening enveloped the warm, lantern-lit stable, and the kitchen with its blazing range and smell of fried potatoes, and made all the simple farmer's family beings in an old saga.

Of course the answer is simple. He had called out those deeper levels of energy which are always ours to tap, and which, when released, transform the universe. People are constantly warned not to over-do. It is only by over-doing sometimes that we learn how much we can do.

3

Though individual and solitary adventure is far better than the soulless and passive gregariousness of the cities, there is also a great need for the other kind of exercise which the 5000 whose leisure was studied so earnestly desired. Sports are one of the most delightful forms of social life. They combine the glamor of the human contact with dramatic action and physical exhilaration. The most delightful of modern clubs is the country club, which adds to the fun of sports the theatrical gaiety of a social scene—bright woolens, lovely natural backgrounds, social form and order. Better exercise can be found by any farmer, but not better social life.

There is a place in every life as in every community for sport socially enjoyed. It is a quite different thing from fronting nature on your own. A good game is not only an artistic but an artificial creation, but delightful just on that account. As we grow civilized, our communities will sprout with tennis courts, swimming pools, municipal golf courses. A start has already been made with the P.W.A. and a blessed start it is. When the proposal was made to build a swimming pool in a little Maine resort town on an island, every one laughed. What! The place was surrounded by seas and shores! Swim, who could help it? Yet as one goes down to the place where with Federal money the sea-water has been dammed in with concrete, and furnished with spring-boards, and lies warm under the sun, in its rectangular wall, one realizes that something is here contributed to the life of the community that all these majestic wild shores could never give. Here among these young men and women, flirting on the wall, swinging from the spring board, splashing in and out, here is social civilization in an ideal form. It is an out-of-door substitute for a ball-room. The sunshine has the glamor of shaded lights. The pool is the town's social centre. One who wants real exercise must still rush out into the sea and ride the surf. That is one thing. But this is something else, and very good, too.

For many people in the city on small incomes more of this sort of thing is available than they realize. Among the forms of self-amusement which I discovered when I began to ask people to confess ways of being happy which they had unearthed for themselves was that of a young woman in an office. She was in her thirties and imagined that she was getting fat, though the increase of ten pounds or so was only what the various weight charts allow for her age and her friends said she was just right. So she conceived the idea of swimming every lunch hour in the Y.W.C.A. swimming pool. Having been accustomed to paying fifty cents for her lunch, she now paid twenty five cents for a swim, and ate ten cents worth of fruit and nuts on her way back. This made thirty five cents. In this very economical way, she said she found her lunch hour twice as much fun as before. The swim set her up for the afternoon. The lunch was really enough and helped her to reduce very slowly—or may be the swimming did that. She had the pride of an improved figure, a better complexion, and a new skill.

Most city dwellers who feel that they cannot afford sports can economize on food, if they choose it rightly, cutting out the superfluous bread and sweets which we all eat too much of, and not afraid to fall back on the good old stand-bys of the food faddists, such as milk, nuts, and cheap dried fruits, which give you lots of calories for your money. Most people have no idea how little it takes to maintain the human organism. To devise some simple and economical way of keeping yourself in training through diet makes all exercise more exhilarating, and leaves a margin in the budget for the expense of organized sports. Even the well-to-do folk on the golf courses of the country clubs would get twice as much fun if they paid their country club dues out of their food. Take a typical member of such a club. He or she is not overflowingly fat, but broad, hard, rosy, and cheerful. Religiously, in all weather he or she is out, fighting the battle of exercise with food, disciplining the fat, pushing it down and making it hard, and trying to forget how hungry he or she will be at lunch. This is all very well, but it is a waste of human energy. If they would eat half as much, their golf would be much less of a discipline and much more of a joy.

And is not that the best that the wholesome art of exercise has to offer—not health, not increased capacity for work, but joy, the sense of having life within you, and having it more abundantly? The first and simplest road to the more abundant life is to get into your own lungs, limbs, and muscles.

The Delectable Art of
Reading—XVI

ONCE there was a man who had no money, and no job. But somewhere he found a book.

> *He ate and drank the precious words,*
> *His spirit grew robust;*
> *He knew no more that he was poor,*
> *Nor that his frame was dust.*
>
> *He danced along the dingy days,*
> *And this bequest of wings*
> *Was but a book. What liberty*
> *A loosened spirit brings!*

Did this happen during the great depression of 1929 and the years following? No doubt. But Emily Dickinson wrote the poem more than half a century ago. The comfort and magic of books is such an old story that there are hardly any words left in which to tell it. They were all turned to superlatives long ago.

Yet it is worth while to think what books still mean to us now, for we are faced with a return of the social conditions before there were books—conditions which many found so good that they have sighed for the good old days before printing, as some sigh now for the days before radio. For printing was the first of those mechanical contraptions, of which radio and motion pictures are the most recent examples, by which individual thought and imagination were canned in large quantities and cheaply distributed. Nearly everything that is urged against radio and motion pictures, as vulgarizers of culture, was once said about printing, and rightly. Even the great cleavage between the Catholic and Protestant churches was largely over the wisdom of vulgarizing a great book by giving it to everybody. The true word of God, said the church, was a living word, coming down from mouth to mouth among those who gave their lives to the understanding of it, and were able to translate ancient phrases and images in terms of the current need. So the Platonic Socrates long ago had said that the true word is the spoken word, "of which the written word is properly no more than an image."

After centuries in which the written word so conquered all minds that education has been made synonymous with reading (a point of view which would have seemed absurd to some of the most cultivated people of the past) we have found a way of distributing the spoken word even more cheaply than the written word. For the price of from ten to twenty books, you may have a little instrument which, for years, will bring the living word hurtling into your house from all over the world at any hour of the day. The president of the United States now speaks right into your parlor. You can go to church or to a concert or to a lecture and never move off the davenport.

And this revives, curiously enough the social use of the spoken word which was superseded by printing, and the passing of which many quite rightly regretted. How were the Greek heroes entertained in the great Golden Age of classical culture? Not by reading, for most of them could not read. They got both education and amusement from professional persons who chanted to them the stories, which were later made into the epics, of Homer. Between the poems and stories there was probably music. And quite likely the traders gathered around the edges and in the intervals cried up their wares—golden trinkets from Mycenae, sandalwood from the East, amber from the Baltic, figs and honey from the shores of the Aegean. How were the more sophisticated gentry of later Athens and Rome trained for political life—by walking out into the market place and listening to the orations of public men, or the disputations of philosophers as we now listen to our public men on the radio. How were the knights and ladies of the Middle Ages inducted into the growing common culture—by wandering troubadours, closely followed by the wandering traders, who stopped in the halls and tuned up of an evening. Even the church carried the living word of God about and brought it into the bed-room and the "closet." Every castle, and even every hovel, had its altar to which the priest might come and hold a service somewhat as you can now go to church in your own home.

When the gentleman of Rome was taught Rhetoric, he was not taught to write daily themes. He was taught to talk. When the lady of the Middle Ages had the gift of words, she did not write stories for the pulp magazines. She took up the story where the troubadour laid it down, and talked back. There were many advantages in this. It encouraged the art of conversation which was nearly killed by print, and it kept music and language developing together as the twins they really are. Great as is the art of printing, and blessed as has been the distribution of books, the Bible, the epics of Homer and Vergil, the Divine Comedy, and the King Arthur stories, and much else that is most valuable in literature, were developed under social situations that resemble not the silent company of the readers in libraries but the family and social group listening in to the radio. So literary culture describes a circle and comes back to where it started.

Yet all the while, books and writing existed. Books could not be printed and distributed in duplicate cheaply, but there was something so precious in them that they were lovingly copied and recopied by hand. To be able to keep and return to the word which, spoken, is so fleeting, to pore over it in quiet, without your neighbor's comment dinning in your ear, and some one just outside trying to sell something, meant much to the finer spirits harassed by the noisy socialization of the common culture. That great invention of writing which was the first of man's many attempts to conquer the immaterial by material means made possible an intimacy between one spirit and another, impossible where flesh and sound must intervene, and gave to the world of thought and imagination a continuity and a lonely magic. Men took refuge in books as they took refuge in desert hermitages against the noisy mediocrity of the crowd. When they thus turned their backs on man, they thought they had found God, and probably they were right.

So to us, deafened as we are by this great new burst of canned and duplicated sound, books have not less but a greater meaning. Writing was always a special and aristocratic art. Perhaps it was a mistake to make it too popular. If the two great means of popularizing literature—the lending library, and the whooping-up of a best seller and wide distribution of a few books through book clubs—should be curtailed because every one is too busy listening to radio, and if people read fewer books, but chose them more in accordance with personal taste, and bought and cherished and displayed with pride all that they did read, would literature suffer? Probably this will not happen. In the past the more everybody listened to the spoken word, the more some people were stimulated to write and to read. The more the troubadours told stories and sang, the more earnestly monks copied manuscripts. And the more we listen to radio, the more we will wish to have hours when, tired of hopping from one subject to the other to the tune of the saxophone, we can relax in peace and follow something through to the end, and wrap ourselves in a great silence with one who speaks straight into our hearts and minds, without sound or static.

2

The first use of books in the radio age is that they allow us to carry to satisfaction that interest which the bombardment of words and names arouses in things of which we have no daily experience. When we read such a book as "Sons" or "The Education of a Princess" it is as if we had taken a far journey into lands we have heard every one talking about. We have lived another life than ours, fresh, contemporary—something going on this minute somewhere else. Contemporary novels have the same value. They take us into kinds of life which are continually advertised to us by pictures in newspapers and magazines, by programs on the radio, and even by the kaleidoscopic view of city and country from the car. Time was when a man, living all his life in one place, could really know all about anything that caught his eye or his attention. Now we cannot read fast enough to keep up with all that is forced upon us, but the more we do read about anything that illumines the contemporary scene the more form and intellectual security is introduced into our chaos. Most of man's life is lived in memory and imagination. Books enlarge this life, and make it beautiful and orderly and intelligible.

Yet there is a real danger in the habit of getting too much of contemporary life from books. Everywhere there are the word-minded people to whom what is evoked in their imagination by verbiage, printed or heard, is the only reality, and who can neither recognize nor enjoy the actual stuff about which books are written when they meet it. How many summer people there are in Maine who read "As the Earth Turns"! But though they buy their milk and vegetables from such families as the Shaws, they have no interest in them, and take refuge from the difficulties of really meeting them on a human ground in vaguely sentimental attitudes derived from books. So with our attitude to negroes, to the different kinds of picturesque foreigners in our midst, to people of a different social class from our own. There are many cultivated older people whose attitude to youth is created not by the many actual boys and girls around them, but by books about youth, tales of their wild doings, professorial discussions of youth as a "problem."

To be really valuable, everything we read should be supplemented by the great art of seeing and of going places. This marvelous world the books tell about is all around you. Read the book, and then get out and look at what it tells about. Your sight will be miraculously increased and your understanding and sympathy quickened. I know a very simple fisherman on the Maine coast, whose father sailed a sloop constantly to foreign shores and has bequeathed to his son, stuck for life in a small village, a habit of going places which makes this plain man's life a constant excitement. Whatever he reads about in the local newspaper, he goes and looks at. Western cattle are being brought into Maine pastures. The fisherman is down at the station to see them land. He knows where they are going. He reproduces in his imagination the parched deserts they have left, and their joy in the lush green that is coming. A whale has been brought into Bangor. His father told him about whaling. He never saw a whale. Now is his chance. Up he goes to Bangor to see the whale and comes back and reads everything in the library about whaling. He reads that a new Federal Bureau has been set up locally. He promptly fakes some business with it, and goes to see the bureau, just to know what it is like. This is what reading is good for—to make life exciting and romantic and give cohesion to disjointed scraps of experience.

3

Another use of contemporary literature is that it teaches one how to live one's own life. Not in superficials. The advertisements, the radio, and the motion pictures now take care of that. Time was when the girl in the village derived most of her notions about the way in which a lovely woman ought to look and live and treat her lover from novels. The movie heroine is her model now, and she can hear her ideal self replying to the proposal of an ideal lover any night over the radio. But just because there are so many superficial patterns, the secret confusion and worry of each individual is driven deeper. We have to tear ourselves loose from this fine spun enchantment of sounds and pictures, and really think out the fundamentals for ourselves. Here is the place for the reading of books on economics and psychology and philosophy, and indeed on the whole art of living. Such books are popular now, and rightly so. There never was a time when for his own peace of mind and personal guidance, a man had to read so much and so seriously. It is sometimes interesting to go back four or five years, and to see how exactly much that has happened was foretold. The books and the serious magazine articles of 1927-28 were full of prophesies of just what happened to us all. Such magazines as *Harper's* and *Scribner's* bristled with warnings. The world war was foreseen and known before it happened. While one man cannot stand against the madness of the world, a steady reading of the more informed and serious books about the business of living protects one from those great waves of propaganda and mass-belief by which many are plunged to destruction. Such reading might even keep one from selling one's house and land to buy Peruvian bonds, or dying too precipitately to make the world safe for democracy. At any rate it might give intelligence to the management of one's own life, and the feeling that one knows where one's own road is going.

In the search for helpful contemporary writing, it is best not to depend entirely on best-sellers and the book clubs. A considerable proportion of the best books do have the luck to sell very well and to be adopted by book clubs. But a considerable proportion don't. Pearl Buck's excellent books about China have been brought to every one's attention by their popularity. But one of the most remarkable of recent books—a book of absorbing interest in view of the recent strikes everywhere—Lauren Gilfillen's "I Went to Pit College" might well escape the notice of one who followed just the most popular book lists. And reading it is an experience not to be missed. The popularity of the best seller has often been prepared by little groups who have found the author's previous books for themselves, and kept alive separate sparks of enthusiasm which, when fanned by circumstance or advertising, suddenly run together and make one resistless fire. There is adventure in the hunt for one's own books among all the new offerings, and pleasure in telling one's friends about them. So much is chosen for us—the programs of the radio, the contents of the monthly magazine. We might reserve the luxury of choosing books for ourselves.

4

Since man's mind has never accepted the limitations of space or time or physical mortality, it is inherently necessary for him to know his own racial past. The beginning of culture, among savage peoples, is the record of the life of the departed, symbolized in permanent monuments, and transmitted, before writing was known, by those set apart to learn from the old and tell to the children, usually in musical chants, the unbroken tale of the tribal history. Ancestor worship is one of the early stages of all human culture. In each house an altar is set up to the vanished fathers and mothers of the family. For each individual ancestor there is an image or a tablet or at least a candle. Once in a red Chinese temple I came on a niche in the wall in which had been set up a block of wood decorated with Chinese letters. The letters read: "Confucius: His Spirit's Place." There is such security and sense of continuing life in this environing presence of all the men and women who have gone before that people cut off from the altars and the graves of their fathers have often sickened and died, like plants cut off from their own roots.

Where we have lost this tribal and family continuity of life, we must supply its place by establishing our own relations as best we can with our whole human past. Books are to us what the altars of the ancestors are to the Chinese. Opening a copy of the "Divine Comedy" can we not say, with the same reverence with which the Chinese bows before the tablet of Confucius, "Dante: His Spirit's Place." In reading very old books there is a satisfaction which has nothing to do with knowledge. It is something atavistic in us—a longing to assure ourselves that this little span of life is not all there is, to be supported, even in our follies and frivolities, by the whole human past.

So every one, for his own deepest satisfaction, should make his daily obeisance to the past in his reading, as the Chinese and Japanese make their obeisance to their ancestors. Such reading may well be formal and ritualistic. A time may be set aside for it—perhaps the twenty minutes before going to sleep. Such reading was offered to our fathers in the Bible. An utilitarian and pedagogic substitute for it has been offered in the Five Foot Shelf, to be read fifteen minutes a day. Such reading is best when it is brief and it is regular—an intellectual routine. It gives something to focus the mind on, something to carry around and relate to the swarming present.

But with all due respect to Doctor Eliot, I think the reading of old literature should not be as scrappy as his choice is. Before he made up his Five Foot Shelf, there was no such bombardment of every one by odds and ends of knowledge and aesthetic experience. Then people had more need of surveying the whole field of literature and nibbling here and there. But now our one need is continuity both in thought and imaginative experience. A mediocre whole is better for us than a thousand samples of the best. So when one reads books out of the past, one should choose big wholes, and go straight through them, ready to take the roughage with the vitamins, to break one's teeth on the pits and chew at the tough skins of the fruit on the tree of knowledge. For one who reads this way, practically all the really significant books out of the past, the ones of which all others are imitations or variations, can be read through in much less than a life-time at the rate of twenty minutes a day.

The greatest of these books are those that give you a whole

civilization between two covers. Such books as these are the epics of Homer and the dialogues of Plato, which tell you not only what one great man felt, but the way cultivated Greeks talked to each other and met socially. Such a book is "The Divine Comedy" which sums up not only the whole mediaeval point of view on life but the best of the still living Catholic Church. Such a book is "Don Quixote" which is not only Renaissance Spain, but the whole tragedy of what we would like life to be set against what it is. Such a book is the Japanese "Tale of Genji," now so beautifully translated into English by Arthur Waley. It is not only ancient Japan, but ancient China—all the fine art of daily living which is behind the lacquer and brocades and porcelain we admire in the Oriental shops. These are old books, but the substance of them is living yet, in our midst, and to read them rightly is to understand what we are, and why we are. Among such books one might include the Bible, which is becoming so unfamiliar to many cultivated people that to read it through as if it were any volume is an experience. Golden texts and sermon texts are very different from what Romain Rolland calls the "salt and bitter savor of that savage old book."

Nor must the American forget that his own true past is not only in England but in his own continent. We slight American literature too much in our schools. Having had it dished up to us in bits, in the grades, we think it is only pabulum for children; and that mature men must look to England for reading. So it has happened that our greatest authors, like Melville and Whitman, have been best appreciated by the English. Though less solid and massive, English critics realize that some of the nineteenth century literature of America is fresher and more truly interesting than that of England. Even in the eighteenth century, when Americans had something more important to do than writing books, there is little in English of its kind much better than the "Autobiography" of Benjamin Franklin. In the fresh life of the American continent, literary forms were revived which had died with the old heroic life in Europe. One of these is the epic. "Moby Dick" is a true epic, the only one spontaneously written in modern times. There is an epic reach in Cooper's novels, in Mark Twain at times, and something of it in "Uncle Tom's Cabin." An epic is a poem whose hero is not really an individual but a whole type of life—a struggle of a dawning culture-ideal with something bigger than itself. Another primitive and heroic form that has burst forth spontaneously in America is the "lay"—the formless, enthusiastic chant of such a wanderer as Walt Whitman or Vachel Lindsay. Even the second-rate books which have dealt truly with the American scene, like those of Eggleston or Hamlin Garland or Jack London have something worth much to the American. They make his fresh, heroic, and romantic land what it ought to be in his own eyes. There are, too, some of those early epics of history, by Parkman and Prescott. If the "Conquest of Mexico" by Prescott had been written in prehistoric times, it would be to us another siege of Troy.

Americans suffer from the fact that they do not know how wonderful their own life is. It takes one who has lived a great deal in other countries, especially in that rather tame and petty Europe from which our fathers ran away, to appreciate it. The recent interest in *Americana* of all sorts is very wholesome. But it has not really touched our own literature. So if you do not really know all of Hawthorne and Cooper, if you have forgotten "Uncle Tom's Cabin" and "Ramona" and "Huckleberry Finn," and such histories as "The Conquest of Mexico" and Parkman's history of the Jesuits in Canada, there is the place to begin to make your daily reverence to the ancestors. With what charm our own domestic past burst upon us in the film of "Little Women". There is a great deal more as good, and some is not so well known. While one is collecting old clipper ship prints for the wall, one might collect old books for the shelves.

5

We spoil our best experiences because, in our rushing life, we do not set the stage for them. Reading needs both a time and a place in household life, and now and then some social ceremony. The most delightful houses are those in which there is not only one place to read, but several. I remember a bookshelf on the stair landing, whither volumes discarded from the lower shelves found their way. What fun it was to sit on the stairs there and read. There were the old books in the corner of the attic, where, with half a dozen red apples for provender, one could journey thousands of miles into fairyland. I know a house where there is a large cathedral-like room made out of a wood-shed where the light from the sea falls with mellowness on shelves of substantial sets, and a couch invites you to lie and read for hours, the dim sounds of the household and guests coming from far away. But in this house there is also a sun-room with tables over-flowing with children's games, and book shelves full of the children's stories. There are books of poetry and novels and current books in the living room. And one of the bed-rooms has reading-lights wired to the bed-posts, and shelves built in the alcove around the head of the bed for reading at night, or during day-time rest periods.

In this house father has always read to the children since they were a year old, dramatizing the favorite characters. The wooden accent he furnished Pinocchio and the smile he put on for the Cheshire Cat are only equalled by the sonorous pomposity with which he now reads the part of Malvolio in "Twelfth Night" or the mawkish whine in which he speaks for Uriah Heep. A new book is an event in this family. Every one reads it, and talks about it, until it is as if one had read it five times, for as each one gets to its most interesting or exciting part, he is sure to have something else to say about it.

Such a family likes to get its books from the library as little as most people would like to rent their clothes. A book is a personal or household possession. Every one in the family, from the youngest daughter to father, has books which are his own and which are not to be borrowed without permission and are lent reluctantly. But there is a great store of books held in common. Every one has a history. You can look at one and think of the day when it was brought home fresh and shining, the reading aloud around the fire, the disputes, the re-reading some quiet afternoon, the journeys it has gone with you, the comments that have been written into it, the markings along the side of some one's favorite passages.

Though public libraries are a blessed institution, a book worth reading is worth possessing. We waste in trivial and unnecessary expenses enough to keep books coming into the house almost as fast as they can be really read. Even the ephemeral ones are worth their price. They look new and sociable on the living room table. They are something to talk about with the friend who drops in. They go out of style, but no faster than one's hats or one's curtains. They are a passing amusement, but they last longer than a box of candy, and fill more hours than a visit to the motion pictures. If you give them to the hospital afterwards, you will have the pleasure of a generous gesture. If you stow them away in the attic, your grand-daughter will find them there some day— and laugh. Any way you look at them, they are worth their price in fun.

The good books, the enduring books, those you will re-read, and see with pleasure on your shelves, are usually worth far more than they cost. Merely as household ornaments they have a value, for books make any home, however simple, look civilized. But a good book is far more than a household ornament. An article on thorough-bred dogs, telling what a friend a dog will be for years, says that a good friend is cheap at $75.00. How much more cheap at $2.50 or $4.00!

The Lovely Art of
Song—XVII

SONG is the oldest language of man. Even before he could talk, man probably advanced against the enemy to rhythmic shouts, and so had a war-song, and women crooned to their babies, and so made a lullaby. Something of those chance articulations to which, making music, men first shaped their lips are retained in the senseless syllables of our choruses, like tra-la-la-la-la. Perhaps language began when men first hit on the idea of giving a specific meaning to syllables they sang over and over.

While words and the immortal continuity of human speech are all man's own, song is a language he shares with the creatures below him. In the multitudinous humming of the field, the z-z-z-z of the grass-hopper, the chirp of the cricket, the buzz of the locust, each species celebrates the joy of life after its own fashion. There seems no vital reason for many of these noises. They are pure superfluity like so much of the love, joy, and beauty in nature. The birds usher in the dawn with music for themselves alone to hear. Long after man and his noises are still, the katydid and the frog still shrill and boom their delight to the majestic unheeding pageant of the stars. But even the stars, says the old book, sang together on the morning of creation, and some poets have imagined they are singing yet, and the rhythm to which they swing, one round the other in unwearied dance, sends vibrations through the ether which might break in music upon some not inconceivable ear.

Song in the beginning was probably inseparable from the dance. To dance is only to sing with the limbs. It is difficult to tell of some creatures which make music by rubbing parts of their body whether they are really singing or dancing. What we hear is a kind of dance made audible. Poetry is only a refinement of singing. All literature began with poetry, and it may be that language as a means of communication began thus, too. Familiar syllables might long have had a fixed association with certain images or facts in tribal songs, before it dawned on the first Brain Trust that they could be taken out of their context and freely arranged to express ideas. Poetry begins in metre, and metre in motion. In the older drama of Greece and Japan poetry is not only sung but danced.

The ordering and development of music was probably the beginning of human culture. This may be why in civilizations like those of China and Greece, which seem to be nearer than others to man's beginnings, music was the basis of education. It was the first means by which man tried to change himself from what he was into what he wished to be. The early Greek curriculum consisted of music and athletics; the early Chinese of music and ceremony, or, as we would say, music and manners. In both cases, the idea was the same. You were to get control and artistic use of your body, either in the sports which the Greeks cultivated, or the various formal social relations which the Chinese valued, and partly to insure this, but partly also for the shaping of the life within, you were to learn music. Music included dancing and the chanting of the poetry which was the first history and the first philosophy, the forms in which the experiences of the past were crystallized and passed on to the young. When you had brought order and harmony into your outer motions and your inner impulses, you were an educated man.

It is worth while to remember these old simple uses of song, because, bombarded as we now are with music, we forget how to select and use it. It pleases us. It dopes us against our own troubles. It makes us one in sounding

gregariousness with our fellows. But, in so doing, it may bring
back the emotional chaos from which human music should
be a deliverance. Yet it is still used by crowd leaders to
discipline groups. It turns a crowd of raw, shrinking boys
into a single fighting machine animated as one soul with
courage—and that the courage of the band. It is used in
service clubs and foot ball rallies and alumnae gatherings
and revival meetings to make one thousand diverse and sometimes unwilling hearts beat as one. For the crowd you have
only to invent a common feeling and turn it into music,
and in five minutes they all have it and think it is their own.
If the soul of a crowd can be thus turned to courage or joy
or fraternity or worship, so, too, can an individual soul. One
has only to be obstinate and lonely and choose one's own
tunes.

It is with music now as with knowledge. It is the instrument of the mass mind, and you cannot escape it. Canned
music is ubiquitous as the printed page and may soon be
even more effective in shaping the common soul. If one is
not to have tinsel emotions and fake hilarity wished on one,
and feel spent and vapid between noises as if one had had a
drug, one must find one's own music. Plato thought some
music was so demoralizing that it could not be allowed in a
properly governed state. He wished to ban some tunes as we
ban opium. He said they "relaxed" men's fibre, and made
them soft and silly. What a radio censor he would have made!

But if the worst music comes over the radio, so also does
the best. Every evening the best feeling of all the world is
ours to share for the turning of a button. Music alone on
the radio has even now the continuity, the complete satisfaction and climax of aesthetic experience which all the
scrappy talking lacks. We have heard more than once the
whole of Beethoven's "Choral Symphony" by our own fire-
sides, with our loved ones around us. We have yet to hear
the whole of Milton's "Paradise Lost." This is because the
greatest music is really more intelligible and universally

appealing than the literature which most nearly corresponds to it. One speaks directly through the senses and the emotions; the other indirectly through the intellect.

2

Since, of all the fine arts, music is the oldest, and the most fundamental to personal happiness and social adjustment, it might well take first place in our use of our time off from work. People with musical training do not need to be told this. Their music is already the solace of personal unhappiness, the voice of their inmost feeling, the means to self-forgetfulness and to tranquillity. But most people have just enough musical training to frustrate their use of it as a means of joy. They had some lessons on the piano, but are out of practice now. They used to sing in school, but they have forgotten the words of the old songs and never learned the new ones, of which the tunes nevertheless haunt them. By attending concerts and incidental reading they are familiar with many of the great pieces, and the best-known musicians, but only in a vague, haphazard way. They dance, but not very well. The irresistible jazz makes their feet tap, quickens the blood, and brightens the spirits, but they feel awkward and unsatisfied when they get on the floor. Still, they like now and then to turn on the dance music. It brings a certain social radiance into their home, lighting up the commonplace with the magic of ball-rooms, bringing them close to the whole gay, metropolitan world. But they exercise no choice, even in this. They take it as it comes and it acts on them passively. They don't know the alphabet of music, as a language. Expressions like "A-Minor," "C-Major," "dominant," "diminished seventh" are jargon to them.

On the whole there are probably more people with suppressed musical tastes than with tastes for reading or scientific knowledge or pictorial art. And the trouble with them often is that they are ashamed to begin again and learn what they wish to know clearly and well. They think music lessons are for children. Since one can hardly make music without some one hearing it, they are afraid that others may laugh at their tentative efforts. They think they can't sing unless God gave them a "voice," that they can't play anything unless they have talent. As a matter of fact, God gave everyone a voice, and if you can speak without giving others a pain you can sing without hurting them, too. As for talent, musical talent is probably the most widely distributed of all the cultural aptitudes. It is more likely that you can make reasonably good music than that you can write or paint or act.

Those who have children in the family are lucky, for in teaching and playing with the young they can rediscover the joys of music from the beginning and save face with their family and friends. For those without children some suggestions may be offered in the hope that they may get courage to shut the doors and the windows and try, too.

3

Every one has a first class musical instrument in his own throat. For people of any age to take singing lessons builds up their self-respect and general sense of well-being, and is deeply, egoistically interesting. And people of any age can make some progress. There are much worse things to do with a little spare time and spare cash than look around for a singing teacher. Nevertheless, without a teacher one may go some distance. Many people can sing well enough to please themselves and not hurt their neighbors if they will set themselves to learn the whole of a song carefully, taking pains to make the sounds pleasingly but naturally, as if they were talking, and to follow the notes accurately. Both tone and ear improve with practice, and with practice they gradually learn to breathe. Practice also gives ease and courage in just letting the voice out. It breaks down that bashfulness and deep-seated emotional repression which hamper many people in singing. If one can practice to a piano, learning one's own accompaniment, so much the better. But the phonograph also offers an excellent accompaniment and has the advantage of setting a real standard of voice production and accent and tone coloring.

The *Christian Science Monitor* once published the story of a boy of eleven who when he came to school sang with great beauty and accuracy and a finished use of his voice. It seems that from babyhood he had sung with his mother to the accompaniment of phonograph records, and had learned in this way to sing fifty different songs, exactly reproducing the tones and quality of some of the great voices. A joyous family singing hour may be held around the phonograph as well as around the piano. It is fun to pick each new record, to learn it carefully, till all can sing it clear and true even without an accompaniment. Paul Robeson's beautiful renderings of the negro spirituals make ideal material for such singing. If any one in the family has a stringed instrument, even a ukelele, an accompaniment may be worked out for each song by playing the record over and over, and carefully experimenting with chords. Since it is often difficult to understand the words of a song, it facilitates the learning if the words of each record are looked up in some song book or music store, and copied out for each member of the group.

One of the greatest hindrances to spontaneous singing, alone or in groups, is that people do not completely learn the words for the tunes they know. In "As The Earth Turns," the typical farmer's family, when they were moved to sing, finally fell back on hymns, because the words for them could be found in the hymn books. Song-leaders know how it facilitates singing to hand out printed copies of the words. To keep in the phonograph cabinet a loose-leaf note-book with typewriten copies, in duplicate, of the songs one likes to sing would help greatly in releasing our suppressed desires.

It is interesting, too, to make one's own anthologies of

songs. Such excellent collections as "Twice 55, Plus, Community Songs," published by C. C. Birchard and Company, and widely used in schools and community singing limit themselves too exclusively to the old popular songs. We need to supplement them with some of the less antediluvian melodies which, whether you think they are great music or not, have already some of the quality of folk music, because they suit the sentimental American soul. Such songs are "Ole Man River," "It's a Long, Long Trail a-Winding," "Gypsy Trail," "The End of a Perfect Day," and "Mother MacChree." Nor must it be forgotten that many of the hymns are to Americans already folk-songs. "Abide with Me" and "Nearer My God to Thee," and many others have associations and meanings for us that have nothing to do with religious convictions. There are lots of jolly new songs from musical comedies which are worth learning and discarding—part of the passing show in which, if we are socially alive, we like to share. The main thing with these, as with others, is to learn them completely and to learn them right.

One determined singer, with a few copies of words to pass around, can frequently be the making of a picnic or social gathering. Most people can sing far better than they think they can, and want to sing far more than they know. For one who gets interested in singing there is a world of community enterprise one can join in and keep on improving all the time. In every little town there is still the church choir and a few people who, if they don't know much about music, nevertheless may know more than you. More and more there are community sings. It is quite an experience to rattle over a country road and join with the local farmers, in some bare barnlike structure, in singing "Way Down Upon the Swanee River" and the "Little Brown Church in the Vale." One of the blessings which the new leisure promises us is an increase in the Musical Festivals which have long been, in many communities, magnificent social enterprises.

4

Closely related to singing, in its release of the emotional life and its personal stimulus, is the dance. Every one should learn to move to music, and to do it often and spontaneously, and I think for modern Americans, the music should be mainly well chosen jazz. Jazz is our own social and popular music. It evokes for us, as no other music of motion does, the social glamour. It suits the rhythm of our modern life. The fact that much of the dancing to jazz is abominable is no reason for not doing it right. To dance well, one must learn to move spontaneously to jazz, under any circumstances, and to move any part of the body. The various setting up exercises, for which instructions can be found in a dozen places, including old copies of *Physical Culture Magazine*, are, when done to some good jazz tune on the phonograph, almost the equivalent of a dance. And they do you good. They make you graceful and physically competent, and clear the blood and the mind.

As for the current dances, it is best to go to a good dancing teacher and learn them properly. One thing we may discover, as we get used to the new leisure is that instruction is one of the cheapest means to enjoyment one can buy. To dance the current steps well is a passport to the most glamorous of modern fun. What adventure there is for those who really like the modern dance in hunting around a big city or in country road-houses for some new place, all lit up like a theatre stage, where one can dance. The pity of it is that many who do this are such repressed Puritans that they cannot silence an outmoded conscience sufficiently to be enchanted unless they waste far too much of their substance and their vital energy on drink. And those who could get along very happily with little or no alcohol are prevented by the same Puritanic repressions from seeking this innocent sport and social adventure. Wine, woman, and song used to be classed together as allurements of the devil. But those who can really enjoy woman and song have very little need for wine.

Many people, unable to appreciate the charm and stimulation of the modern modes, are for reviving the old country dances which were, in their day, just as objectionable to persons like them. There is much to be said for the old dances. They are a good romp, and a good game. Where they can be revived, they vary the social picture. But they are no substitute for our own kind of dance. Theirs is a set pattern, a social enterprise for many. Ours is essentially an improvisation in which two people devise, almost by unconscious agreement, their own dance together. This type of dance has nothing really to do with jazz. One could make formal patterns and social romps to syncopated music if one wanted to. And one can make an improvisation in the modern manner, with the modern steps, to much of classical music. I knew two couples at a houseparty who used to turn on classical pieces every night, and make beautiful two and two, cheek to cheek, improvisations to them—nor was the music less ennobling for getting so into their blood and their nerves. To do something like this to music is really to dance, and comes nearer to the essentials of this great art than following any set pattern.

But beyond this simple social dancing, there is the whole of the great art of the dance, and no space in which to discuss it. It is an interest in itself, and opens up worlds of aesthetic experience.

5

Into the larger aspects of music, it is impossible here to enter. One may approach them in many ways. One may, without learning to play a musical instrument beyond picking out notes and chords on the piano, study music as one might study literature, learning the ABCs of musical form and theory from books or from a teacher, studying the works of the great musicians, and familiarizing one's self with them by listening, as we grow familiar with literature by reading. Once this would have been difficult to do without great expense for concerts and long trips to big cities. Now so much of the world's great music is to be got for the phonograph, that, piece by piece, you can come to know it almost by heart, and so much comes over the radio that sooner or later you are bound to hear anything you become interested in. This kind of study is particularly suited for older people who are bashful about learning to sing or play, and want interests which may be quietly pursued at home.

There is, of course, the steady mastery of an instrument. It is absorbing. It may and ought to be undertaken at any age by one who is able to give time to it. Many older people could do far better with music lessons than the children. But modern life has put great difficulties in the way of the piano, once the great centre of social life and a universal means of domestic culture. We move around so much and live in such small quarters that it is difficult to make a place for this large and expensive piece of property. It is a pity, for there never was a piano made which was not the means of many happy hours for some one. Yet, valuable as instrumental skill is to one who can get it and keep it, the difficulties in the way of becoming a skilful performer have too often been allowed to block the whole impulse to make music and to share in it. One must not forget the many simpler ways of dedicating one's limbs and one's ears and one's heart, if not one's fingers and one's breath, to this most appealing of the muses—music.

The Beautiful Art of
Decoration—XVIII

THE largest surplus in
this world is the surplus of beauty. Everywhere Nature throws
it in with a lavish hand, and changes the picture while you
look and makes another. De Maupassant tells of an old priest
who thought that everything God had made, He had made
for a purpose. He was for ever looking around and saying,
"what is God's reason for this?" and usually he found it. But
when, one evening, he walked into the moonlight, he was
baffled. What reason could there be for this great flood of
glory, this expense of solemn magic on a sleeping world?
Then he saw two lovers embracing as if this silver universe
were all their own, and they the Adam and Eve that would
found a more angelic race. The old priest was satisfied. The
moonlight, he perceived, was made for lovers.

Yet in the terrible winter of 1934 there were moonlit mid-
nights in the north when the temperature fell forty below
zero, and the snow was piled ten feet high, and the wind blew
sixty miles an hour. Then, if one were still alive, one might
see the moon riding high among a glittering rack of clouds
that blazed like a sunset, and, below, great hills of snow moving and shifting, breaking beneath the wind into fiery foam.
For whom was all that passionate and solemn glory?

There is something else about this superfluity of beauty
which, when one thinks about it, is very strange. Much that
we call beauty seems, as one might expect, but the outward
manifestation of joyous life within—the flush on a young
girl's cheek, the gold of the orange, the fresh green of the
trees. But there is another beauty which has nothing to do

with intrinsic character. It comes from somewhere else, and lifts the most sordid things to dignity, and lays on ugliness an alien and inexplicable grace. Such is the beauty of a great city like New York at twilight. The fairy glitter of these tall towers springing into light from within is something very different from all that is at that moment going on inside— the closing of deals and locking of offices, the washing of hands, and putting on coats, and lighting cigarettes, and descending in elevators. A fishing smack is a rather ordinary creation of wood and ropes and cloth, smelling rankly and operated by men whose talk never gets much beyond the size of their haul and the price of fish. But see her out on the water, when the wind is in her sails, and the blue waves smack against her sides, and she flies like a bird straight for the far horizon. Is there not a beautiful life in her that has nothing to do with men and sea-food?

Yet, as if he were not contented with this great out-pouring of beauty, man never ceases to try to add to it something of his own. Sometimes he seizes on Nature's rough sketch and finishes it for her, as in landscape gardening, and in growing fine vegetables and fruits and flowers and domestic animals, which are creations man has arrived at by observing Nature's methods and then bettering her. Sometimes he deduces from many imperfect forms, the ideal pattern which she must be aiming at, and makes it for her. Such art is that of the Greek sculpture which shows the kind of human body Nature would produce if she were only equal to it. The Greeks to whom art was mainly the finding of the original patterns of things, puzzled a great deal about this idealizing faculty of man. Plato fancied that man's spirit might have come from some pure other-world, in which existed the originals of the things Nature seemed to be reproducing so badly. Sometimes, observing a constant recurrence of color and pattern, man undertakes to work entirely on his own, making exact repetitions of form and color, with those regular lines and measured spaces, and perfect duplications which Nature in her carelessness disdains. So he arrives at formal decorative art. Sometimes he reproduces a world of his imagination in forms for which Nature gave him the hint, as in the great Italian paintings of saints and angels. And sometimes, as in modern art especially, he is fascinated by that other beauty, which interposes between him and even the ugly forms of things, and so paints a wrinkled old woman peeling apples or the steel girders of a modern city that he makes permanent on canvas that eerie and evanescent loveliness, which is the product of mood and circumstance, and yet suggests some solemn and unknown meaning in the commonplace of life. For great as is the beauty of the world, it seems but a striving for and an imperfect semblance of a beauty that is greater still.

2

If one has nothing else in life, one has always beauty. One can reach out anywhere and take it. One can spend a life-time searching it out and looking at it, in those lovely forms of nature which are all about, and are never to be seen twice quite alike in all one's three score years and ten. One can spend hours trying to reproduce it with pencil or paint or camera, or to find words which will evoke it for another's inner eye. One may go happily from one modern exhibition to another. One can spend years studying the many forms of art by which are preserved what eyes have seen long after the eyes themselves are dust. And one can be busy all one's days trying to turn the details of one's own life to beauty.

Few have seemed more continually satisfied and happy than such men as Wordsworth or Thoreau, who have made themselves connoisseurs of the beauty of Nature. "For many years," says Thoreau, "I was self-appointed inspector of snow-storms and rain storms, and did my duty faithfully." Wordsworth speaks of his youthful joy in Nature as a "giddy rapture" which with age was "matured into a sober pleasure." The sight of a mountain water-fall, of daffodils blooming be-

side a fence, was not only to be enjoyed but to be put away
against future moments of blankness or ennui, until the mind
should be as a storage place for all sweet sights and harmonies.
He says of the daffodils,

> *And oft as on my couch I lie,*
> *In vacant or in pensive mood,*
> *They flash upon the inward eye,*
> *Which is the bliss of solitude,*
> *And then my heart with pleasure fills*
> *And dances with the daffodils.*

So he decorated the walls of his memory, as another rich man
might decorate the walls of his house. It is an inexpensive
form of decoration and available for every one.

To seek out the beautiful in the life of man and in his creations is more difficult. But there are many choices here, and
all of them interesting. There are lovely older forms of building and of life, as in these white, elm-shaded New England
villages, which make beauty out of "a noble neatness." There
are those new creations of architecture and furniture and
streamlined machinery, whose weird and visionary beauty
seems a ghostly evocation from the great Not Yet. One may
collect odds and ends of old decorations—old lace, old china,
old prints, old glass. One may become a connoisseur of human
beauty, and of the beauty of life and manners, and support
one's self, in one's search, with literature and pictorial art
and even with history, contemporary and ancient, by which
this is recorded.

As for the actual study of pictorial or plastic art or of architecture and landscape gardening, or of the various crafts, the
field is manifold. There is the interest in the techniques of
reproduction or production. There is the interest in what is
told of the life of other places and other days by pictures
which are, as it were, windows into some other life. There is
that strange consciousness of the other beauty, comparatively
weak in classical art, but intense in some of the art of the

East which seems, to the novice, merely decorative, and so
great in modern and American art that as our material creations become ever greater and more daring our own vision
of them seems to become more ghostly.

The great Italian artists of the high age of painting, like
Raphael, took an other-worldly subject, and painted it carefully and roundly and solidly in terms of this world. The
modern artist, at his best, takes a subject from this world,
often trivial and casual, and paints it in the light of some
other-worldly vision. In a European art-gallery I passed rather
suddenly from the Renaissance room into the modern gal-
lery, and my eye transferred itself from a round, solid, buxom
Madonna to an American picture of an adolescent girl under
a tree in the sunshine. For a minute I hardly realized it was a
picture. It seemed like looking out of a window into the sunshine, and seeing a spirit, a wraith emanating from the fresh
verdure and disappearing into it again. This creature was
neither of paint nor of flesh and blood—just a transient vision.
But how warm and real and solidly human she made the
Virgin Mary look!

The study of the art of the past in schools and in woman's
clubs has been made dull because it has been made too literary. One was to memorize the name of the artist, the date of
his birth, the "school" to which he belonged. One was to look
painfully at poor prints of his innumerable works, good and
bad. All this is sterile. It is interesting to follow the artistic
work of the past in historical sequence, but far from necessary
to understanding, or to imaginative participation in another's
vision. The only use one can see in much of the school teaching of the history of art is that it might make one whose taste
could survive it seem rather bright and informed when he
entered a European art-gallery. But European art galleries
are full not only of beauty but of rubbish. To study the art
of the past or the present, the best thing to do is to begin with
the one thing that speaks, for some reason which you may not
even know, to your own imagination, and proceed to any

further inquiry or observation which it leads you to. Going on, in this way, from one thing you love to another you can really understand and care for, you might, if you lived for ever, come upon all the beauty in the world.

3

When our grandmothers were girls, they all sketched and painted. Indeed a girl was hardly ready to be married until she had hung her flower-piece on the wall, and collected along with her hope-chest a few dozen versions of some old ruined wall or tumbled down cottage. The most dashing of the young men painted, too, though not generally with the approval of their families who thought they should go into business. Would Charlie, of "Eight Cousins" and "Rose in Bloom," have been such a beau ideal in the young lady's eyes, if he had not had "talent"?

Probably it was a good day for all when this kind of leisure pursuit was laughed out of existence. Now our popular damosel, seeing a ruined cottage, does not sit down on a wall under a sun hat and sketch it. Instead she rents it or buys it for nothing, and with her own hands, she not only scrapes and mends, but paints it. This kind of painting is quite rightly considered a better use for her decorative talent. But now that the dream of Ruskin and later nineteenth century reformers is realized and the interest in decoration has turned to making beautiful the articles we must perforce use, one may still be permitted a passing tribute to the old sketch book, and the studio in the attic where the one talent of the family tore its hair and splashed the paint.

What tensely happy hours they represented, what sketching trips into the country, what union of talented souls in seeing the beauty denied to the vulgar, what dramas of effort and climaxes of despair, and efforts bravely renewed! Trying to paint is the romance of that generation of American and English youth which Louisa Alcott represented and Kipling a

little later depicted, not without sarcasm, in the tragedy of
"The Light That Failed." Perhaps, after all, that feeble light
of genius among all these striving but ultimately defeated
young things did not fail. Perhaps it lives again in the wonderful new burst of decorative beauty in the modern world.

As we settle happily into our almost universal competency
in domestic decoration and the use of color, which distin-
guishes the high period of an art as against the struggles and
defeats but larger efforts of its beginnings, we may find again
a use for the sketch-book and the water colors. If in the effort
to record the observed forms of the world, not much is got
on paper, a great deal is nevertheless painted into the walls
of memory and imagination, and more truly than the amateur's daubs would ever indicate. Everyone can learn to draw
if he really tries. Some of the great early artists taught themselves. But, in this, as in the other arts, instruction is now
more sympathetic and intelligent than ever before, and good
teachers are a good investment for one's future leisure time.
Nor must one neglect those beguiling new materials which
have been developed to make children artistic. A finger painting outfit might well make an adult as happy as a child, and
these colored modelling clays make the fingers itch to be at
them.

While in the arts of practical decoration, in the design and
coloring of useful things, of the interiors of houses, of fabrics,
of women's dress, we have made wonderful progress, there is
a field of decoration which lies open and empty for the use
of the new leisure. In an editorial in *Leisure* magazine Sydney
Greenbie suggests that children, studying art in the schools,
might decorate the walls of their own school rooms. Writing
on the art-projects of the P. W. A., which has set many unem-
ployed artists to work painting pictures for the interiors of
public buildings, he suggests that much of local unused talent
and desire for pictorial expression might be lent to making
our own towns and villages beautiful. People could build
and decorate civic halls, play-centres, community rooms of

all kinds, each one giving his modicum of talent to carry out some portion of a great design, as in the Middle Ages the people built their own cathedrals, each receiving his task, but using his own imagination and ingenuity in the way he carved his particular regiment of saints or made his own gargoyle look devilish.

Of the personal use of decoration it seems hardly necessary to speak. Magazines are full of suggestions for painting the furniture and choosing the curtains, and making an ensemble of the dress, and designing your own Christmas cards. There are a hundred activities of this sort, and all of them delightful. If the new leisure could lead us out from these domestic decorations to larger community enterprise in depicting our common vision of our lovely world, how beautiful our Main Streets might yet become!

The Magical Art of
Make Believe—XIX

THE land of Make-Believe was once a wonderful place. When children ran away from it, to escape the dullness of having to pick up their clothes and learn their lessons, indulgent elders smiled. Grown people who walked with one foot over its borders, and only one on the stony path of reality, were believed to have "temperament," to be of just a little finer clay than their fellows.

Now the psychologists have given us a rude shock. Day-dreaming, they say, is "just a flight from reality", and so a source of daily unhappiness and social maladjustment. Building castles in Spain is a prime source of incompetence. And as for that lovely land of Make-Believe, it is really inhabited not by fairies and angels, but by divorcees and ruined speculators, by the down-and-outs and the permanently unemployable. The slums were once described by a psychoanalytical social worker as the marshes of Neurotica, bounded on the north by the black holes of Moronia—which are only territories of Make-Believe. If you get so far over the borders of the country of Make-Believe that you cannot get back, you are not a genius. You are mad.

It is with make-believe as with all those illusions which, in their place, make life worth living, the illusion of sex, of social contact, the unfailing illusion of one's own importance. One must take it out of the practical business of living and make an art of it. The arts are all means by which one may safely live in that larger and more glorious world which our own idea of ourselves seems to call for. The difference between make-believe as a practical way of life, and make-believe as an art is the difference between a lie and a novel. Just in proportion as the borders of Make-Believe are sharply defined and guarded, and ruled from within by its own laws, may we safely take all our vacations in it, and come back happy, and free, and reconciled to the quite different laws of physical and temporal reality. Maybe, as the great mystics have suggested, this other world we hanker for and in which, in one way or another, we manage to spend much of our time, is the true reality, and this small prison of space and time and flesh and blood an illusion. But, whatever the case, the two are quite different, and the sooner we realize it, the more safely we learn to live.

This perennial problem of that other world of dreams and desires was well expressed long, long ago by a quaint Chinese sage, whose words I have paraphrased thus:

I dreamed I was a butterfly.
A lotus petal on a stream
Is not so lovely as that dream,
When down the world that little I
Went floating, bodiless, all wings
Above the broil and toil of things,
           Only a butterfly!

And now I wake, and lo! I am
A thing of flesh, propelled on feet,
And weighed to earth, and forced to meet
With every cow or pig or lamb
On terms of low equality.
Compared with what I thought to be,
           Look what I am!

And yet, perhaps, it may be I
Am dreaming now—a butterfly
That has a nightmare and believes

It is a thing of shoes and sleeves.
A man who dreams that he can fly,
Or insect, sleeping, which am I?

To keep make-believe from getting loose among banks and corporation directors and politicians and social life, and making some more of our late trouble, it is well to give it free and public rein within the limits of all the arts, but especially of that art of the drama in which it takes its most social and dazzling form.

2

The necessity of finding some public means of periodically purging the body politic was the beginning of western drama. The first effort of this sort was the public orgy. The early Greeks apparently allowed a yearly orgy in honor of Dionysius, the god of wine, in which people compounded for the necessity of being sober citizens most of the year, by one grand, noisy, disreputable release of all their suppressed desires. This method of letting off the social steam is a very old device, and has been tried by many civilizations. In some cases, liquor was the symbol of the release, in some cases sex; and Eastern temples even provided religious prostitutes who helped to satisfy and so to sober dangerous social impulses, within prescribed limits of time and circumstance, as a service to the gods. A relic of this old institution of the orgy survives in the Mardi Gras carnival of the Latin countries, in which people are allowed an opportunity to get the foolishness out of them, under the gaudiest social auspices, before settling down to self-discipline during Lent.

It seems incredible that a yearly orgy, refining itself into a yearly carnival, could have culminated in anything so noble as the Greek public drama. But so it was. The dances and rituals in honor of Dionysius were given a more and more dramatic form, until Dionysius dropped out entirely. A speaker was introduced to explain the evolutions of the chorus or the meaning of a ceremony. Then two speakers. When this was expanded to three there were all the characters the Greek drama, at its height, needed to have on the stage at any one time. Finally there developed the great yearly display of drama, for which the plays were chosen in a competition among poets and playwrights, and the choruses and actors were trained and the stage set created at public expense.

The function of this great drama was what Aristotle called a cathartic, applied to the social consciousness. It was a means of making the people do, what the psycho-analyst gets his patient to do—call up their buried wishes and suppressed memories and unconscious fears and parade them publicly in a great and gorgeous display. This display was inevitably a tragedy because tragedy is what most of such suppressed material leads to when converted into physical reality.

It is worth explaining this Greek catharsis in greater detail, because the problem of the Greeks was, in a singular way, our own at present, and the motion pictures are blindly dealing with the same sub-conscious fears and sinister figures through which the Greeks found a way of achieving social catharsis. While the Greeks had arrived at a clear-sighted and intelligent democracy, and moderately intelligent and humane laws, they were haunted by the remnants of older and cruder forms of rule and of life in their midst. There was, for example, the haunting fear of incest. There was the blood revenge corresponding to our Kentucky mountain feuds, and always an underground antagonist to public justice, somewhat as lynch law still is in the West and South. So, finding that these things were still alive among the people, as their corresponding impulses are in our own democracy, the Greeks did not say, "We won't give publicity to such things. We won't talk about them." They said, "All right! We'll show you. We'll show you these things undertaken by great and gorgeous people, people whom you can really love and admire, kings, heroes, beautiful ladies. We'll show them carried right through to a beautiful, pitiful, terribly tragic end. In the end you may be desperately sorry for these heroes of your antiquated imagination, but you will be cured of wanting to do anything like that yourselves."

So one of the stories told and retold in Greek drama, year after year, was the story of Oedipus, who killed his father and married his mother. Another was the great family history of adultery and blood-revenge which Eugene O'Neill translated into modern terms in "Mourning Becomes Electra." And just as the plot material of tragedy was frankly morbid, so that of comedy was deliberately obscene. Obscenity was another thing people had to get out of their system. It could be translated into humor, and the psyche purified by laughter. That was the catharsis of comedy.

So fundamental was the Greek choice of subject-matter for both tragedy and comedy that in the long centuries since there has been very little great, popular tragedy whose subject-matter was not morbid crime, and very little socially effective comedy which was not at times salacious. So when moralists object to the motion pictures because they deal with gangsters and crime and unlawful love, and to stage plays because they are bawdy, they might as well object to vinegar because it is sour or pepper because it makes you sneeze. Great public drama, when it really touches the whole people, must deal with popular fear. The difficulty with the bad motion pictures about gangsters is not that they have the wrong subject, but that they are not carried through to the true catharsis. You cannot show as hateful on the stage what the people ought to hate but don't. You must show it as lovable, even as grandly lovable, until reason wakes up with decision and says, "but impossible."

Now and then life furnishes us with a denouement which is a true catharsis. Such was the death of Dillinger. No public trial could have been so conducted as to prick the balloon of his glory. But being shot like a rat in a hole while running away, did.

Just as tragedy or any serious drama of large proportions and fundamental popular appeal deals with sub-conscious public fear, so comedy deals with social rebellion. Almost all our modern social comedy turns on the subject of marriage. It ought to. That's what we are rebellious against. As for bawdiness, when properly employed it has its social value. There is only one universal moral rule for it, and this is: "Let the wit be greater than the dirt."

We have in the motion pictures the possibility of great popular drama. Despite the sickening succession of trite and trivial variations on the old and necessary themes of popular drama, again and again it rises to something like its real function. It belongs to our age. It may be universal and seen by everybody. It has the epic reach which the American scene and imagination in particular demands. It has even some great figures. There never was a comedian who better understood the pathos and inevitable glamor of make-believe than Charlie Chaplin, or who could more deftly explode the social dream and send one back sobered and resigned to reality. The good people who ask that motion pictures should be only pure and wholesome, that they should give them back only pretty versions of their social ideals, are asking what vital drama, appealing to all classes, can never do. If it does it will be only a parlor amusement for the genteel. The be-glamoring of dangerous social impulses, which was never so sinister and so threatening as at present, can be fought not by denying them or putting them out of sight. One can only meet fire with a back-fire. To do this the creators of motion pictures need not be moralists or preachers. They need only be what mostly they aren't, real dramatists.

We have not only a potentially great popular drama; we have what, for two centuries, the western world has lacked, a true stage drama. Its proper field cannot be tragedy, or even serious drama, for only truly popular drama can be that, and the stage-play is limited, of necessity, to small and sophisticated city audiences. The only great tragedy that ever was written was that of the Greeks and of Shakespeare, when drama was really for the man in the street. One might add to this the great tragic drama of Christendom to which the Catholic church has given its full theatrical embodiment in the image of the crucified Christ, and in the ritualistic drama of the Mass. The circumstances of the modern stage limit its field to social comedy. But in this it is now very much alive. George Bernard Shaw helped to restore social comedy to its true function by taking the various pretty make-believes— domestic and moral—of sentimental Puritanism, and exploding them one after another, as one might pop the children's balloons. Now a large number of competent stage plays do the same job for us, year after year, and a wholesome and exhila· rating job it is.

Perhaps as the new leisure brings more and more people into the motion picture theatres and the legitimate theatres, the audience, without getting more pious, will become more aware of what drama is for and what it can do for them.

3

But there is a lovelier and less dangerous side of make-believe. There is the legitimate idealization of ourselves and the world we live in, a picturing to ourselves of all that we should like to be, and an inspiration to be it. This element, as has been said, enters into all the stage-sets and costumes and rituals of social life. Personality is unstable. We make ourselves anew with every act. The oftener we can achieve outward manifestations of that beauty and happiness to which all life is blindly groping, the lovelier life is. And no one is content to limit himself to the hands and feet and color of hair and social luck he happens to have. The power to imagine ourselves in the place of others, to live mentally through many other kinds of life is not only a joy. It is also an essential to social understanding and social adjustment. Much that we imagine may be, for the time, impossible, but it is nevertheless desirable. By picturing it to ourselves, by realizing it in make-believe, we bring it nearer to realization in fact.

All putting on of amateur plays, glorifying of local history in pageantry and public ceremony, has a great value for us. It satisfies our desire to be something besides ourselves. It gives us importance and glamor in the eyes of others. It makes our own place and circumstance lovely and impressive in our own eyes. There are some towns which are always trying to blow themselves up into big cities by getting more factories to come, by advertising and boosting. They might better express their patriotism in pageants and festivals. They may make believe that they are big cities from now till the next depression but they won't be, because the favoring circumstances are lacking. Those who take this make-believe seriously will waste a lot of money in development schemes. But to set themselves forth charmingly as a place with a history, as a charming little bit of town and country to come to, as the place one is happy to live in, is a make-believe which, to all satisfied citizens, is nothing but an idealization of the truth. It might conceivably even attract more friends from outside than commercial boosting.

So the little theatres which have spread all over this country are ways of making people happy where they are, of bringing into their own circles romance and gaiety and experience of the world, of acting those parts they dream of performing on the larger stage of life. For this there is already a world of instruction and help. And the desire to give a play is so universal that one has only to say, in any group, "let's put on—", and have some concrete suggestion and the ball begins to roll at once.

Mary Pickford, in the interview with her by Sydney Greenbie, published in the April, 1934, number of *Leisure* magazine was asked what could a talented girl do who wanted to get into the motion pictures but couldn't? She promptly replied, "Develop her personality." Many of the young men and women who hanker to go on the stage do not know what it is they really want. They don't want the drama of the footlights. They want the drama of real living. The beautiful girl doesn't want handsome movie actors making imaginary love to her. She wants one real man truly adoring her. She doesn't want the acclaim of audiences. She wants the affection and praise of friends. So with the young man. He doesn't really want to rescue a movie heroine from an imaginary bandit. He wants some real girl who thinks him the bravest and noblest of men. He wants to be successful, competent, admired. The thing to do with this natural desire is to consider how the motion picture folk must labor to attain charm and poise and adaptability and the power to win others' allegiance, and figuring it out, to practice it on the real people all around. To speak well, to move gracefully, to act with precision and assurance in all the crises of life, to be as loyal, generous, and self-sacrificing as the stage folk are, when they are acting, is a worthy way of turning make-believe into the real stuff of life.

Every social relation is a drama, and every one if he tries can learn to act it through with beauty and with sincerity and loyalty to that ideal aspect of things which is the higher reality behind all make-believe.

The Absorbing Art of
Making Things—XX

WHEN with real devoutness, people believe in what isn't so, they are believing not in God or Heaven or Love, but in money. Money is the gauziest of the human fictions. But now that we are slowly coming to our senses after our late disastrous adventures in the land of financial Make-Believe, the witch-fire that we followed into the marshes of idleness and poverty is being blown up again into a pretty new flame, and that by people who purport to tell us what to do with our leisure. Use your leisure to make things, they say—new things, pretty things— and somebody will immediately buy them. Then into your house will flow the golden streams, money and yet more money. One organization, which says it is non-profit-making, spreads the gospel of what it calls "leisure," but its *real* theme is easy money.

A typical story of this kind, which you may have heard yourself over the radio, runs something like this: Ikky Ikstein is in his little flat one evening with Mrs. Ikky and little Ikky who stands with his nose flattened against the window, whining periodically a request for money to go to the movies. But there is poverty in the house. The last great tragedy has happened. They cannot let Ikky go to the movies when he ought to be in bed, and Ikky, who apparently knows no other way of being happy, and was never told not to whine, is suffering audibly in consequence. Mrs. Ikky's heart bleeds for her young. But Mr. Ikky is absorbed in a new leisure-time pursuit. He is trying to fit an electric fixture to the top of a little aquarium. Suddenly he calls for an electric light bulb. It is attached. The light goes on. Mr. Ikky has a lamp. Mrs. Ikky is delighted, and even little Ikky almost forgets the movies for two seconds. Does this show that an intelligent man can find ways of amusing himself with making things, can even please his wife by decorating the living room, and can distract little Ikky from morbid fixation on the beautiful gangster in the pictures? Not at all. For Mrs. Ikky places the aquarium-lamp in the window to show it off to the neighbors. Mrs. Rosenberg, passing by, comes in to admire. Here we have the social uses of such pursuits. They interest other people. They set them to finding ways of making their own lives prettier and more entertaining. But no. Listen! Mrs. Rosenberg wants to buy the lamp. She will pay Ikky five dollars for it. Five dollars! Ikky goes off in the dream which dollars alone can create. Five whole dollars! Others come in. The idea ripens. We have it! Ikky will start a company, make lamps for sale, have a big business, set up a store on Fifth Avenue. And so, gentle reader, he does, just like that. And the climax of all this new craftsmanship, wealth, and social vision is—and this is the authentic ending of a particular radio program on leisure—that little Ikky now at last has "two bits" to spend at the movies!

This is not burlesque. It was offered, in all seriousness over the radio, and well supported fore and aft with the most pious generalizations about the new leisure. And so we are to swallow it, hook, line and sinker—the very same dope that nearly killed us last time!

There is much to be said for this new epidemic of making things, and even a faint gleam in it of economic hope, but we can never find the real happiness and even the material well-being it promises unless we prick the big balloon of easy money the very first time it goes up. For the cold truth is that not one in ten thousand, making things by hand in his leisure hours, can hit on a product which can be marketed in sufficient quantities, at popular prices, to make even a minimum living. And not one in a million who has the real capacity for

craftsmanship will also have the financial shrewdness, the gift
for salesmanship, and the sheer staying power that it takes
to form a company, create or raise capital, and keep going
till he makes a million. If he has all the necessary qualifica-
tion for thus jockeying the dollars out of other people's
pockets, he could probably do just as well at it without a
craft to set him off. It takes a lot more than a bright idea
to make a million.

Yet if we leave dollars and cents to the myth-makers, and
think of wealth in terms of actual things to use and to enjoy,
undoubtedly there is the promise of new riches in the use of
leisure time for making things. There is even the possibility
of actual cash earnings among people so situated that cash
can be used, not for subsistence, but for a margin of luxury.
Such are the New England country people among whom some
successful and promising new movements in handicrafts are
being started. The state of New Hampshire has a League of
Arts and Crafts, subsidized by the state, under the direction
of a paid manager, who is teaching the country people how
to make things which will be interesting and distinctive
enough to attract buyers among the summer people. Similar
projects are being started in other New England states, and
in various places in the South and elsewhere. Against the
radio promise of a fortune one may set the results of the Arts
and Crafts Fair of New Hampshire at the Crawford House
in the White Mountains. Representing years of amateur experiment, and trained professional guidance, sponsored by
the Governor of the state, and by a lady of wealth and social
influence, this Fair was a great success; *for nearly $2500.00
worth of hand-craft articles were sold!* This would not keep
Ikky Ikstein a year in that station in life to which the movies
had accustomed little Ikky. But, distributed in small sums
among the new craftsmen in New England country families,
it represents wealth which has a kind of fairy-tale quality.

For this money was earned by people who were getting so
much fun out of it that it would have been worth while to

them if they had done it for nothing. It had meant new interests, new ideas, new things to talk about, and to do together, through the long, bleak winters. Men who had been wont to whittle by the fire and tinker at the work-bench through the long winter days had learned how to make beautiful furniture, putting into it that absorbed patience of one to whom something to do with his hands is salvation from ennui. Women who, year after year, had met to stitch quilts which they did not need, having piles of them already in the closet, were taught to turn their fine stitches to smocks and children's clothes and things which the summer people really would buy. These country folk had that deep and desperate love of craftsmanship common to those to whom it is the one resource against stagnation. But it had run in stereotyped and out-moded channels. To unblock it, to give it new hope and direction, means in happiness and hope something that cannot even be measured in money.

But in addition, there is the cash. If you are a rural New Englander in winter, and have a tight roof over your head, and a house banked with fir from the forest against the winds, and a roaring fire of wood from the wood-lot, with plenty more wood in the shed, and vegetables in the cellar, not to mention maple syrup, milk from the cow, eggs from the hens, pork put away from the fall killing, and apples in the barrel, and if you have an untold number of quilts and a hot stove lid to go to bed with, and suddenly you have, in addition, cash you "didn't calculate on"—then open the mail order catalogue some fine evening under the lamp, and you will know what one whole dollar can really mean! Every penny in that dollar is a shining road to the more abundant life.

2

What the new craftsmanship means to the New Englander, it means to many other people, in many different ways. It is no substitute for earning the necessities of life by the well tried roads of industry and agriculture and professional activity. Except in rare cases, it cannot usually be a living. But it is luxury. Once a highly trained professional man, disappointed in a large opportunity through the chances of the depression, walked out of his office in a fury of frustration, and suddenly began tearing the wall paper from the walls of his lovely but run-down old colonial house. He had hoped to pay for expensive redecorating. Now, just to tear something, just to vent his energy on something concrete, he fell on the room himself. His wife, coming in two hours later, found him whistling as he rubbed away with sand-paper at the old beams of his house. "Dear," she said, sitting on his step-ladder, and watching him, "this is building fortitude and patience into the very walls of our house." And so it was. He redecorated that room himself. It cost so little in materials he said that he was ashamed to mention the price. In the end all the disappointed family fell to and worked with him. It tided them all over weeks of stagnation. He did not make in this way anything to feed and clothe the family with. But what he did make was luxury, and it was also character. The lovely room when it was done had an air of wealth and comfort which it would take a good deal of money to buy. And what they made within themselves couldn't be bought for dollars.

So it is with all the things one can make. If you make dresses, material for a good winter dress will cost about eight dollars. But for eight dollars you can buy a pretty and well-made dress which keeps you just as warm, and looks, superficially, smarter. But if you have taste enough, and skill enough, what you will have for that money will not be a duplicate of the very pretty and adequate commercial product that every stenographer can buy. It will be such a dress as only the woman of wealth can afford to have especially made and designed for her. What your skill will have brought you is luxury. So with food. Even if you grow your own tomatoes, you can hardly can them, using commercial fuel, at sufficient profit to compete with the commercial canners. But for only a fraction of their commercial cost you can have such jellies, and fine pickles, and syrups for cooling drinks, and marmalades as only an epicure's table is furnished with. So it is with hand-made furniture, with metal work, with interior decorating. On the level of common use there is no way of making our hands compete with machines. But they can go further and do better. The products for use must be made by mass-production methods for a mass-market. The products of luxury remain individual, expensive in time and attention, lovely in special detail. Only the wealthy are the purchasers of the hand-made furniture, the especially designed dresses, the hand-knit woolens, the professional services of decorators. If you can do these things for yourself, you may not make a living, but you may become wealthy. The wealthy can afford to have a surplus of linens and of jellies, a hand-wrought lamp at the garden entrance, a hand-tended conservatory opening off the living room. So can any enterprising family with taste and spare time and love of making things.

One effect of making your own luxuries is that the money spent for luxuries can be saved for things which only industry can make. If you paint the house this spring yourself, and lay the garden walk, which you can do with a little practice and taste, enough money is saved for a first payment on the new car which you can't possibly manufacture yourself. In your actual possessions and the quality of your social living, the effect of using leisure in thus creating your own environment is the same as if your cash income had been doubled.

3

This is to suppose that every one can make things, and make them beautifully. It is a large assumption, but one abundantly justified by experience. Within the last three decades, a general spread of knowledge and of taste in craftsmanship has quite kept pace with machine development, and

the machines themselves have come to the aid of the crafts-
man. Any one who wants to work in metals, in colors, in
wood, in fabrics, in foodstuffs, or in almost anything else that
makes material living rich and beautiful, is now provided by
industry itself with materials and tools that are almost fool-
proof, and with excellent instructions. You can't go wrong if
you follow directions, and such good examples of everything
one wants to do abound not only in shops but in private
homes, that one inevitably acquires taste by just trying and
doing. The information supplied by industry with its materials is generally reliable and so worded that it is often better
than that of books and articles not directly interested in
selling things. Housewives often marvel that the recipes enclosed with cans and boxes of food are really better than the
recipes in the standard cook-books. So with enclosed instructions telling just how to use the paint or care for your tools.
If the world is now everyman's school, this is one of the departments in which the pedagogy is uncommonly good. In addition, there are various centres in the city which teach
craftsmanship for very small fees, and in the country the farm-
bureaus are excellent free centres of learning.

Years ago manual training was introduced into the school
with the idea of helping pupils to find remunerative voca-
tions. With the new point of view of life, born of the depression, we are beginning to see another and greater value in it.
It is a preserver of the character and the means of personal
happiness whose loss has been so disastrous to us within recent
years. If Latin and Algebra are to be retained in the schools
because they are an intellectual discipline, manual training is
even more needed because it is a moral discipline. It brings
home the necessities of things as they are. It brings an immediate retribution for shoddy, insincere work. If you don't put
on a roof honestly, it leaks. If you don't sew honestly, the
garment comes apart. If you don't cook honestly, you can't
eat what you cook. One can bluff and slip by in a class in
English or history. One can't bluff with hammer and nails, or

knives, or paint. Again one must learn patience, and ingenuity in surmounting obstacles, and a humble readiness to scrap what is done badly and do it again.

In the good life craftsmanship is the necessary complement of the fine arts. In the fine arts one learns to give form and limit and meaning to the world of dreams. In the practical arts, one learns to get rid of dreams in dealing with the physical stuff of life. One learns that a fine idea is nothing until with slow patience and experiment one has somehow bent the innate cussedness of metal, and fabric, and wood, and paper, and paint to its realization. An eager young author, who, having had one book published, was burning up with a desire for fame and money, and much cast down every time she got a rejection slip, was sewing one afternoon. "I like to sew," she said, looking up with an uncommonly tranquil face, "It always reminds me that life must be made the way a dress is—stitch by stitch."

The Peaceful Art of
Growing Things—XXI

GARDENING is one
of the leisure time pursuits that always make people lyrical.
There is a poetry in Nature which inevitably colors anything
one writes about her, and human happiness is so organic, and
so akin to the great contentment and apparent joy of all the
lower creation, that one can hardly do anything which brings
one back into harmony with the rhythms of plants, animals,
and the seasons without being happy. Moreover, in civilized
life, we are starved for that variety of sensation in which
children and animals revel. To get out at four o'clock some
rainy summer morning, and transplant the cabbages, gives a
lot of nerve-centres the delight of being set to use once more.
It is true that farmers often seem as dead to sensation as city
men—or at least the city-man thinks they are. But I have
never seen office-workers look so alive and contented as most
hay-mowers or wood-choppers or plough-men look, at least in
the earlier hours. The trouble is only that they get too tired.
If farmers could do what the old knights of Europe were said
to do, "plough in the morning and joust in the afternoon,"
they would be a happy race of men. Even so, good farmers
are no objects of pity. Some of them, even now, enjoy nearly
everything they do.

Now and then a smart guy on a newspaper falls for the
"back to Nature" idea, and when his tomatoes mildew, and
his chickens get the pip, and he has acquired ten calluses
and a back-ache, he returns to his typewriter and explodes
the great fallacy. All this means that, in growing things the
first time, you can't score much higher than in playing golf

the first time. If you plunge into haying with a set of urban muscles, you will come back feeling the way you do if you ride a horse all day without previous practice. But that is nothing against horsemanship as a sport, nor against growing things as a sport either. Thoroughbred chickens will die if you don't handle them right, and so will thoroughbred dogs. If half the energy that is spent in becoming an expert at the country club, or the kennel club, were spent becoming an expert on the farm, you would have just as good sport, and at least a little for your money.

There comes a time, in the evolution of every cultivated people, when the necessary labors of primitive times become the sports and arts of leisure. What is now happening to farming happened to the earliest American means of livelihood, hunting and fishing. So while farming is being consolidated into a mass-industry, it is also becoming an art for leisure-time. While, with one hand, the government directs the ploughing-in of cotton and wheat by professional farmers, with the other hand it is encouraging the amateur to raise everything from a cow to a cauliflower in the back-yard. In this the government is merely anticipating, and easing off for the individual, a development which was coming about anyway.

Growing things as a professional is very hard work for very poor pay. Growing things as an amateur is pure fun, and three hundred per cent profit. It seems strange, but so it is. For in some kinds of growing, mass-production, instead of being cheaper, is dearer, because it must make expensive work out of what Nature and man's natural instincts take care of individually. Take, for example, the transportation of red raspberries. If you pick them yourself, and carry them in from the garden as you need them, you don't know that you are doing it. But if they are transported from the places where they must be grown to the city where they can be eaten, there is expensive over-sight and an immense loss through spoilage. The ideal then should be, "Every man his own raspberry bush." It is with growing things as with craftsmanship. The more a product is a luxury, the more it pays to grow it yourself. Such comparative luxuries as strawberries, asparagus, raspberries, and celery are among the cheapest and easiest things for the backyard gardener to produce for himself in quantity and quality to dazzle an epicure. This is because the cost in the market comes from circumstances the private gardener does not have to contend with.

One of the fondest dreams of the Roosevelt government is the idea that social security can be achieved, in part, by getting people to enjoy the peaceful art of growing things in their spare time for their own use. Being a leisure-time farmer himself, Mr. Roosevelt has that generous zeal in sharing his own fun with which bounteous nature seems to inspire her votaries. Besides its own unique gift of health and happiness, growing things in leisure time has the same moral values that belong to craftsmanship. It takes the nonsense out of you, and the egoism. It makes you settle down and work patiently with things as they are. It brings home, as nothing else does, that august law which, in the Orient, they think is the foundation of all ethics—the law that every act has a consequence, that whatever happens to you to-day follows, as the night the day, from something you did formerly. At any time in gardening, and to a lesser degree in the care of animals, what you get to-day, or suffer to-day, is the result not of to-day's actions, but of what you did some time back. You didn't spray the potatoes last June. Now, in October, the potatoes are rotten. You carefully dug in the manure last April, and tested and treated the soil. Now in July you are feasting on green peas. You neglected to cut off your expensive new tea-rose as directed, and mulch it down. Your rose is dead. It is not for nothing that great statesmen, in our own and other lands, have been farmers or country gentry, that a sound and thrifty farming population is the backbone of a sound state. Such myth and poppycock as that on which Wall Street fattens and which ever and again runs us into the ground is taken out of

the grower of plants and beasts by wind and rain and para-
sites and the daily ups and downs of things.

2

For the enrichment of life, growing things is even a surer
substitute for cash than craftsmanship. There is almost no
way of losing money on a backyard vegetable garden. Under
the worst circumstances, enough comes up and matures to
equal the low cost of seeds and labor. Sufficient vegetables to
feed the average family all summer and much of the winter
can be grown for less than $10.00 for seed, ploughing, and
spray materials, with an average of one hour a day of labor.
And it is mainly delightful labor, not hard enough to give
even the muscles of a bank-clerk a pain, that kind of putter-
ing, miscellaneous employment out in the sunshine amidst
his own possessions, which is of all employments the one man
instinctively enjoys. It is so opposite to the hard, drive-in-one-
track, never-think-of-anything-else labor on something you
don't own and can't control, which most factory work and
office work consists in, that it has for the city-worker the
exhilaration of a sport.

Similarly, most fruits, large and small, cost little to plant
and are a delight from the day they burst into honey-filled
sprays of bloom to the day when they come heaped and glowing to the table. Is there anything around which pleasant
memories gather more surely than around the old apple-tree?
Its grandmotherly arms invite children to play in it, and its
delicate rose-petalled blooms call lovers to pause beneath it
in the moonlight of May. Its very fruits lean down to you, on
the bending boughs, as if they would fall into your mouth.
An orange tree is as lovely in its clime in a more delicate,
aristocratic fashion—its flowers the symbol of brides, and all
that is most pure and fragrant in the young dream of love, its
fruits the golden apples of Hesperides. And what if these
glamorous things with their fairy-gifts must be maintained by

such sordid efforts as spraying at intervals with stuff that
smells to the blue heavens? That is the way with all the
beauty of life.

Nature is incredibly bounteous. One cannot grow things
without gratitude and amazement at that over-flowing fountain of all good things which it is man's to tap. Every
September, as the flood of fruits and flowers and vegetables
rolls in from the garden and I think humbly of how little I
have done for it all, I marvel how any man can be poor in
a world like this. It does not seem reasonable that a five-cent
package of cabbage seed should turn into two hundred big
cabbage heads—enough to feed a family for a winter; that
ten cents worth of celery seed should now be one hundred
and seven bunches of celery ready to go down into the cellar,
and turn into such white and nutty delicacies as no market
can supply, for that kind won't keep under market conditions. What is true of the vegetables is true of the flowers.
Once I had a birthday gift of a dozen tea-rose bushes from
the gentleman I most appreciate. Every morning, year after
year, from early June till the first of November those rose-
bushes punctually deliver a half a dozen new roses at breakfast time—as if they were a permanent order at the florist's
shop.

And for all this one has very little to do but be faithful.
When people fail in growing things, it is not because the
work is too hard or the techniques difficult to learn, but because they do not know how to be faithful, faithful always
and in little things. They think the spraying won't matter
this time, and overnight the green worms eat the cauliflower,
and mildew turns the delphinium to gray dust. They think
they don't have to pull the witch-grass out by the roots,
instead of cutting it off like a weed, and its roots soon spread
underground like a mattress and take the whole garden. They
don't notice that the iris must not be planted deep. They
drop it into whatever hole in the ground they happen to
make, and are aggrieved when it rots. When their gardens

fail, they do not say, "I am slack, and haven't sense enough to boil an egg." They say, "I have no luck." There are people like that in other pursuits than gardening, but generally civilization is more patient with them than Nature is, and the fines not so heavy and so immediate.

3

Our good paternal government is not only encouraging gardens as leisure time pursuits and substitutes for cash; it wants again to make the cow and the pig and the chickens household pets. There are difficulties with maintaining animals, in this free motor age, when sometimes you want to be home to feed and care for them and sometimes you don't. But on the other hand, the horror of domestic animals which some people have derived from memories of the smelly old barn-yard is not justified. One can keep useful animals as clean and neat and healthy as one's pet dog. And it would not be hard to revive, in modern families, the love which used to be lavished on the more useful domestic pets. Nathaniel Hawthorne and his whole family used to dote on their chickens. Hawthorne was never tired of watching the hens. He said the hen was one of the most amusing of animals. There was something "so laughably womanish about her." Once a day the whole Hawthorne family used to go in a procession to feed their chicks. The family of the president of a successful industry, settled in their country home outside of New York, used to have a cow that was a family pet. The daughters were pretty and sophisticated young buds, but they enjoyed playing dairy-maid, and even named the cow after one of them. She was Betty, and the cow was Betty Moo.

If we are to keep domestic animals, we must restore some of this love for them, and family play about them. Only this will make the mess and responsibility worth while. But this is just as true of dogs. Sometimes it seems that there might be an advantage in pet animals that didn't share our own

houses with us, that didn't shed hair on the davenport and
have to be shooed out of the dining room at meals. The pet
animal is, in a special way, the symbol of household affection
and responsibility. But this affection might extend beyond the
dear creatures that jump on us, and sniff our guests, and bark
themselves into apoplexy every time the door bell rings, to
the less bumptious producers of eggs and milk.

As for the smart Alecs who invest in a great deal of farming
machinery and lay out a great deal of capital, and then blame
the good art of growing things for not giving them back
their money multiplied, who ever said that was the way to
farm? Growing things doesn't need a vast outlay and a lot of
gadgets. It needs love, and patience, and faithfulness. As for
capital, there is only one safe way to get it in farming—grow
your own! One seed that turns into a score of cucumbers is
just as good as one dollar that turns into twenty. When Shy-
lock tried to explain what he did with dollars, he could only
turn to growing things for his example. He said that he
made them breed. Helping plants and animals to breed is an
older road to the more abundant life than bankers know, and
probably a better.

The Dangerous Art of
Thinking—XXII

MOST people think
that they like to think. Almost all favorite indoor games, like
puzzles, card games, checkers, and chess, are an exercise of
the wits comparable to the exercise of the body in out-door
sports. Few things give more social exhilaration than a chance
to show how bright you are.

For all this, real thinking is a pursuit not lightly to be
engaged in. One must make sure ahead of time that one is
not going to be torn limb from limb for it, or boiled in oil
for it, or given hemlock to drink, or nailed on a cross. All
this has been done to thinkers before, and it may quite likely
be done again. Because thinking has always been mortally
dangerous, there are some old and well tried disguises for it.
Every one who wishes to be brighter than his fellows ought
to know about them.

One of these is the mask of the buffoon. At the very dawn
of history the First Brain Trust was made to know that man's
brain was something Nature had not calculated upon and
didn't wish to allow. It upset the whole organic balance of
things. It sent a shudder to the very centres of creation. It
punctured the grandiose content in which life had thus far
evolved, each creature the center to himself of an enormous
dream, but furnished with mechanical tricks for surviving
which developed and worked almost automatically. The first
brain played havoc with the decent order of things. It took
the devastation of the lightning and made it permanent in
fire. It tore off the skins of animals, and put them on man.
It was terrible and incalculable. So the human crowd which,

as distinguished from the individual man, remains even to-
day a species of lower animal, instinctively massed itself as
one against this new catastrophe of brains, ready to rend and
tear like any other beast at bay.

Then the first brain had another bright idea. It said to
the crowd. "There! There! You are bright, not I. See I am
only mad! I ate an herb and went crazy. I was walking on
the moor and was moon-struck. Don't believe anything I say."
So he pretended to be very silly, but kept on telling them in
jest just what had scared them in earnest. Since individuals
are human, but the crowd is an animal, the idea quietly
lodged in a mind here and there, and surreptitiously, under
a mask of foolishness, he gathered in a little support for his
first ideas.

This method of disguising the ticklish art of thinking was
so good that it has been used ever since. In the Middle Ages
kings used to have court fools who, under the cover of buf-
foonery, made very pointed and helpful remarks on what was
going on. Whenever they said anything that was dangerous
because it was true, the king and the court could drive them
out with a great fuss, and then act on it in quiet. This kept
the king and his councillors from being driven out themselves for having the identical idea. On the same principle,
some Japanese newspapers, wishing to print more truth than
the crowd will tolerate, keep one editor to go to prison for
the rest. Nowadays Will Rogers serves as fool for the American public. Under the cover of a joke, he says a good deal
that he couldn't say with such popularity in earnest. Once
when the crowd tried to rise against him and get him fired
from *The New York Times* he asked blandly what had come
over people when they took comedians seriously, and thought
Senators were a joke?

This simple disguise is often used even in childhood. A
child that naturally sees through things, and so seems to evade
or to be antagonistic to that series of fictions by which the
young crowd is swayed from one violent group activity to

another, is often cruelly persecuted. But often he learns that he can turn their fury off by giving them some obvious excuse for teasing him or feeling superior to him. This is why so many geniuses are incompetent in practical ways and why professors are absent-minded. They learned early that amiable incompetence was a valuable means of self-preservation for the person who carried around the dangerous gift of brains.

Some lucky intellects have been lodged in homely bodies. Socrates' chunky form and snub nose, Voltaire's small size and monkey visage were comic masks that they accepted with glee and paraded for a laugh from the handsome and the tall. It is a lot of trouble for naturally good looking people, like George Bernard Shaw, to work up so effective a front. Even great statesmen, who happened also to be men of special and therefore dangerous mental keenness, like Disraeli and Lincoln, have made good use of social peculiarities or disabilities as something to draw off the attention of the crowd. One of the advantages of being a woman is that Nature gave the softer sex a mask ready-made, and from the dawn of history clever women have known how to use their wits behind it.

Another mask for brains is that of the medicine man. If the average man were persuaded that ideas were a very special thing, a revelation from on high, a sacred tradition handed down from the past to people specially designated, he felt himself excused from the necessity of having them. A modern medicine man is Einstein. His operations are not half so mysterious as he makes out. But he keeps himself popular, and safe, by disappearing into the secret shrine of knowledge and coming out with something no one can understand. Most of the professions still protect themselves by this method, and they need to. When a lawyer like Judge Lindsay or a physician like Doctor Robie lays aside professional secrecy and invites the public to read their case-histories, all the hells of primitive fury are unloosed. So the Catholic church, protected by the old mask of mystery, has never had to make the concessions to the mob that Protestantism has been driven to.

A third adaptation of the man of brains is a reassuring kindliness. The public must be assured that this queer and startling bearer of brains means well. Loving-kindness of the most supreme quality did not prevent Christ from being nailed on a cross for His thinking, nor Joan of Arc from burning in flames for hers. But a deliberate geniality, radiating often from a warm heart, but well and dramatically focussed on the crowd has helped many a sage, from Socrates to Mark Twain, to get by. It is always a pity when people of great common sense and useful social insight, like Joan of Arc or Napoleon, get started upward to spectacular heights too young, and have too much luck. With a little slower going at the outset, and more chance to age in the wood, their brains might have been preserved for the public good. This is why an obvious personal handicap, either of straitened opportunity in youth or of health and looks, has often been of great assistance to men of genius. The American public now gives its very charming and intelligent president more chance to use his brains than it might under other circumstances.

If the necessity of deliberately disguising every sensible and useful idea for the improvement of general living were better understood, clever people would be saved much pain and some martyrdom, and changes that are good for everybody could be made much faster. For those who, in their own families and private circles, wish to enjoy the freedom of action of those who really know where they are going and the inner excitement of really using their wits, the first use of thinking should be to find a way to keep the individuals with whom they deal from being scared by ideas or knowledge into massing themselves as a crowd. Cultivate something amusing. Acquire humility and bland good nature. Say you don't mean it. Run when they boo, and come back, unperturbed, by some other path, the way Voltaire used to do. Be as meek as

Benjamin Franklin tried all his life to look. If you are young, be very young, and look up to your elders. If you are old, take to the shelf before you are put there. It's as good a place to think as any. If you are a woman, be pretty and lean on the sex that is wise and strong and thinks it runs the world. If you are small or foreign or handicapped, thank God for it and make the most of your chance to think.

The greatest protection for thinking is laughter. Only man laughs, for only man really thinks. Laughter is the explosion which the rays of intelligence generate among the fumes and gases of man's unconscious. When the crowd glowers and gathers and draws together to spring as one beast, the man of wit can deftly pop-off its emotion in an explosion, which we call a laugh. Laughter is the great catharsis. Rage, fear, envy, can all be popped off in a laugh, leaving the psyche cleansed and exhilarated. Wit and humor are sure, shining arrows in the quiver of him who wants to keep the liberty to think.

2

For thinking is worth all the trouble it takes to protect it. It may leave you a little disillusioned and lonely when all the crowd go "whooping" by you in pursuit of the impossible. But it saves you also from their blind catastrophes and nightmare despairs. In the midst of the impinging darkness in which man is set to run his course, it makes a narrow road of daylight for his own feet, and gives him some grains of knowledge to comfort him for all he cannot possibly know. The utmost of all that man's thinking can master of the forces that control his own life is very little, but that little is better than nothing.

Thinking sets bounds to that chaos of dreams and illusions of which nine-tenths of the wisest life must consist. It helps a man to lay aside, for practical purposes, ideas which are not for this world, even when they meet the instinctive reachings of the heart. Such an idea is that of infinity. The imagination and religious longing cannot dispense with it, but practical man must. To believe that corporation stocks will go up, up, up to infinity and never come down, that sales can be increased more and more and never reach an end, that one can grow richer and richer and richer—these are very dangerous delusions. To believe that one's own success will mount for ever, that next year one's parties or one's business or one's clients or one's fame will be bigger and better, and the next year bigger and better still, is madness. There is almost nothing that acts that way in what the Christian Scientists call this "world of mortal affairs," except cancer. The possibility of more and more and more cancer tissue seems to be unlimited. Once set going the stuff doubles, triples, quadruples, multiplies exactly like a speculator's dream of money. One comes away from a cancer laboratory with a wholesome respect for and contentment in the limits which the very constitution of things seems to put on everything in this life but cancer.

Fine arts assist the effort to fit man's vision of the illimitable into concrete limits. Narrow and exact limits are a challenge to the artist, and, in general, the stricter the limit the finer the work of art, as in a sonnet. If we could only work with money and time and human strength and human capacity the way an artist works, accepting the inevitable limits, and making all we can within them, we should all be materially better off. The sky is nobody's limit. The utmost distance any one has gone into that sky is not a dozen miles.

Another idea that is dear to the human imagination and belongs of right in his world of dreams and of God, is the idea of the fixed and unchangeable. How we long for it! How we try to make it! And how in this world we are baffled! Nothing stands. Everything flows. What we are now we inevitably will not be to-morrow. Permanent standards can only be imagined. Permanent laws and institutions cannot be made. We are up; we are down. We are happy; we are miserable. Round goes the wheel perpetually, and we with it. The most bitter quarrels between the men who do the thinking and the crowd at large turn on this. The man of brains, perceiving change, wishes to change with it. The crowd as a whole clings, with desperate delusion, to the idea that what it is used to is, was, and always will be. To live on this flowing tide of life, one must swim. Make yourself rigid, act as if the stuff under you were solid, and down you go. But throw yourself on it easily and completely, relax and breathe, and go with it, and lo! it bears you up.

Yet the idea of the Infinite, the Eternal, and the Unchangeable are essentially noble ideas. They belong to man's mind, if not to his flesh. They enlarge his spirit and give him vital assurance. It was when man took them out of the cathedral into the counting house that he went wrong. One of the effects of allowing no time or place in modern conceptions of life for the old religious retreats is that ideas which belong to religion and can satisfy on that plane alone are used in material business to displace common sense. What you can serve nobly in the spirit is sometimes destructive if you try to make it serve you instead in the flesh. Such an idea is destiny. Applied to the whole grand necessity of things, to all that is "world without end, Amen," it is very grand. But whatever may be the larger destiny which mankind fulfils, for practical purposes, from moment to moment, man is free. Crude people are always speaking of their own faults and disabilities as if they were part of a sacred plan arranged by God. Father always had indigestion. So therefore must you. Fat runs in the family, what use to look after your pounds? "I am so sensitive, just like my poor mother." "Others may, but I can't." They act under compulsions. "I don't know why I did it." "Something told me to." One use of thinking is promptly to dissipate ideas like this. What we think is destined, we can change. What we want to do, we can, by just doing it.

Another idea which the greatest religious spirits reject but which is at home in some of the lower and brighter realms of fancy is the belief in fairies. We all believe in fairies. Sure!

Somehow or other, if you don't do your work, a fairy will come and do it for you. If you lose your job, a fairy will get you another. If you neglect your health, you won't get sick. A blessed influence will suspend for you in particular all the observed laws. To many people God has been nothing but a big Fairy. Some faith in the general beneficence of things is undoubtedly justified. This old world has muddled along for an indefinite period with things so bad in it that you would think it would blow up in a day. Somehow or other the spark of physical life in each one of us has come down in unbroken succession, through wars, famines, earthquakes, and floods. If all our ancestors survived to maturity, back through untold ages, to the first vital cell that ever was, it is quite possible that we and our children will survive also. But as for fairies, looking after our particular selves, on particular occasions, it is best to believe that there aren't any.

3

The more important anything is to our health, social security, and peace of mind, the less we are willing to think about it. We don't really want to think about ourselves, and so discover that we are not heroes of the universe, but just scraps of organic life among millions just as important as we are. We don't want to think about other people. They wear a beguiling illusion which makes the charm of love and social contact, but which in many concrete dealings must be laid by.

One of the things we are particularly unwilling to think about is money. One would suppose that this, of all things, belongs to the hard, simple world of things as they are. But it doesn't. We surround it with pretenses. It is loaded for us with an inexplicable embarrassment, so that in transactions between friends we "hate to mention it;" in paying the doctor we discreetly pass it not to him but to his office assistant, in meeting one to whom we owe a debt, we are shame-faced, and in trying to collect we often feel strangely humiliated.

Though money is obviously limited and gives out, we like to pretend that it doesn't. Even when banks close and we can't get our own funds, we feel as if it were somehow our fault and are ashamed to ask credit or admit that we have no cash. Most people will not tell how much they make or have. The fiction is that a bright flow of fairy gold descends in unlimited quantities on them from some mysterious source on high. Though this world could not go on a day without work, most people feel humiliated in asking for a job, or admitting that they are dependent on anything so mundane as a check. The depression has been prolonged and made needlessly painful because of all this complicated fiction about money. What is true of money applies to most of our economic thinking. Some day some of the present arguments among the wise-acres about production and consumption and the gold and silver standard may look as idiotic as the old arguments of the theologians about the number of angels that could dance on the point of a needle.

Another thing we don't like to think about is the birth of children. Since preserving life and reproducing it are the basic necessities of any organism, it would seem that they should be the very things we ought to use our heads about. But because these functions are older than man's brains, they are the ones that resist him with the blindest determination. This is illustrated in the perennial problem of birth-control. One would think that every one who could not accept and make sincerely his own the Catholic ideal of continence as a personal discipline and fecundity as a social duty, which is at least consistent, would immediately follow his common sense to the possession of hygienic, safe, and psychologically unobnoxious contraceptives. But every year or so when revision of our laws comes up, we have a great burst of solemn nonsense from doctors, from celibate priests, from law-makers, from "hard-headed" practical folk. We are told everything that a happy and experienced mother, sitting at home among her flock of beautifully "spaced" children, with health, happiness, and love all safe in her own person, knows isn't so. And the law that doesn't allow anything frank and sensible to be said on the subject permits large, glowing, and mysterious advertisements on "feminine" hygiene, which give some very inadequate information, in fairy tales that play with woman's tragedy. Yet while the majority of marriages still flounder in the bitterest misery and confusion, perfectly adequate contraceptives exist and are quietly used to enhance and preserve the highest purposes of marriage—but here thinking must put on the brakes under the stop light marked DANGER, lest we should all be arrested before we get safely over into the next chapter.

The Dubious Art of
Doing Good—XXIII

ONE of the many things man is not satisfied with is being confined to one life. He wants to live all over the map and be everybody. Fortunately, outside of drama and fiction, there is a way in which this may be accomplished. In so far as we can share others' lives in comradeship and sympathy, can work with our fellows to some common end, we multiply our own living. Marriage is a very blessed way of living double, and children, especially as they grow older, multiply one's own life through many experiences and interests. So in friendship, we extend ourselves into other kinds of living, and in all self-forgetful effort among other people we are living not our own lives alone but the lives of others.

Herein is the difficulty. To share another's life, as an extension of one's own, and with due respect to that other's right to live his own life, is one thing. To live some one else's life as a substitute for living one's own, and sometimes as a means of hiding the fact that one can't live it adequately, is quite another. Doing good is often an easy road to a very fine state of mind that one hasn't a right to. For the trouble with doing good is that it is not half so pleasant to be done good to. In a world where it is more blessed to give than to receive, there is bound to be considerable inequality.

The curious thing about doing good is that while it is singularly interesting and makes you feel wonderful, there is a notion that you ought also to be able to claim the martyr's crown for it. Just why this should be is difficult to tell. Most professional doers of good, such as social workers, missionaries, and the priests who are true pastors, have romantic and adventurous lives, and many more really fine moments than can possibly come to salesmen and bank clerks. The Orientals have a beautiful idea, often followed with great success. The idea is that a man should marry early, make his fortune, and then, when his family is growing up and he has had his fill of the struggles and triumphs of this world, he should lay it all aside, and going forth penniless, with his begging bowl and his hermit's robe, take thenceforward all mankind for his family, and all life for his portion. It is thought that in this way he gives up nothing, but rather escapes. He has paid his debt to society. Henceforth society is properly his, to study, to adventure in, to take or leave as he pleases. In lands where the great majority of men are still very poor, and very miserable, there is always much to do which will give such a man the great exhilaration of doing good, and at the same time be socially useful. The difficulty will be some day to find this very delightful use of leisure time in a society which, on the material side, is run the way it ought to be. The poor we have always with us. But we ought not to have them, and when we don't, what shall we all do?

2

So without whooping up the charms of the benevolent life, which seem alluring enough without advertising, it is only wise to consider the very great difficulties in the way of it. We may begin with the ideal of self-sacrifice. Self-sacrifice is a fine thing for the one who does it. But how can it be enjoyed justly? Not in families, and among friends. In families, one can not long sacrifice one's own personal wishes or pleasures without making the other person sacrifice something in turn which is very much more important than personal pleasure—his own right not only to be unselfish but even to be just. In the long run unselfishness among equals must be made into a social gesture, a fine art. It must consist only in little gracious social adjustments, and in offers of self effacement which cannot honorably be accepted. And along with this must go, in the end, a scrupulous justice. Even in social life, the kindest way of doing a service is tactfully to open the way for the recipient to do a service, and even a greater one, to you in turn. It frees him from the burden of obligation; it transfers from you to him the glow of generosity.

The minute unselfishness among friends and equals is carried beyond justice and a fair exchange, it takes very ugly forms. There is a suppressed determination to be repaid, as when the mother, having sacrificed herself for her children unduly, thinks that they in turn should look after her for the rest of her life. There is the demand for gratitude. It is a debt that, in the eyes of some creditors, is never paid. Once when Mark Twain lent money to a young man, he said, "Understand, you owe me money, and some day when you can, you will feel better if you try to pay it. But you don't owe me gratitude. Gratitude is a kind of interest on money I am never mean enough to want."

Still there are some kinds of unselfish service which, it seems, must be unequal. One is the service to children. But was there ever a normal child who did not pay his way from the first moment when the baby fingers, clasping helplessly around the hand, clutched delightfully at the heart? Children are worth all they cost, in fun, in love, in the freshness and gaiety they bring into life. No true parent can talk of self-sacrifice. Whatever he gave up, he merely substituted one satisfaction for another.

Sometimes self-sacrifice, though undertaken sincerely, may be only a common sacrifice to a false god. These farm parents who slave to send a son to college or a daughter to Normal School, these working class people who are determined that the children shall enter professional life, these wives who work themselves to death that the husbands may save and get rich or have a "career," are often only enslaving all concerned to ideals of social snobbery. Sometimes such efforts are for the whole family only a social investment, and are justified as such, but not as self-sacrifice. Sometimes they only substitute nervous tension, and worry, and pretense for honest and healthy work and happiness. Whatever glory once attached to self-sacrifice for an education is now outmoded. Anyone can now get an education anywhere, if he really wants it, and the sooner he looks these delusions of the "best school," the "fraternity," the college in the face, and discards those for which he cannot easily pay, the better off he will be. They are delightful luxuries, but those who miss them may, by appropriating the knowledge they are everywhere free to take, go just as far in this world and be just as wise.

3

But if self-sacrifice as a virtue, or even as a very large possibility in families and among equals, somehow evaporates, there is still the need of much good work among the poor and the outcast and those unable to help themselves. That such work is interesting to those who do it is unquestionable. Social settlements are exciting places and full of human adventure. But bit by bit the pious glow is being taken even out of this. Sadly we must abandon the luxury of that love with which Saint Francis kissed the leper, admitting to ourselves the futility of maintaining human rubbish and the needlessness of seeing it multiply. What we must do for it or with it becomes not a matter for good will but only a grim social necessity. On the other hand, there are conditions which must be met by human kindness, but which ought not to be allowed in a civilized state. Every year *The New York Times* publishes touching stories of the deserving neediest. In practically every case the difficulty is a family handicapped by illness. But a society which casts the innocent victims of family illness on charity is still barbarous. While the great flow of Christmas kindness is a blessing to those who feel it, and good fortune to the very small number who can benefit by it, this sort of charity too often keeps people blind to conditions which call for basic social re-adjustment. Again it is a very pretty thing for the debutantes to give a fashion show, parading superfluously expensive dresses, to raise money for little children who have no clothes. But it would seem that only a calloused social consciousness could quite enjoy this.

Things being as they are, all the good and the tender-hearted can do is to throw in what strength and money they can to help here and to help there, like one rescuing victims from a burning ship. But their natural joy in the good part they have the luck to play should not blind them to the fact that ships should not be on fire.

4

If doing good will have to be surrendered as a personal luxury and taken on as routine business by society as a whole, and as routine penance sometimes for things ill done socially, there still remains the great happiness of sharing. To work with others to a common end, to create together, is to expand one's little span of life many times. It is to live more largely by being part of a larger community than that which purely personal affection and social choice can build. Even on the levels of well-to-do life, where what has been called "charity" is not needed, the life of the individual expands thus in co-operation. The alumnus of a school for the well-to-do, who was happy in his youth there, extends that happiness through his life when he keeps on taking an interest in it, or lives again his boyhood in the person of some lad he is able to send there. Such generosity is one of the pleasantest of luxuries. So the Garden Club, working to make the town beautiful, is not doing anything very noble or pious. It is merely improving its common property, in the town in which, being land-owners of substance and pride, the members have a considerable stake. It is a happy thing to do, and multiplies the individual joy of gardening.

To apply to community or co-operative effort the test, "Am I happy in doing this?" seems a selfish proceeding, but it is a means of keeping such effort sincere and useful. If we took our names off the miscellaneous charity subscriptions which we are often bullied into signing, and avoided all committees which bored us, most of us could still find plenty to do which would be an extension of our own genuine interests, a sharing in something to which we could bring intelligence and experience. And probably the common weal would not greatly suffer. Increased leisure time might well create the democratic equivalent of that leisure class which, in countries like England, formerly furnished the men of public affairs. Every one could be a man of public affairs in his own community, interested in its welfare, concerned for its health and its beauty and its freedom from distress.

Such a use of leisure time is offered in the various service clubs. But, though these are kindly affairs and a means of education and entertainment for the members, they cannot under present conditions make their candles throw much light into the social darkness of our communities. Apparently they cannot even insure that when one of their members has federal funds to administer for sorely necessary purposes, he should really be able to read English. An almost universal inability on the part of the local administrators of federal mortgage, loan, and relief funds to read the English on the numerous necessary blanks correctly and to interpret instructions with anything like common sense has unnecessarily aggravated a great deal of misery for which relief was in sight. Nor can the best "whoopee" of the service club do away with the lies and pretenses, economic and social, behind which misery cowers at their very doors. Nor can it somehow prevent the plainest social justice and community necessity from assuming the humiliating guise of charity, or get together the victims of morbid individualism in the simplest co-operation for their own salvation.

In a lovely little town, inhabited only by Americans of the

ancient English stock, and well subsidized by comfortable and well-to-do gentry of the kindest intentions, much of the benevolence of the town is exercised on two families, and their many collateral relatives. One family which has always been "on the town" has eleven children, and yearly adds another sickly baby to the population. They are all physically and mentally weak, but with good care they keep on living and multiplying and being supported. Another family produces the town's bad boys in endless succession. They get hauled up before the court periodically. A policeman is maintained, at town expense, with the sole purpose, apparently, of keeping them in order. But with careful and kindly supervision they are kept out of the reformatory and have not yet added to the world's stock of major criminals. Such families are the community's charge. It looked after their ancestors and will probably continue to look after their ever-increasing descendants. Every town has inherited something like this, often something much worse.

When we go out with the beautiful old sentiments of good will and charity to right the wrongs of the world, we are painfully like Don Quixote. The feelings and the code of action are very fine, very noble, so sustaining to the soul that, like the good knight, to the very end we are loth to give them up. But what has happened to the world that they no longer seem to work?

Yet, for our own happiness and the fulness of living, we must not be wearied in well doing. Perhaps, in the end, the only persons we shall do much good to are ourselves. The social end of benevolence is only justice. At the point where the innocent moral glow of good will dies out in a saddened perception of things as they socially are, a new and perhaps higher experience opens, for at that point one begins really to think.

The Supreme Art of
Living—XXIV

EVERY now and again,
in the history of human affairs, there comes a generation, or
several generations, which must bridge the gap between an
age that is dying and one that is waiting to be born. Such
were the generations when the Roman Empire was breaking
up. The barbarians were knocking at the gates; the strong
new plant of Christianity was coming up under ground, but,
try as he might, man could not make the virtues and the
methods which had made Rome great work again. So it was
at the end of the feudal period, the tragedy of whose passing
was made into a magnificent farce in "Don Quixote". The
trouble with the poor old don was that he was born too late.
His poor stiff body and rusty sword and shambling steed were
symbols of a decrepitude which had overtaken ways of life
which had once been just as grand and inspiring as he thought
they were. Some believe that we are living in such a period
of transition now; that capitalism, once so fresh and blooming and able in its way to make the earth bloom, too, is sick
of its last depression. The fact that it has recovered from other
depressions is not to the point. A man might recover from
a disease several times, and still die of it. It may even be
possible that the business man's loud cry for "confidence"
is only the expression of a failing spiritual vitality which no
government and no external methods can restore. Perhaps
men have lost faith in the ideals that under capitalism they
used to live by, not always unhappily. Perhaps they don't
even want again what they had in the great age of prosperity.

The abandonment of a particular concatenation of ideas

and of systems of social life which for convenience we may call *paganism* or *feudalism* or *capitalism* does not mean that there never was and never will be buying and selling and investing of money except under capitalism nor chivalrous behavior except among the knights. It only means that at a given time something is built upon one department of human activity which tries to be a working religion for the whole of life. So long as self-defense was the primary need of every little social group in a disordered world the virtues of the knights could be the ideals of everybody, and the feudal age flowered. The minute men had evolved sufficient safety for industry and commerce to grow up and prosper, their attention turned to other things, and new ideals were built on the new activities which we call bourgeois or capitalistic. Perhaps capitalism has, in a similar way, done its work. It is for the future to show.

But certainly men are casting around for other ideals to live by than those which seemed supreme a few brief years ago. And in groping for them many have seized upon the idea of transferring their enthusiasm from work to the use of leisure time, from making a fortune to maintaining a security. The minute everybody begins to believe something, it is probably wrong. The most dubious thing about the idea of the new leisure is that it is so suddenly popular. But the avidity with which it has been seized upon nevertheless is the sign of a great hope and a great need. And so, proceeding rather tentatively, and not pretending to speak gospel, we may consider what it may mean to us in the greatest art of all—the art of living.

2

No life can be good or beautiful till, on its simplest animal basis, it is secure. What we have been awakened to is our terrible, unparalleled insecurity. Slowly we have come to think of all the goods of life in a single term—cash. So long

as he has enough cash, a modern man may live a charmed
life. He may live in a beautiful house or apartment, with no
gun on the wall to repel an enemy, for unknown powers
whose working he hardly inquires into protect him. He does
not have to build a fire. He turns on a radiator or an oil-
burning furnace, and heat is delivered to him, and even regu-
lated by a magic he calls a thermostat. He does not have to
make or wash his clothes, or go out and get his food. He picks
up the telephone receiver, and anything he wants appears
at his door. He does not even have to amuse himself. He pays
money and every kind of gaudy entertainment is his. While
the bright flow of cash continues, all is so smooth, so gay, so
easy, that he is lulled into a beautiful illusion. He thinks
that this condition of affairs is and was and always will be.
He almost forgets that he even has to do anything for it.

True he surrenders something for it, but he does this
under such slow enchantment, that he scarcely realizes what
he is losing. He does not notice that one by one all the little
centres of sensation all over the body are growing duller and
duller and failing to deliver those many and various small
delights which organic life, not only in men but even in
animals, has developed through the long centuries. He ceases
to feel the exhilaration which comes from the quickening of
the heart against danger, from the tensing of the muscles
against labor, from the impact of wind and water and cold.
Some of this, if he is wise, he keeps in his sports and his arts,
and much of it he forgets. Life insensibly becomes a little
flat, but he takes this for the natural condition of life, and
gives himself a "kick" with stimulants for which, as for everything else, he pays with the magical cash.

But suppose the cash ceases, ceases as in the worst days of
the depression, because of something over which he has no
control, something as magical and not-to-be-understood as
most of the other conditions he now lives by. When he cannot pay for it, the light goes out, and there is not a stick in
sight to make even a torch of. The fire goes out, and not even

grass or leaves anywhere to be lit. The water is turned off, and in this world which flows with rivers and is flooded with rain, there is not even a rill or a trickle for him. He is put out of his house, and no cave anywhere to crawl into. He has no food, and there isn't a fish to catch nor a wild berry to pick. Nature, when most savage, never treats her children like that.

And worst of all, he has nothing to fight. In the cruelest deaths in the open, or even in war, a man may fight and struggle to the end, and feel in the jaws of death the wild joy of a fast beating heart and a battling will. But how many have sat during the depression and felt stagnation like an evil enchantment falling on them, binding them closer and closer, cutting them off from every help, unseen, impalpable, in a slow nightmare from which, maddened, some can leap only to suicide. So men who have jobs, which means cash, cling to them in terror. Over every job hangs the horror of the day when it might end. And people who have saved money have, in the past, turned with piteous trust to the great magic which made all life for them and said, "Keep it for me, and make it more," and have wakened from their dream to know that all magic is not good and some fairies not all-powerful.

Some on whom the axe fell early in the depression now think they are lucky. They are out of the enchanted wood now, and they got out partly on their own steam. And they can look only with pity on those who are still in it, and think it is heaven and will always last. While the dons and pundits of the New Deal try to find ways of making the very fine world which capitalism built for a few somehow safe for everybody, it is best for every man to look around and see how to make it safe for himself.

This is what the arts of leisure promise. They promise various small securities to supplement the security of cash. They release love and happiness and the ultimate ends of life from domination by money. If men stop paying money and struggling to get money to pay for what money properly can't buy, they can stretch their money much further over the things it is really good for. When money is taken out of the world of magic and reduced to its place, and with it the means of money, which is a business or a job, it may become a substantial though limited and indispensable reality. Then at last men may really appreciate it and let it go only for something substantial that can really be lived on, instead of letting it be juggled out of their fingers for immaterialities or surrendered to those who will play hocus pocus with it.

During our late unhappy experiences, the countries or sections of countries which survived with the least agony were those that knew what money was worth, because they had built economic security on much besides money. In the United States such people were the rural New Englanders. They suffered enough, but it is a platitude that they suffered less than the rest of the country. This was because the rural New Englander seldom spends money till he has done what he can to get what he wants without it. In the ancient economy of the New England countryside, one can somehow have a house and vegetables and fruit and wood without money. One may even live in a pretty little town with great dignity and self-satisfaction, and have a round of pleasant associations with one's neighbors, and never own a car or go to the movies. Nowhere do people care more for appearances, but they somehow make their own—by keeping the house neat and planting flowers and general tinkering. Their political, financial and social thinking may remain incredibly stupid when it is expressed in generalities. But they are like the Chinese, who get along without a good government, because they have a good way of life which is independent of any government. But no one appreciates hard cash better than the rural New Englander. In making a little money go a long way, he treats every penny of it as if it were a dollar.

Another kind of people who have survived the debacle of capitalism with less agony than most, though with trouble enough, are the French. This is because they have many arts by which they preserve economic security, independent of money. In such arts as cookery, costuming, and conversation they get social effects and satisfactions for little or no money, which are the equivalent of social luxury elsewhere. But they, like the New Englanders, know that money is indispensable for some things, and they take good care to keep it safe for its own purposes.

The first aim of a good life should be to get as wide and solid a material base as possible independent of a job or a specific business. This is found in mastery of the fundamental arts of life, gardening, building, cookery, craftsmanship, which may be pleasurably pursued in leisure time. It is also found in the maintenance of health and personal fitness by such pleasures as camping, and those outdoor interests and pleasures that do not involve large fees to country clubs or athletic centres. They restore areas of pleasure which are deadened by civilization, and they make a man safe against despair when civilization fails. Security is found also by investing spare cash in genuine material comforts which are enduring, safe, and free from debt. Many people during the depression, who saw their savings go up in smoke, and their stocks go down to nothing, nevertheless were able to maintain much of the habitual comfort of life because they had also bought good clothes, good cars, good furniture, and household conveniences which kept them going a long time without actual loss of a civilized standard of life. However, in a civilization so bemused by advertising and salesmanship as ours, it is easy to go too far in purchasing even these things. If one buys only what one has a genuine need for and cannot get without money and really uses and enjoys it, the arts of leisure are again a protection. Some people make more real use of one old car in going on picnics and taking long trips, than other people make of three. The more the energy is released from the driving necessity of getting more and more and yet more things that are half used, and is turned to making a good life out of what one has, the less there is that psychic dependence on the means of livelihood which makes the typical "worry" of the business man or salaried man.

Within limits, things which are really used and enjoyed, and so appreciated that they will be preserved a long time, save one from the temptation to take money out of present use and comfort for investment in an uncertain future. Some saving is, of course, wise; but a man's best securities against the future are his own habits and those of his family. For example, many people keep themselves unnecessarily poor by carrying too much life insurance. Insurance is a necessity for safety against the unavoidable hazards of life, such as fire and accidents. No one can be sure that he will not be killed by a wild car on the road or have his life bumped out by a brick falling on his head. No one can be quite secure against fire. Therefore fire and accident insurance seem necessary. But accident insurance is nothing against the huge weight of general life insurance which in hard times is a delusive security for, if you cannot pay the often heavy premiums, you are sure to lose half of all that you have put into it. Now a sound and healthy habit of life ought to make it fairly certain that one will not die of any ordinary illness. Short of extreme old age practically every fatal disease is the result of long continued carelessness and physical ineptitude, poor diet, lack of exercise, lack of rest and recreation, chronic constipation, and the like. A man who is a good risk for a life insurance company ought to be a reasonably good risk for himself. Means of living a healthy life, in all the leisure pursuits that make for health, ought to limit, at least, that tremendous anxiety which keeps some families loaded with more insurance than they can carry. Some of the insurance money would be just as good an investment if it were put into land for a garden or a vacation to rebuild the health.

Again there are family habits which are life-insurance.

One is a way of life which preserves for the wife of the family
such means of livelihood as she may have had, and so in-
creases general culture, social contacts, practical experience,
and physical competence that, short of extreme old age, she
could very well look after herself. Another is bringing up
the children to such health and competency and such an
attitude toward life that, thrown out on the world in early
youth, they could still find their way and make a good life
for themselves as others have done. All the leisure pursuits
that build health, hardihood, competency, and independence
of the lures of the crowd and of expensive amusements are
an investment equivalent to life-insurance.

Another way in which money goes for immaterialities is
in heavy interest on mortgages and instalment buying. People
who can build happy lives for themselves as they go, who
constantly extend and improve their environment and the
quality of their social living, are saved from some of the
temptation to assume too much debt. One can so genuinely
enjoy the old car that one does not strain one's self to make
payments prematurely on a new one. One can keep one's self
so busy improving a simple and inexpensive house with one's
own hands that one does not hasten to take out a mortgage
on a palace. One can have such a happy family life and so
many friends and social good times of one's own that one
never cares whether one keeps up with the Jones family
or not.

3

The essentials of food, clothing, and shelter are easily
earned. What people passionately labor for, and pile up
more and more money for, is something beyond that—a good
life, a handsome, care-free, drudgery-free life, a gay life,
with many friends and much admiration, an honored and
successful life. Sometimes, too, they are really only working
for love. The beautiful but not impossible She who will some

day be his keeps many a young man striving. The wife and
the children are the sweet bosses which most of our hard
business men really serve. And sometimes, though they do
not know it, men are really working for God—for some
"well done" no human voice need utter, but which has an
echo in their own consciences, some ideal which they dimly
see as human service, some ultimate goal of sheer perfection.
These are beautiful ideals and the true ends of living, but
is any job big enough to encompass them?

One of the many ways in which men have been betrayed
in the great profit era is that they have taken the best they
had, their human love, their striving for something more
than human, and have been persuaded to give it all to some
corporation, some business, which in turn drained it as gold
into the coffers of invisible owners, and left them nothing
against a rainy day except the need to look for another job.
Salesmen and cub-reporters are whipped up for their work
with talk that is just the old revival stuff revamped. Even
now, when we are more chastened and temporarily skeptical,
in gatherings where business people discuss their problems
together there is still a kind of talk and a kind of look on
people's faces that can't possibly be suited to the discussion of
anything less than the fate of their immortal souls. But what
is being talked of in this high and holy strain is usually how
to sell more shoes, or more tooth paste.

Leisure time rightly used should take out of business and
the job some of the emotions and some of the idealism which
the humdrum business of making a living can never satisfy.
There are better ways to love the wife and the children than
slaving in an office for them. The work will not suffer if
the free time is used to build happiness at home. As for
that larger striving, who does not know that even the best
work for a living is a constant compromise with the ideal?
Some area of life should be kept where the ideal, and that
alone, is served, in the fine arts, in the pursuit of knowledge
or skill for its own sake, in human service which is not an-

other name for selling somebody something, and in activities which, whether of a traditional religious form or not, are turned to some ultimate beyond the partial and inadequate scheme of things as they are.

As for the good life, the gay and gracious life, the fun, the glamour, and the admiration, they will come just as surely from social activities that need take no large amount of cash, from forms of self-enhancement which make one admirable and good company, independent of what must be done for a living. Where there is surplus money for these things, it is best spent first not in the goods that perish, but on that inner wealth which lasts as long as life. Such an investment is travel. Such are books which are really read, and, if possible, owned. Such are the social accomplishments and the artistic skills. Wealth buys these things, and the wealthy, in general, make some effort to achieve them. But they may be achieved without wealth, if one uses one's wits and one's time. They are a surer entrée than money to what is called "good society." And they can't be frozen in a bank or go down to zero when Wall Street goes down. Even on the material side, if what is spent for the support of social pride, for the saving of face, for the building of prestige could be saved because one is the kind of person who can command these anyway, a good deal of money could be secured for such humble utilities as bread and butter.

As for the feeling that the job or the business is one's great opportunity to make good, is the test of one's worth as a man—that is even in the best professions a delusion. It is true that the people who are happiest are those who can make a secure income in work they like to do and can do well. But apart from a very few people of very exceptional gifts, most people have no exclusive vocation. They can and ought to earn a living at almost anything that turns up. In most cases, they can turn from one thing to another with zest, and learn the simple tricks necessary to carry on most of the useful work of the world if they try. If the sense of

social pride and of exclusive vocation were taken out of the
training for work, and a man built his claims to honor
and distinction on something outside of the work he did
for a living, some problems of unemployment would solve
themselves. There are too many mediocre doctors and law-
yers, too many specially trained people waiting helplessly
for the one chance that does not come. Even in the highly
skilled professions, a competent person can turn his training
to some quite different use if he tries. No one should be such
a specialist that he does not have one or two subsidiary interests which, at a pinch, could be turned to remunerative purposes. The lawyer need not spend his leisure perfecting his
special field of law. If he uses his working time well, *it* should
be sufficient for that. He should reach out into general study
of politics, of finance, of economics, or psychology. It may
serve him, at times, in his own profession, far better than
more reading of law; it may open other fields of activity for
him. In any case it will make him a happier and rounder
human being. So a dealer in building materials might well
study architecture for amusement, or a dealer in food stuffs
agriculture.

Again, since all work that is done for a living is bound,
at some time, to force a compromise with the ideal, one ought
for one's own psychic health to have something one does
entirely for its own sake, something which fulfills the desire
to do as well as possible, to carry through to perfection, to
follow one's own taste and inspiration with subservience to
nothing except the inner voice. There should be some art,
some knowledge, some well doing, which has no personal
end, something that is its own sure and unceasing reward.
For some, very simple hobbies serve this end; in this way
they do work of lasting good and glory. It does not matter.
It only matters that in this avocational activity, whatever it
is, the spirit is wholly free.

To build a good life, filled to the brim with all that life
can bring from youth to old age, as little hampered as pos-

sible with sickness and poverty and lack of love, is no easy thing. There is no hard and fast formula for it. If this golden calf on whose altars so many of us have been burning ourselves to ashes seems a particularly foolish god, we shall if we are not careful only set up something else just as bad. One touch of nature makes the whole world kin, writes Shakespeare; and many quote the words with simpering sentiment, not noticing what he says that touch of nature is. It is that men, one and all, "run after foolish baubles." Even now many are talking of leisure as if it were a new god, a kind of cross between Santa Claus and the great god Pan, piping on a shepherd's pipe, and dancing a jig, and carrying on its shoulders a sack full of shining new hobbies. Leisure is not necessarily this and it is not that, even though there are twenty-five good arts in this book which might, conceivably, fill some hours. Perhaps the most it can do for us is to lead us to pause now and then in the inevitable day's work, and say, "Life is a mystery I do not understand, and probably I never shall. But the first free shining hour that comes my way I will seize and start on the great adventure of finding what it is all about." It may be we shall never find out. But what does it matter? In an adventure like that one is bound to have a good time all the way.